"Danny Collum's *White Boy* brings a fresh pair of eyes to the real-life drama of the South in the civil rights era of half a century ago, and it's as if nothing— not even the clock and calendar—has changed. In this sentient and tightly ratcheted novel, the past is still present, along with the blood, sweat and fear."

— John Egerton, author of numerous books about the South, including *Speak Now Against the Day: The Generation Before the Civil Rights Movement in the South*, winner of the Robert F. Kennedy Book Award.

"A fine, sensitive novel, daring in concept, mythological in structure, an unsparing picture of what it meant to be white and young and male in Mississippi at the time of the civil rights revolution."

— Susan Richards Shreve, author of thirteen novels, most recently, *A Student of Living Things*, and the memoir, *Warm Springs: Traces of a Childhood in FDR's Polio Haven*.

"Rock-a-billy, blues, Elvis and Little Richard—icons of a Southern boyhood—collide with lynching, freedom rides, sit-ins and car chases in this fast-paced story of race and redemption in the Deep South. This debut novel is as much a celebration of popular music as it is a tribute to the dangers of one young man's commitment to his morality journey. Heart warming and riveting, it is a provocative and satisfying read."

— Anthony Grooms, author of *Bomingham* and *Trouble No More*

White Boy

a novel

White Boy
a novel

Baltimore, Maryland
www.apprenticehouse.com

ISBN: 978-1-934074-67-1

Printed in the United States of America

First Edition

Cover Photo: Courtesy *The Birmingham News*
Cover Design: Caroline Valentino, '13

Published by Apprentice House
The Future of Publishing...Today!

Apprentice House
Communication Department
Loyola University Maryland
4501 N. Charles Street
Baltimore, MD 21210

410.617.5265
410.617.2198 (fax)
www.ApprenticeHouse.com
info@ApprenticeHouse.com

For Polly, at last, with all my love and gratitude

- One -

It was a warm Friday night in the spring of 1955, and Tommy Jackson was sailing. He and his friends Jack Gerard and Wade Suggs were out cruising the country roads near their hometown of Calhoun, Mississippi in his folks' old pale green 1948 Chevy. It was during that tiny sliver of the Mississippi Delta year when it was warm enough to drive with the windows down, but not yet hot enough to sweat. In the fields there was water standing between the rows of last year's dead cotton stalks. The moon reflected off the water so that it looked like an ocean all around them.

Tommy had just received his driver's license a few months before. The fresh, new document read "Thomas Jefferson Jackson, Born 1/12/40, White, Blonde, Blue, 5'10", 180."

Jack Gerard was sitting shotgun. He was the tallest of the three, well over six feet and still growing. He was toothpick skinny, with overlong arms and legs, and he had a shock of red hair that was liberally greased but still untamed.

Jack put his head out the car window as they barreled across a bridge at the edge of town and picked up speed. His red hair broke loose completely and flew in the wind. He looked like a scarecrow that had just caught fire. Jack yelled out the window to the fields and distant farm houses, "Wake up, morons! Here we come!" He banged on the roof of the car and yelled, "Faster! Faster! We got to go faster!"

Jack was the wild one, the kid who would steal anything, jump off any tree, and stay out later than anybody, just to prove that he could.

"Are you going to ride on the roof?" Wade Suggs asked from the back seat. "There's people in those houses, and one of them's liable to call the cops."

Wade Suggs always rode in the back. It was the short man's burden. Wade was also a little plump and pear-shaped. He had a great big butt, like his mama. He also had his mama's turned up nose and unnaturally long eyelashes.

Wade was looking over Tommy's shoulder at the speedometer. "How fast you going to go?" he asked. "Can you drive good enough for this?"

"Yeah, sure," Tommy answered. "There's nothing to worry about out here."

Jack banged the roof again. "Faster! Faster!" he repeated.

Tommy had never driven really fast before that night. It was a new thrill and he was curious how far it would take him. He'd started speeding on Highway 8 when they were making their way back to Calhoun from Greenville. They ended up making the 50-mile trip in only 35 minutes.

Tommy and Jack and Wade had been over in Greenville that night for a live music show. A new guy named Elvis Presley had played in the National Guard Armory. Presley was making a big racket that year all over the Southern states. People called him the Hillbilly Cat because you couldn't tell from his music if he was supposed to be country or black.

Tommy had talked his two friends into going with him. Tommy was a nut for rhythm and blues and had been since he was 12. He played ball like everybody else and read books more than most. But he was really alive when he was by himself at night, listening to rhythm and blues on the radio. The music brought him a secret world of wise and free black people who sang about sex and liquor and cars and dancing and made it all sound like the stuff of eternal life.

But that world only existed on the radio. What Tommy saw that night in Greenville was real. There were hundreds of white teenagers there, people just like him. And when Elvis walked on stage, spread his legs, and slammed his guitar, they all went crazy together.

There was one moment from the show that Tommy carried with him down Highway 8. Elvis had just sung a slow song and he stood in the spotlight with his head bowed, waiting for the cheering to stop. When the hall was almost quiet, he slung his guitar down low by his right hip. He raised his right arm high and slowly twirled his pointed index finger in the air for a long teasing moment. Then the arm slammed down as if to call the start of a race. The drums crashed. Elvis threw back his head and hollered, "Have you heard the news? There's good rocking tonight."

Elvis lived in Memphis, but he was born and raised in Tupelo. He was a Mississippi white boy, just five years older than Tommy. The things Tommy saw and heard that night filled him up with a strange new sense of what might be possible for a Mississippi white boy. As he drove the Chevy into the night, he kept seeing flashes of Elvis slamming down his arm and announcing the news. He kept hearing the roar of the music and the crowd in his head.

The feelings made his heart race and his face get hot. They made his arms and legs restless. He hammered the steering wheel in time to the music on the radio. When the hour was late, they tuned in WLAC from Nashville for John R.'s rhythm and blues show. Every time the tempo of the music picked up, Tommy pushed the accelerator a little closer to the floor. Soon he found himself flying down the highway faster than he had ever dreamed.

Of course on Highway 8, Tommy was always having to get around slow-poking cars and lumbering pick-up trucks. The vehicles cluttered the road like static on the radio dial. But every once in a while it all came clear; then it was smooth sailing, Fats Domino, "Ain't That a Shame."

When they got back to Calhoun the boys weren't ready for the trip to end, so they headed across the bridge and out Moriah Road. Nothing could stop them out there. Tommy pushed the accelerator down until it brushed the floor. The surge of power ran through the car and Jack yelled, "That's the stuff, baby!"

Without looking away from the road, Tommy said to Wade, "It's almost all straightaway from here to Moriah. It's like a drag strip." He wasn't sure if Wade heard him over the roar of the engine and the wind.

Moriah Road began at the Calhoun city limits. In town it was called The Boulevard. The Boulevard started at the Calhoun River, which divided the town into good and bad sides.

The Boulevard was just what the name indicated, a wide shady street lined with ancient oaks and two-story mansions. The houses had pillars and balconies and elaborate gardens. They'd been built a century before by plantation families, and descendants of those same families still lived in most of them. The Boulevard represented everything that was old and unchanging on the good side of town.

But The Boulevard ended at the Little Muddy River and so did the town. Once you crossed that bridge, it became Moriah Road, and all bets were off. All distinctions of good and bad fell away before the barely-tamed wildness of swamps and cotton fields. The road ran open and free for ten miles until it reached the dying little town of Moriah.

Moriah Road was the place that teenaged boys in Calhoun, white ones anyway, went to race their cars, drink and fight on the river bank, or park with their girlfriends in the turnrows. It was a place so laden with mythical sexual conquests and exaggerated alcoholic adventures that, among the white boys of Calhoun, a reference to "going out Moriah Road" always brought a mixture of giggles, smirks and reverence.

So on this warm, wet and moonlit night, with a head full of Elvis and a tank full of gas, Tommy and Jack and Wade were sailing down Moriah

Road to freedom. A couple of miles down the road, Tommy pumped the accelerator hard. He got the speedometer up past 80. Finally Jack pulled his head back inside and put his hands forward on the dashboard. "This is the life, man," he said. "Let's just keep going!"

Wade was still leaning over the seat to watch the speedometer. He periodically reported their speed, like a radio announcer. "Up to 88 and still climbing," he said.

The radio played "Maybelline." Jack reached over and turned the volume all the way up and they began to sing along. It was perfect. Tommy felt omnipotent and invincible and free. He pushed the pedal a little bit harder until he thought his foot would go through the floorboard. The needle inched up a little bit more until it was hovering just under 100.

"God, this is great!" Tommy hollered over the wind and the radio. "I think if we could get it up to 100, we might take off and fly." He held the steering wheel lightly with both hands. The old car had never travelled more smoothly. It felt as if it were driving itself.

Jack just yelled back, "Push it harder, boy! Push it harder!"

There came a long, gentle curve in the road. Tommy started feathering the brake and bringing the speedometer down. Halfway around the curve, there was another car coming. It was going almost as fast as Tommy was. The other car's left wheels had creeped over the faded white line in the middle of the road.

Tommy saw the other car coming, and he leaned the old Chevy a little bit to the right to avoid a collision. The oncoming car didn't waver. Tommy gripped the steering wheel harder. His hands were sweaty and the wheel felt slippery. He turned it a little further to the right, just a fraction of an inch, he thought. But when he did, the car lurched. The right wheels bolted off the edge of the pavement. The car jerked and hit the loose gravel on the shoulder of the road. The oncoming car was beyond them and Tommy tried to steer back onto the pavement, but the car was ignoring his commands.

He heard his friends screaming words he couldn't understand.

The car wasn't on the road any more. When it hit gravel, the green Chevy took off and flew. It went sailing off the road and hung suspended in midair over the cotton field like a redneck Hindenburg. For one terrifying moment, Tommy could picture them bursting into flames like the Hindenburg. Instead the car came down on all fours in the damp cotton field.

Heads banged on the car ceiling. The boys were shaken to the bones. Tommy sat for a few seconds, stiff as a board, with his hands glued to the steering wheel. He couldn't make himself move. He tried to think but his mind seemed frozen, too. He was conscious of the sound of voices. But they were distant and confused. After a while one of the voices emerged from the babble. It was the voice of John R., the disk jockey, reading a long advertisement for Ernie's Record Mart.

A thought formed in Tommy's mind. "The radio is still playing. We must be alive." Next he tried to speak. "Hey, is everybody still here?"

He heard Jack's voice mutter back, "Yeah, we're still here. What the hell happened?"

Wade chimed in from behind, "We ran off the damned road, fool! That's what happened. The question is, what the hell are we gonna do now?"

Nobody answered him, because nobody knew. After a moment of silence, Tommy tried his door. It opened. He got out and walked around the vehicle. His legs were trembling and it took a few minutes for his eyes to focus in the dark. But as he looked around, the car still seemed to have all of its parts, though the tires were sunk a few inches into the mud. Tommy got back in and tried to restart the engine. It turned over and caught. As the motor hummed and the headlights shone, the boys began trying to plot an escape from the cotton field.

Jack had the bright idea that they should angle the car up the embankment that led back to the road. So they tried that. In low gear the car rolled forward out of the mud easily enough, but the angle of the embankment was too steep. When they headed up it, they got a sick rollercoaster feeling. The car was leaning backward. Wade started to holler, "Oh God! It's about to flip! It's about to flip, I tell you!"

Tommy gently backed the car down the slope. Jack and Wade got out and rode on the front fender to try and give the car some ballast. But under their weight the wheels sunk into the mud and began to spin. The boys hopped down to give the car a push out of the mud. But when they did, it started leaning into a roll again.

Tommy backed down onto level ground and said, "I think we're better off taking our chances with the mud." He turned off the headlights and drove along through the field, parallel to the road, until they came to a farm house. He drove slowly through the yard and into the driveway.

Quiet as they were, the sound of the car still woke up the chickens and they began to squawk. A dog started barking. When they looked back from the road, they saw a light come on in the farm house. By then it didn't matter because they were safely back on blessed asphalt and Tommy was driving back to town at the legal speed limit of 40 mph.

The boys didn't speak. They were still scared. They only stopped once to empty their bladders on the shoulder of the road. When they crossed the bridge back into town, Tommy drove up The Boulevard for six blocks, hung a right on Parker Road, and pulled into Mackey's.

Mackey's was what they called a beer joint. It was also a cafe that did a pretty good lunch trade during the day. But at night it was taken over by white teenagers as a hangout. It was a very popular place because the owner, Jerrold Mackey, sold beer to minors. No questions asked, as long as they could see over the bar. In 1955 Mississippi was still officially a dry state, though everyone knew where to find anything they wanted. Since all liquor sales were illegal, selling liquor to minors was not really any more illegal than anything else.

At Mackey's, Tommy, Jack and Wade sat down to reconstruct their composure. Wade and Jack had beers. Tommy abstained, saying, "I've got enough to cover for when I get home without having to worry about my breath."

Tommy also secretly felt that perhaps, in return for being snatched from the jaws of death, he should turn away from his sins. He had that same exhilarating, washed-clean feeling that he'd had after his total immersion believer's baptism four years earlier. That feeling was appropriate. After all, he had just been saved, again.

After recounting their adventure a couple of times to the crowd at the bar, the boys went outside and pulled the car up under Mackey's neon sign to get a good look at the damage. Miraculously there was none. There was mud caked all along the underbelly of the car. But they kicked a lot of it off and got the rest with a hose from the gas station next to Mackey's. When the mud was gone, it was as if nothing had happened.

The boys headed home. Tommy dropped Jack off first. He lived on a side street on the good side of town. His family wasn't very well off. In fact, his father was a notorious drinker and gambler. His mother drank, too, but she was somehow related to the Parkers who were one of the big old plantation families, and that connection was enough to keep them on the right side of the river.

Tommy had been friends with Jack since eighth grade when they had almost failed shop class together. Tommy was no good at mechanical things. Jack was good with his hands but couldn't resist making a joke out of everything. Halfway through the term, Tommy and Jack were teamed up by lot and assigned to build a desk lamp together. They constructed a wood-based appliance that was shaped like a penis and seemed to ejaculate light. The teacher confiscated the project and gave them an "F." Tommy and Jack had been good friends ever since.

After saying good night to Jack, Tommy and Wade crossed to the other side of town together. Wade got out at the house on the edge of the downtown business district where he lived with his mother. Wade's father had disappeared when he was little.

Since Wade and Tommy were almost neighbors, they had been friends since they went to Robert E. Lee Elementary School. They used to spend long days together riding their bikes all over town and wandering out into the surrounding fields. They swam in the river and played baseball and shot BB guns together. They spent nights at each other's houses telling scary stories about goblins and girls. When they were 12, they started smoking together.

After dropping off Wade, Tommy bumped across the railroad tracks to the Jackson home. He slipped in unheard and unnoticed and slept the sleep of the just.

- Two -

The next day was a Saturday and that afternoon Darrell Farmer and his cousin Willie were hanging out in front of Mr. Woodside's general store in the town of Moriah. The store was on what remained of Moriah's main street. The railroad ran through the town and the stores on the two-block strip all faced the tracks. Behind the main street were scattered a couple of dozen broken-down houses and two churches.

That was the town. By 1955 most of the people had left Moriah and moved in to Calhoun. The only things still alive out there were the churches and a gas station and Mr. Woodside's store. Hayden White, the benevolent lord and master of Calhoun, Mississippi, owned all the land in and around Moriah. The town served mostly as a trading post for his tenant farmers.

Darrell Farmer was a 14-year-old black kid from St. Louis. He had come down to visit his uncle Hosea Farmer, who worked a section of land on the White place near Moriah. Darrell's

parents were both school teachers in St. Louis. But they came from the Delta, and most of their people were still around Calhoun. So they sent Darrell down to visit whenever there was a school holiday in St. Louis.

Darrell and his cousin, Willie Farmer, were sitting on the curb in front of Woodside's store drinking Cokes when a red pick-up truck drove into Moriah. In the truck was a 14-year-old white girl named Elaine Kimbrough, her mother and baby sister, and her 16-year-old cousin, Barry, who was driving.

The Kimbroughs were poor white folks from way back. Elaine's father, Jake, owned a little patch of swampy land that bordered the White place near Moriah. The land was so bad that the Whites wouldn't buy it from him at any price. Jake worked it for what cotton he could get. He also worked in town when he could, and stayed drunk when he couldn't.

Elaine's mother took solace in the Pentecostal church. She had the plain appearance of a strict Holy Roller woman whose faith prohibited make-up, flashy clothes and haircuts. Young Elaine followed her mama in the faith. She was always right beside her whenever the doors of the church were open. She never went to the movies and she dressed according to the Holy Roller rules of modesty. But she was also a young girl full of life and hormones and flesh that was busting out all over. She could be a smart one, and sometimes a little bit of a tease.

The Kimbroughs' truck pulled up to the gas station near the store, and Barry got out to fill the tank. The mother and the baby stayed in the truck, and Elaine walked across a vacant lot full of high weeds to Woodside's store to buy groceries.

When Elaine walked up to the store, Darrell and Willie were sitting out front on the curb drinking their Cokes. Elaine walked straight toward the two black boys and made a point of stepping up onto the curb right where they were sitting. Willie immediately scrambled up and retreated across the sidewalk as the white girl approached. But Darrell was used to sitting where he pleased, so there he sat, on the curb, knee-high to Elaine Kimbrough's skirt.

Elaine stopped and stood on the curb right beside Darrell and said, "Ain't you gone move aside for a lady, nigger?"

"I will when I see one," said Darrell.

"Well, I swear, I never heard such!" said Elaine, and she gave Darrell a little kick in the side of his butt with her worn old, blunt-toed shoe. Darrell didn't say anything. He didn't even move. He just sat on the curb and stared straight ahead. Willie ducked behind a corner at the side of the store. But Elaine kept quiet and went inside to do her business.

When she came out of the store with an overflowing bag of groceries, Willie and Darrell were sitting on the railroad tracks all the way across the road. Elaine saw them and called out, "Hey, you, nigger boy, come tote this sack for me."

Willie jumped up to comply. But Elaine called back, "No, not you, the other one, with the smart mouth."

Darrell stood up and walked across the road toward Elaine and said, just loud enough for her to hear, "I'm not your nigger, and I'm not carrying anything, you low-class bitch."

Elaine spat in his face and stormed away toward the gas station, clutching her grocery bag with both arms. Darrell calmly wiped his face and retreated back to the tracks where his cousin stood. He thought that was the end of the story. After all, things like that happened all the time up in the big city, where all kinds of people bumped up against each other.

Willie knew better, and he dragged Darrell off toward home before he could get in any deeper. Elaine rode away in the red pick-up truck. While they were riding home, she told her mother and her cousin all about what the black boy had done and said.

That Saturday night, the lights were out early at Hosea Farmer's house. It was a long trip to the New Hope Baptist Church, and the first service started early the next morning. So Willie, Darrell and Hosea were all bathed and bedded down by 9:00.

Darrell and Willie had not dared tell Hosea what happened at the store that day. Hosea slept peacefully in the front of the two-room house. Willie tossed restlessly in his bed in the back. Darrell was settled in on a mat on the floor of the back room. He wasn't even trying to sleep.

Darrell was not used to this early-to-bed stuff. He missed the city life and city noises. He was playing the radio at a low volume under his blanket, listening to the Rufus Thomas show on WDIA out of Memphis.

Nobody else heard when the red pick-up truck pulled up in the yard. Only the two boys in the back room heard Hosea's scream as two white men with burlap bags over their heads kicked in his door. The shorter of the two men carried a small shiny silver pistol. The taller one carried a flashlight and a brand new, store-bought axe handle the size of a small baseball bat.

The tall man shined the flashlight in Hosea's eyes. "Where's the boy?" he demanded.

"What boy?" Hosea asked.

"You know what boy," the shorter one said. "The smart-mouthed little Yankee nigger you got staying here."

"Ain't no boys here," Hosea answered. "They out. I don't know where. It's Saturday night." Hosea was a big man and still strong in his mid-50s. But there was nothing he could do to stop the white men in his bedroom. They had a gun, and a lot more, on their side.

The two men looked around the room, trying to search in the dark through their narrow eye slits. The short one found the door to the back room. He threw the door open and the tall one aimed the light through it. Willie was hiding deep under his covers. He had been holding his breath since the front door broke down, and he would have held it until he died if necessary.

Darrell Farmer was sitting up on the floor looking into the light like a deer trapped in a poacher's spotlight. He was wearing his fancy red pajamas with the little horses' heads on them. On the mat beside him the radio was still on, softly playing Guitar Slim's "Things That I Used to Do."

- Three -

On Saturday, the night after he ran the car off Moriah Road, Tommy was again out driving in the pale green Chevy. This time he was alone, killing time, slowly creeping around the streets of Calhoun and listening to the Rufus Thomas show on WDIA. He was thinking about all the strange and frightening things that had happened the night before. The screaming crowd in the Armory. The sensation of flight. Elvis. The sudden disaster. The arm calling down thunder. The nearness of death. The crash of the drums. The sweet feeling of resurrection. "Have you heard the news?"

Tommy replayed it all obsessively while he drove laps around the Calhoun town square. On the radio Rufus Thomas played "Things That I Used to Do" by Guitar Slim from New Orleans. Tommy liked that one. Slim's guitar wailed like the angels of hell. Tommy swore that it was the loudest and ugliest sound ever recorded. And all the way through it, the piano kept ticking away high-note triplets, like the second hand of a clock.

After a few more passes around the square, Tommy cruised down River Road along the south side of the Calhoun River. The radio played "Maybelline" and he was suddenly inspired to drive back out Moriah Road and revisit the scene of last night's disaster. He thought it would be interesting to see if there were any signs of the wreck left behind.

It was about 10:00 when Tommy cruised out Moriah Road driving about 50. When he came to the beginning of the curve in the road, he slowed down and stopped and turned off his lights. He got out of the car and walked ahead until he came to the place in the gravel shoulder where there were ruts from his tires. He walked down the embankment and into the field. The moon was bright, and he could clearly see the deep tracks in the mud where his car had landed and where they had tried to climb the slope back up to the road. There was a shallower set of tire tracks through the field leading toward the dark farm house.

While Tommy was standing in the field, looking down at the tracks he'd made toward Calhoun, there was a thump of tires behind him. His heart jumped at the sound and he skipped a breath. Slowly Tommy turned. Off at some distance, there was a pick-up truck, with no headlights, driving across the bare, muddy cotton field. The truck kept going until it reached the line of small trees along the banks of the Little Muddy River about 200 yards away.

Tommy squatted among the cotton stalks to avoid being noticed, and watched the scene by the river. He was scared. A truck with no headlights seemed like trouble. And even if it wasn't trouble, he'd rather not explain why he was out alone in a cotton field in the middle of the night. Tommy wanted to leave. But the sound of his car would attract the attention of whoever was in the truck. He squatted in the shadows and watched.

Behind the trees Tommy saw two men take something long and large from the back of the truck. It took two of them to carry the object and they stumbled from its weight. At river's edge, they dropped the thing on the ground. Then one of the men retrieved another, smaller, heavy object from the front of the truck and dropped it beside the large thing.

One of the men held a flashlight while the other kneeled and worked over the two objects for a while. Tommy could hear their voices talking to each other but he couldn't make out what they said. They seemed angry. One of them raised his voice for a moment and Tommy made out the words, "Goddamnit, Billy, hurry up..." There was more, but he couldn't make it out.

Finally the two men dragged the objects on the ground over to the edge of the water, and pushed them in. They got back in the truck and started driving back across the field. When Tommy heard the truck engine crank, he lay out flat on his belly in the muddy field. He cocked up his head enough to see through the dead cotton stalks as the truck passed on its way through the field.

The truck still had no lights on, but with a longer and closer look, Tommy made out more details. The truck was red and old, and he knew that he'd seen it before. It was exactly like the truck that his high school classmate Barry Kimbrough drove around town sometimes on the weekends. It was a truck that belonged to Barry's father, Billy Kimbrough.

When Tommy couldn't hear the truck anymore, he scrambled back up the embankment and jumped into his car. He made a turnabout in the middle of the road, and didn't turn on his headlights until he was almost back to Calhoun.

Tommy was terrified. He wondered if this stretch of Moriah Road was cursed. There were nothing but bad things out there at night. He was ready to swear that he would never cross the Little Muddy River again. He was worried because Billy Kimbrough was bad news, and everybody in town knew it. He had been in and out of jail most of his life. Three years ago, he was in the state penitentiary at Parchman doing a stretch for burglary. When he got out, Hayden White had hired him as a handyman on his plantation, mainly because he felt sorry for Kimbrough's family.

Billy Kimbrough had kept out of trouble since then as far as anyone knew. But nobody would have been surprised if he'd ended up in jail again. Everybody said that he was just naturally mean. Tommy knew that his son Barry was naturally mean. He was the biggest bully in town and had been since elementary school. Tommy had spent much of his childhood hiding from Barry Kimbrough. Now he was worrying about the father, too.

As he drove home, following the speed limits to the letter, Tommy tried to tell himself that whatever he'd seen couldn't have been important. And it certainly didn't have anything to do with him. But inside, Tommy knew that just seeing whatever it was he'd just seen made him a part of the thing, whatever it was, whether he wanted to be or not.

This was a lot worse than what had happened the night before. Car wrecks can only kill the body. This kind of stuff could eat up your soul. There was no sense of release or feeling of redemption for Tommy at the end of this night. There was only the bone-chilling dread that whatever it was that had happened might not be over yet.

- Four -

Monday morning life started up again as if nothing had happened. By 7:45 Tommy was in the parking lot at Calhoun High School. He was leaning against the hood of a car, squinting into the sun and smoking the day's first sweet and intoxicating cigarette. The sun was warm but the cars were still damp with a layer of dew. Jack and Wade were in the parking lot alongside Tommy. Together they were telling a circle of other guys from their class about their Friday night adventures.

When it came to the wreck, Wade did most of the talking. He loved to dramatize things. At the part where they ran off the road, he leapt across the parking lot himself and held out his arms like airplane wings to describe how they had hovered in mid-air. Wade was on his third telling, and each time the speed got faster and the flight got higher and longer.

Finally Jack got bored and said, "Wade, stop talking shit. You hid behind the seat from the time that we got above 80."

"Did not," Wade answered, "and besides, what do you know? You were the one who liked to turned us over with your bright idea about driving up that slope."

Wade and Jack each stomped out their cigarettes and squared off facing each other at arm's length. Wade and Jack didn't like each other very much. They were thrown in together because they were both friends with Tommy.

Tommy intervened by changing the subject. "None of it would have happened if it hadn't been for Elvis," he said, "he is really something, I tell you. We left that old Armory so pumped up that we just had to fly."

As Tommy spoke, he was half-listening to another conversation taking place somewhere behind his right shoulder. There Barry Kimbrough was leaning against the side of his daddy's old, red pick-up truck, holding forth to a gaggle of his redneck buddies. Kimbrough was spitting tobacco juice and grinning a squinty-eyed grin. In bits and pieces, Tommy could hear him discussing the hidden parts and secret doings of some of the girls gathered around the front door of the school.

"That one yonder," Kimbrough said loudly, "that Darlene Shaw, well she may look like a blonde but she's brown down where it counts. Take my word for it. Now that one next to her, yeah, the cheerleader. I hear that she did the entire boys' basketball team on that road trip over to Sharkey last month."

Kimbrough's nasty talk reached a climaxe when Cheryl Parker got out of her mother's car and walked across the parking lot. Cheryl Parker was the homecoming queen and the reigning Miss Calhoun. Her father owned 2500 acres of cotton land and the biggest bank in town. Kimbrough looked at her across the rows of cars, snorted, and spit. "Now that rich-assed little bitch won't drop her drawers for any white man. But I hear she's sucked every nigger dick on her daddy's place. Can't get enough of it..."

Cheryl Parker stopped and got into a shiny, red Thunderbird belonging to one of her rich boy friends. As she disappeared from view, Kimbrough's voice trailed off and his circle of friends grew quiet, lost in thought about Cheryl Parker and the oral act. It was during this lull in the action that Kimbrough heard Tommy Jackson three cars away, describing Elvis Presley's performance.

"...yeah, it was great," Tommy was saying, "They did all the songs on his records and a lot of Bill Haley and Big Joe Turner, too. The kids were going wild. You couldn't hardly hear the music over all the screaming..."

Kimbrough swaggered over and planted his fireplug of a body in the midst of Tommy's friends and classmates. He was wearing a white T-shirt with the sleeves rolled up and blue jeans with big cuffs. He had a very short flat-top haircut. A plug of tobacco in his left jaw stuck out from his otherwise smooth and squared-off head.

Kimbrough walked over to Jack Gerard and abruptly pulled out Jack's shirttail. He grabbed the cigarette from Tommy's mouth and said, "So you and your little fag buddies went to see that greasy white nigger Presley? I bet you liked that. I bet that wiggle-assed sissy got you boys real hot, didn't he?"

Tommy looked at the pavement and said only, "I kind of like the music is all."

"Music, hell," Kimbrough snorted. "It ain't nothing but nigger music." He got right up in Tommy's face, spraying tobacco juice with every syllable, and said loudly, "Nigger music for nigger lovers!" He spit a big, brown tobacco gob right in Tommy's face and walked away.

Most of the kids scattered around the parking lot had watched this confrontation. They got quiet as Kimbrough walked back to his group of friends. Wade handed Tommy a handkerchief, and he wiped his face as best he could. His eyes stung from the juice and the anger, but he didn't answer back. He was afraid to get into any trouble with those Kimbroughs.

When Tommy's eyes cleared, he saw the group of rich boys and girls gathered around the red T-Bird watching him. They all looked away when they caught Tommy's glance, all except Dicky White. Dicky White stepped a couple of paces toward Tommy and stood, staring, with a pained look on his pale, thin-lipped face.

Dicky was a junior at Calhoun High. His father was Hayden White, the big planter. Tommy didn't really know Dicky. He was a quiet guy. He had lank, sand-colored hair, and was slim and fragile-looking, with arms and legs like long pipe-cleaners. He mostly stayed close to a small circle of other rich kids and didn't take part in school activities. But Dicky knew Barry

Kimbrough, since Kimbrough's father worked for his father. Dicky looked at Tommy across the distance, as if he were trying to say something, but nothing came out. Their eyes locked together for a moment, and Tommy looked away.

Two weeks passed, and the days grew hot and long. Tommy kept his ears wide open but heard nothing about any bad business out Moriah Road on a Saturday night. He almost convinced himself what he'd seen was just an illegal trash dump. Then, a few miles downriver, at Johnson's Crossing, the truth surfaced like a bad dream.

Some black boys were swimming in the river on a hot Saturday afternoon when a stinking, bloated corpse floated down the river like a barge. The terrified boys scrambled out of the water and one of them fetched his mother. She called the sheriff. An ambulance took the body to the morgue at Calhoun Hospital and the sheriff sent word to Darrell Farmer's mother.

On the night that Darrell had disappeared, Hosea Farmer had driven to a neighbor's house and called the sheriff. The next morning, a deputy had come to the house and heard Hosea's report of two men with burlap hoods and a red pick-up truck. Willie didn't say anything about what had happened at Woodside's store, not even to Hosea.

That same day Hosea also made a long distance collect phone call to Darrell's parents up in St. Louis. Mrs. Cordelia Farmer came to Calhoun on the next train, and had been there ever since. Cordelia Farmer was a big woman, tall and large-framed. She wore floral-print dresses and big hats. She spoke in a deep theatrical voice and bit off her words with precision.

Every weekday for two weeks, Cordelia Farmer stopped in at the sheriff's office and asked if there was any news about her boy. Every time the sheriff sat in his swivel chair, wearing his straw cowboy hat, and said, without looking up from his desk, "Nope, nothing's turned up." Finally one day the sheriff laid his hat on the desk and looked straight at her. He said, "Girl, did you ever think that maybe the boy just ran away? Maybe Hosea just made up that stuff about the men with the hoods so you wouldn't find out that he let your boy get away?"

She answered calmly, "No, that has never occurred to me." She turned to leave the office and slammed the door on her way out.

Cordelia Farmer didn't see the sheriff again until she met him at the morgue. The morgue was a windowless room at the back of the hospital where they kept the air-conditioning up extra high. The sheriff was waiting in the hall outside with one of his deputies and the county coroner. They led Cordelia Farmer into the room. The coroner passed out surgical masks to keep out the stink and the germs from the corpse that lay on the table. There was a white sheet over the body. The coroner pulled the sheet back from the head and torso. "Is this your son?" he asked.

The body had been in the water for two weeks and was badly damaged. The parts were all intact, but they were swollen and discolored and out of proportion. There were torn places in the skin and flesh. The eyes were swollen shut and the mouth was collapsed inward. The head was enlarged and lumpy. Patches of hair were missing, and there were tears in the scalp and cracks in the skull.

As she looked at the head of the corpse, Cordelia Farmer felt hot bile and acid coming up in her throat. But she did not turn away. She kept looking, trying to focus on the face. She kept trying to see in that face someone who had once been. She stared at the face until her stomach started to turn. She looked away and closed her eyes tight. When she turned her gaze back to the corpse, she looked down at the swollen flesh of the torso. A few patches of clothing remained on the body. The fabric was shiny and red and bore a horse head design.

Cordelia Farmer choked when she saw that. She tried to speak, but her throat locked shut. She tried again, but no words came out, only a long moan. Behind the moaning flowed out a torrent of tears. She ripped the surgical mask off her face and placed her hand on a piece of fabric that lay over her son's heart. She cried until she was shaking. Finally the crying subsided, and she said, "That's my boy. That's his pajamas. He was wearing them that night."

The sheriff nodded. The coroner removed Cordelia Farmer's hand from the corpse and pulled the sheet back over the head. The sheriff put his hand on the mother's shoulder to lead her away. But she turned from him. She went down on her knees beside the coroner's table and screamed at the sheriff, "What did they do to my boy? How did he get like this? Who did it? Tell me! I know you know!"

The sheriff turned to his deputy and said, "Get her out of here." He left the room and waited in the hall. When Cordelia Farmer finally emerged, he looked her in the eye and said, "It looks like a drowning. The coroner's report will be in tomorrow."

"But his body, you saw it, how did it get so beaten up?" she asked.

"Collisions with tree branches and river debris," said the sheriff, "only thing it could be."

Cordelia Farmer straightened herself to her full height, held back her tears, and said sternly, "The truth is not in you people. When can I take my boy away from here?"

"Soon as the coroner is finished," he answered, "say 5:00 this evening?"

"I'll be back then," she said. She walked slowly down the corridor and out into the blinding sun.

Hayden White was in his office at the big plantation house that afternoon when the sheriff called. He was sitting at his desk going over the spring allotments for his tenants. He picked up the phone, and, when he heard who it was, he put his pencil down and turned from the ledger books.

Hayden White was a tall man, about 6'3". In his mid-50s, he had a full head of totally white hair. His face was pale and thin-lipped with watery-blue eyes, like his boy Dicky. His body was long-limbed and lean. He usually stood ramrod straight, like the aristocrat that he was, but he crumpled down low in his office chair as he listened to the sheriff.

"Mr. White," the officer said, "You remember a while back old Hosea on your place reported his nephew missing? Well, he's found. His mama, from up in St. Louis, just identified him." The sheriff was silent. Hayden White said impatiently, "Yes, so..."

The sheriff continued, "Looks like a drowning, sir. He was floating in the Little Muddy River down to Johnson's Crossing. He was in the water for a long time and he was pretty messed up, but the mama recognized his clothes."

There was a long silence. Finally the sheriff added, "Just thought you'd want to know, since it's your people and all."

Hayden White sat with the phone to his ear and his eyes gazing blankly at the ceiling. "Yes," he said softly, "thanks for calling." There was another silence. Hayden White hung up the phone without saying goodbye.

He swiveled his desk chair around and looked out the big double window of his plantation office. He was troubled by this whole affair with the Farmer boy. He had been from the start. The day after the boy disappeared, he had heard whisperings among his workers about night riders. He had bided his time, hoping that the boy might be found alive. But in his heart, Hayden White knew all along that bad things were happening in his hometown.

He had half-expected something like this, what with all the wild talk going on since the Supreme Court decision last year. Hayden White was for segregation. At first he had even joined the White Citizens Council with the others, but the talk bothered him. There were too many speeches about over-sexed black boys coming after pure little white girls. It just raised people's temperatures, he thought, and it made some of them a little crazier than they already were.

Through his office window, Hayden White saw the banks of the Little Muddy River off in the distance. Between the house and the river, tractors were out pulling plows in the fields. The motors hummed in the background. They were turning under the old stalks and digging up the ground for planting time.

Hayden White stared off toward the river for a long time. He thought about that boy floating in it, and about the grieving mother, and about his old friend Hosea. Hayden White had known Hosea Farmer all his life. They had played ball and ridden horses together when they were little. He decided to drop by the Farmer cabin that evening for a talk.

If Hosea Farmer said that his nephew was killed by night riders, it was so, and action would have to be taken. Hayden White was no crusader. But this involved one of his people, on his land. That made him responsible, and Hayden White was not a man to shirk responsibility.

- Five -

The Calhoun coroner ruled the death of Darrell Farmer to be an accidental drowning. He said that Darrell sneaked out of the house, got lost in the dark, and fell into the river. Darrell's family admitted that the boy couldn't swim, and that was in the report. Their testimony about the two men and the red truck was not.

When the official report came out, Darrell's body was already on a train headed north along with his mother, uncle and cousin. Cordelia Farmer called the St. Louis NAACP to help get some justice for her boy. The NAACP sent a doctor to the funeral home to look at the body before it was embalmed. This doctor said that there was no water in the lungs. Darrell was already dead when he hit the river. The doctor also said Darrell's skull was broken in several places, and concluded that he was killed by blows to the head.

The NAACP also sent a lawyer and a private investigator to interview Willie and Hosea. That was when Willie finally told the complete and true story about the incident with Elaine Kimbrough. The investigator took pictures of Darrell's body. The lawyer sent a package, to all of the St. Louis newspapers and wire service offices, that contained the doctor's report, the transcripts of the interviews with Hosea and Willie, and "before and after" photographs of Darrell Farmer's face. On the day after Darrell's funeral, the story was in all the local papers and went out on the wires nationwide.

The wire service story about Darrell Farmer turned up in the Memphis papers. That was as close as the story came to Calhoun. There was a daily paper in the town, but it completely ignored the death of Darrell Farmer. The story was also mentioned on television. But not many people had TV sets.

Tommy Jackson's family didn't get the Memphis papers or own a TV. But Jack Gerard's family did. Tommy and Jack and Wade were smoking in the parking lot before school when Jack mentioned something he had heard on the Today show that morning.

"They're making a big stink up North about some nigger that was killed in Calhoun," he said. "First time I've heard mention of Calhoun on TV. But there it was, nationwide, on Dave Garroway."

Wade said, "Yeah, I heard something about that. It had to do with him cussing a white girl, didn't it?"

"They didn't say," Jack answered, "How did you hear about it? You don't have a TV."

"Aw, folks have been talking around town the last few days, you just don't know the right people," Wade said.

While his friends were bickering, Tommy's stomach rose and his head started feeling light. Something told him that this story might answer some questions he was afraid to ask. Tommy didn't press his friends for details. That would look suspicious. Instead he spent the rest of the day worrying and wondering.

When the last school bell rang, Tommy quickly walked the six long blocks to the drugstore downtown. Inside the store he looked through the rack of newspapers until he found one that had a story about a dead black boy. It was the *Memphis Press Scimitar*. Tommy paid his nickel and took the paper outside. He stood on the sidewalk, under the shade of the drugstore canopy, and leaned against the red brick wall.

Tommy read the story carefully. It was in the bottom left corner of the front page. Above the article was Darrell Farmer's eighth grade school picture. The Memphis paper didn't use the picture of the corpse, but the story described the damage to Darrell's body. It quoted Hosea Farmer's account of hooded men bursting into his house on a Saturday night, and it gave Willie Farmer's version of what happened at Woodside's store.

Tommy stopped reading when he reached the words "Elaine Kimbrough." When he saw her family name, Tommy was struck with the full weight of what he had seen out Moriah Road. It struck him so hard that he was sure the weight of it would push him down into the sidewalk if he stood still for another moment. His face was red and his heart was pounding. People were walking by on the sidewalk, and he thought that every one of them was staring at him. He quickly folded the newspaper and hid it in one of his school notebooks. With his eyes fixed on the sidewalk, he began walking home.

On the way home, Tommy's feet moved carefully and deliberately forward as the business district gave way to houses, first brick, and then wood frame, all with big front porches and some degree of wear and tear. As he walked, Tommy's mind raced back to that night out Moriah Road. Those murky events on the river bank were suddenly all too clear. In his mind he saw the small stand of trees and the red truck. He heard the voices mutter and curse. He saw the large object and the smaller one. But now the large object was a boy just one year younger than himself. The boy had a face. He was smiling and dressed for his eighth grade picture.

It had been dark that night out Moriah Road, but now the light was shining. Billy Kimbrough and some other man had killed Darrell Farmer that night because of what he had said to Elaine. Tommy had seen them dumping the body. This dead black boy was on the front page of the newspapers, and even on television, and Tommy knew who one of the killers was. He was a witness.

Tommy arrived back at his house out of breath. His mother was home from her job at the dry goods store. Through the side window, Tommy saw her working in the kitchen. There was white powder on her face and he could smell the biscuit dough.

Everyone except the preacher and door-to-door salesmen always came into the Jacksons' house through the back way. But that door opened into the kitchen, and Tommy didn't want to talk to his mother. So he walked all the way around and quietly came in the front. The front hall was still and dark. Tommy followed it down the length of the house toward his bedroom, which was the last door on the right.

When he neared the kitchen doorway, Tommy walked rapidly, on tiptoes. His mother was at the counter by the stove. She was wearing a red and white checked and flour-dusted apron over her office dress. Her reading glasses were pushed up into waves of dark brown hair. She was cutting out biscuits with the floured rim of a water glass and lining them up on a cookie sheet.

As Tommy passed the door in a blur, his mother said, without looking, "What's your hurry, son? Something wrong?"

"Naw, nothing. Just a lot of homework to do," Tommy said.

"Well, good," she called down the hall, "get it done before supper. Josie and Robbie are coming over tonight." Josie was Tommy's 20-year-old sister and Robbie was her husband. They were the center of attention at Tommy's house in those days because Josie was expecting a baby.

Tommy didn't answer his mother. He was already in his room. He pushed a chair up against the doorknob and spread the Memphis paper on his bed. He read the story about Darrell Farmer over and over at least a dozen times. The paper said that the body was bloated and beaten beyond recognition. His own mother didn't recognize him except for some scraps of his clothes. The story also said that the Farmer boy had used a curse word to Elaine Kimbrough earlier on the day of his disappearance. It didn't say what the word was.

The Calhoun sheriff said that he didn't know about any incident with a white girl, and he stood by the conclusion that Darrell Farmer's death was an accident. The story ended with a St. Louis preacher at Darrell's funeral saying, "The state of Mississippi will not know peace until it gives equal value to the lives of all people, regardless of color."

There was no peace any more for Tommy Jackson, that was for sure. He read the story until his eyes wouldn't focus anymore. He laid back on his bed and held the paper at arm's length above him. He looked at Darrell Farmer's face in the picture until his head ached. He dropped the paper onto his chest and lay still. He stared at the flaky plaster ceiling of his room and listened to his thoughts running wild.

Tommy knew that there were rules about how black and white people acted with each other. He knew that if black people broke those rules, they got punished. He also knew that one of the rules was that you never took sides against another white person when a black was involved. He'd learned these things from the time he was a child, from the time that he was taught to say "sir" and "ma'am" to grown-ups, but not to colored people. He was taught that they were somehow not as good as the white people.

But he knew that the colored people were people, too. As Tommy lay there on his bed with the newspaper over his chest, he thought of the days before his family had moved to town. They had lived on a farm until Tommy was nine, and there was nothing but black people out there. Their only neighbor was a black family that lived a short walk down the gravel road. The children of that family were his only playmates, especially when his sister Josie was off at school.

Tommy remembered that once, when he was in the first grade, the father of that black family up the road had come to their house at night to pick up a sofa. Tommy's grandparents had passed down their old couch so Tommy's parents were passing their even older one down the line. The black man came into the Jacksons' house through the front door and took his cap off. It was night time and it was chilly outside. Tommy remembered the rush of cold air while the door stood open for the couch to get through. Tommy's father said, "Hope y'all can get some use out of this thing."

Tommy jumped in and said, "Yeah, it was good enough for us, it ought to be good enough for y'all."

When the words left his mouth he knew that he'd done wrong. The black man just looked at the floor and murmured, "That's right, Mr. Tommy." Even a little child could see that he was hurt. Tommy's mother said, "Be quiet, boy." Tommy ran back to the bedroom and cried. Later his mother came in to comfort him. She said, "Tommy, we treat the colored people different, but we don't treat them bad. They can't help being colored. They've got feelings like us and it's wrong to hurt them."

As the almost grown teenager lay on his bed that afternoon, he became the little boy again. He felt guilty and scared. He kept thinking about that poor dead black boy. Tommy knew that nobody deserved to die for saying a bad word, no matter what. That was wrong. He wanted to cry. He wanted to go in the kitchen and tell his mother all about it and have everything be alright. But he couldn't find his tears anymore, and he couldn't tell anyone what he knew, not even his mother. It was all too dangerous and scary.

Finally Tommy curled up on the bed and pulled the pillow over his head. He put his little bedside radio under the pillow with him and turned it on low with the speaker right up against his ear. He lay there like that for a long time, until his mother called for supper, losing himself in the stream of rhythm and blues music that came rushing down from Memphis. He lay there and listened and said to himself, "Jesus tell me what to do. Jesus tell me what to do. Jesus tell me what to do."

For the next week or so, there were reporters and film crews all over Calhoun, Mississippi and the surrounding area. They came down from St. Louis and Chicago and even New York City. They took pictures of Hosea

Farmer's house, and the courthouse, and they went hunting for really poor shotgun houses to show how the black people suffered. Moriah Road looked like a Hollywood film set, there were so many big movie cameras trucking back and forth.

After the first round of stories, the Calhoun sheriff stopped talking to reporters. Desperate for local white reaction, reporters took to stopping people on the street downtown and asking them what they thought about the Darrell Farmer case. Most people either wouldn't talk or said they didn't know anything. Some people said things like, "The nigger had it coming." They were the ones who got on TV.

Sometime during this frenzy, Hayden White agreed to an interview with a reporter from the *Atlanta Constitution.* White had quietly stepped into the case the night after Darrell's body was found. That night the planter had stood on the porch of Hosea Farmer's house and heard his boyhood friend swear that his nephew was taken by white men wearing burlap hoods.

When the connection to the Kimbroughs came out, that brought things even closer to home, since the girl's uncle worked for the Whites. Hayden White had questioned Billy Kimbrough about the case directly. But he had denied knowing anything.

Hayden White knew that somebody in the Calhoun community must know something. Somebody saw or heard something, either that night, or since. But nobody was doing anything. The sheriff claimed that there had not been a crime. Hayden White hoped that a public statement from him, acting as the conscience of the community, might make it easier for someone to come forward. He knew that rarely happened with such cases in the South, and never in Mississippi. But he thought that the times might be changing. So he spoke out, and hoped for the best.

The results appeared in the *Constitution* a few days later, but nobody in Calhoun ever saw that paper. A few more days passed and the Jackson, Mississippi paper reprinted a quotation from the interview. The quote read, "This incident is an insult to the good white people of Calhoun. If the Farmer boy did anything out of line, we have laws to deal with it. We have laws to deal with a killing, too. The men responsible for this must come to justice, right here in Calhoun, Mississippi."

One cloudy May morning, a few days after that quotation appeared, the white people of Calhoun, Mississippi walked onto their porches and found a piece of paper. It was the same piece of paper stuck into the mailbox or door handle of every home and business on the white side of town. At the top of the paper was a crude drawing of a rat. Underneath the rat was a typed message that said:

"Lately the names of certain prominent local persons was seen in the papers making threats against the Defenders of White Southern Womanhood. These prominent persons claim to be speaking they lies for the White people of Calhoun. This person is a traitor to the White Race. We call a traitor to the Race by the right name. They are rats. This so-called prominent citizen is a stinking rat. Anyone else who speaks out against the White Race and it's Defenders is a rat. Any White man who comes out for the dead nigger, Darrell Farmer, is a rat. IT'S RAT KILLING TIME!!!

Signed-- The White Knights of the Imperial Order of the Ku Klux Klan, John C. Calhoun Chapter."

At Hayden White's office downtown by the cotton market, the paper was nailed to the door along with a real, stinking, dead river rat. The nail was hammered through the rat's thick tail.

Tommy Jackson's parents grabbed the paper off the front porch before he saw it. But Jack Gerard was the first one up at his house. He had a copy of the paper at school that day. So did a lot of other kids. In every class all day the papers were passed around to secret snickers. They called it the Rat Sheet. Tommy's head burned every time he saw it. It was as if everyone knew that he knew and the whole town was secretly stalking him to see if he would crack.

At lunch Wade Suggs told Tommy and Jack about the rat on the door to Hayden White's office. That made Tommy feel relieved. It reminded him that this episode wasn't about him. Nobody really knew that he knew. They couldn't unless he told them. The White Knights didn't know he existed. They were after Hayden White, and Hayden White was big enough and rich enough to take care of himself.

Tommy knew Hayden White. Everybody in town knew him by sight, and half the town had business with him. But Tommy felt that he really knew him because Hayden White taught his Sunday School class at the First Baptist Church.

On the Sunday after the Rat Sheet appeared, the six boys in the class were seated in the usual circle of old wooden folding chairs. They had on their coats and ties and were carrying their Bibles and their Sunday School lesson books. But Mr. White was late. One of the boys said, "I bet he ain't coming. I bet he's staying in his rat hole today." And some of them laughed.

Tommy just sat and tugged at his necktie and looked at the floor. Wade Suggs was in the class; Jack Gerard was an Episcopalian. Except for Wade, the boys at the church weren't Tommy's friends. They were just guys that he knew. Most of them lived on the north side of town. He was always uncomfortable with them, but this week being in the class was physically painful. The old chair seemed to hurt in new places, and the small room seemed to be shrinking. He wanted to scream and jump out the thick frosted-glass window. Instead he opened his book and pretended to be reading the lesson.

Finally Mr. White walked in and folded his long frame into the tiny chair nearest the door. He looked around and said, "Well, men, how was the week?" There was silence. Every head in the room was turned to the floor except Hayden White's.

Finally he spoke again. "Well, I've had quite a week. You've probably heard about some of it. This isn't the place to talk about that. But there is one passage of Scripture that I've been drawn to all week. I feel that I should read it to you this morning, and let the Lord speak as He will."

Hayden White opened his Bible to the spot that was marked by a long red ribbon. "It's in the Gospel of John, chapter eight, verses 31 and 32. Will you follow along with me, please?" All the boys opened their Bibles. The rustle of pages filled the room as Mr. White waited for them to find the place.

He began to read, "Then said Jesus to those Jews which believed on him. If ye continue in my word, then are ye my disciples indeed; and ye shall know the truth, and the truth shall make you free."

There was a long quiet moment. Then, as he did every week, Mr. White said, "Bow your heads, please," and he led an opening prayer. "Lord," he prayed, "please guide each of us with the light of your truth, and show us the way that we should walk in the paths of our lives. We pray in Jesus' name. Amen."

"OK, men," he said, "let's get onto the lesson."

Tommy Jackson didn't hear another word that was said that morning. Somehow he made it to the church service after Sunday School. He sat in the balcony with Wade, but he didn't hear anything that Wade said or anything that happened in the service. All that he heard that morning, over and over, was, "The truth shall make you free." Jesus had said it, so he knew that it must be right, but that Sunday morning Tommy Jackson knew the truth, and he did not feel very free. He just felt more guilty and scared than ever before.

He couldn't deal with this. The Klan said they would kill people who said anything, and Tommy knew that they would. All week the kids at school had been telling stories about the Klan. Seemed that years ago a white man came to Calhoun who was living common law with a black woman. The Klan hung that white man from an oak tree and put out one of their "messages" about it to make sure everybody knew.

If they didn't kill a young boy like Tommy, they would at least run him and his family out of town. Just last year the Kaplans, who had a shoe store in the colored section, were run out of town because people said they were giving money to the NAACP. Tommy knew about that. The Kaplans had a daughter at Calhoun High, and she just disappeared one day. Off to New Orleans, people said.

Now here came Hayden White throwing Jesus at him. Sitting in the balcony of the First Baptist Church, Tommy thought that Hayden White and Jesus would have to take on the Klan by themselves.

- Six -

In the summer of 1955, Tommy, Jack and Wade all got jobs. Tommy worked at the building supply company where his father was a clerk. Jack was on a construction crew at the Parker place. Wade had a cushy, air-conditioned job packing groceries at the Piggly-Wiggly. For the first time in their lives they all had money in their pockets and a license to drive. Most week nights they were too tired to do much. But from Friday afternoon to Monday morning, they were almost free.

What they did most of the time was drink. Usually Tommy collected Wade and Jack in the green Chevy after supper. They would stop at Mackey's for a while, and stick around if anything was happening. When Mackey's got dull, they would get back in the car and head for the country. They rode around like drunken sailors floating unsteadily through the sea of cotton fields. Some nights they sailed so long that they almost lost their land legs. Then they would sneak back into their houses and sleep it off.

By Sunday morning Tommy would be queasy and cotton-mouthed from all the beer and cigarettes. Sunday nights he always stayed home and went to bed early. He needed rest because his job was physically demanding. He worked in the yard outside the company warehouse, loading and unloading, and stacking the shelves with cast-iron pipe and lumber and steel. He spent much of the week in a boxcar or truck, loading and unloading heavy crates of nails and bundles of roofing. By mid-day the temperature was usually above 90 degrees. In a boxcar it could easily top 120. By lunch break on Monday, the poisons of the weekend were all sweated out.

Tommy didn't mind the work. It made him feel like a man. This was what men did. He was even starting to develop muscles and lose some of the roundness in his face and hands. Tommy's father had worked in this same yard for years until they moved him inside. Tommy and his father rode to and from work together every day. They said very little, but it was the closest connection they'd had since Little League baseball.

In the yard, Tommy could forget everything that worried him and seemed to set him apart. He could be just one of the guys. The guys talked about baseball and cars and women, and Tommy listened and laughed along. As the summer wore on, he even managed to forget about Darrell Farmer, once in a while.

Hayden White's efforts in the Farmer case did some good. The sheriff changed his mind about the accidental drowning theory, and was conducting a murder investigation. That quieted things down for the summer, even though no one, black or white, really expected anything to come of it.

For Tommy, the most interesting thing about working in the yard was getting to work alongside the black men. The white guys were fun, but they were just grown-up versions of the kids he knew in school. He had not been around black people this way since he and his farm friends were separated and sent to school. Tommy was especially fond of a man named Edward Banks. He was in his late 40s and always wore dark green khaki coveralls, like a mechanic's uniform, with a matching cap. He smoked unfiltered Pall Mall cigarettes all day long, except right before payday when he'd sometimes roll his own from a tin can of Prince Albert tobacco.

Edward Banks had been a sharecropper on the Parker plantation until a couple of years ago. When the Parkers went to tractors and mechanical cotton pickers, they started phasing out their tenants. With all the new equipment, one man could work hundreds of acres almost by himself. That's when Edward Banks came to town and got a job at the building supply house.

The week of the Fourth of July holiday, Tommy was working with Edward Banks up in a stifling hot boxcar. They were unloading 50-pound crates of roofing nails, using a hook to hoist the cartons by their metal bands. The sweat poured off of them in waterfalls. After working for ten minutes, every inch of their clothing, down to the socks, was soaking wet. Edward Banks was filling the enclosure with smoke from his Pall Malls. He lit a cigarette and never took it out of his mouth until it burned to the nub. Then he spat it out through the boxcar door and lit another one. The sweat dripping from his face dampened the cigarettes and he had to puff furiously to keep the fire alive.

They were alone in the boxcar, and Tommy seized the opportunity to ask a question. "Hey, Edward," he said, "You know anything about the blues?"

Edward Banks laughed deep and loud and said, "Naw, except I've lived them almost 50 years."

Tommy said, "No, I mean the music."

The black man laughed even louder and said, "There ain't but a breath between the living and the singing. Just a breath. Like breathing in and breathing out." He demonstrated this with a gust of air that filled the freight car with stinging blue smoke.

Before Tommy could think of a reply, Edward Banks continued, "I know what you talking about Mr. Tommy. I heard you talking to them other fellows about that Elvis and all." He smiled a big yellow-toothed smile, with the stub of a cigarette stuck in one corner. "You one of them hep cats, ain't you?"

Tommy said, "Well, maybe. I don't know what it is. But I just can't stay away from that music."

Edward Banks put down his hook and walked to the boxcar door. He spat out his cigarette and stood in the fresh air for a moment. He leaned back and began to speak, "Well, Mr. Tommy, the blues ain't going to cause no harm. Blues is good for everybody and everything. They make an old man hard and a young man easy. Make the bacon lean and the chicken greasy. Make the young girls shine, bring eyesight to the blind. They cure anything except piles, and make you forget about them, too, for a while. If you young white peckerwoods start messing with the blues, it might do y'all some good too."

"How you mean?" Tommy asked.

"Oh, everyhow. Make you see what folks are really like, that they all the same. Make you horny and drunk so you don't get so much money all the time."

Tommy laughed and said, "I don't have much money. I'm just working, same as you."

Edward Banks turned grim. He looked down at the boxcar floor and said, "Uh, huh." He went back to the end of the car and picked up his hook.

They resumed swinging the crates. For a long time, they worked in silence. Finally Tommy straightened up from his work, and asked the question that was really on his mind, "Tell me Edward, where could somebody go to hear rhythm and blues bands play here around Calhoun?"

Edward Banks started working faster, and puffing harder on his cigarette. He answered without looking up. "Oh, no sir, Mr. Tommy, I wouldn't know about that. I don't go to them kind of places. They ain't for decent folks. If you want to hear the colored folks sing, maybe you ought to go to church. Folks would be glad to have you come hear the singing at church. I go to the Zion Missionary Baptist right around the corner from here. We've got a fine choir. You could come around some Sunday afternoon. But you ought not be asking about them juke joints. That's dangerous."

Tommy was embarrassed and confused. He didn't want to go to any church. He tried to think of another way to ask his question. But Edward Banks had turned away from him. He was working at a faster pace and had begun to sing, right out loud, "Leaning on the Everlasting Arms."

One Friday night in July, Jack, Wade and Tommy were drinking beer at Mackey's. Tommy and Jack were sitting on one side of a booth along the wall. Wade sat across from them, on the side that faced the door. On the table was their second pitcher of draft beer, three mugs and an ashtray. They were talking about work. The jukebox was playing. The place was loud and everything was normal. Then Tommy noticed Wade staring toward the door with a scared look on his face. Tommy turned toward the door. Jack turned, too, and by then the whole crowd in Mackey's had noticed the arrival of Dicky White.

Dicky stood in the doorway dressed in a polo shirt and khaki trousers with cuffs. His clothes were baggy and made him look even skinnier than he was. When he walked into the joint, everybody stopped talking and stared. He had never been to Mackey's before. Dicky looked around at the people one by one. His direct gaze embarrassed them into minding their own business. Tommy and Jack turned back to work on their pitcher, but Wade was ignoring them. He kept staring right over Tommy's shoulder, toward Dicky White.

When he entered Mackey's, Dicky turned right and walked down the row of booths along the wall, until he reached the booth where Tommy and Jack and Wade were sitting. He stood for a long moment, right beside their table, staring at Wade.

Dicky's face had the same hurt look that Tommy had seen in the school parking lot after his encounter with Barry Kimbrough. He looked like he was trying to say something to Wade. Then he just walked away. Tommy and Jack exchanged sideways glances. They didn't say anything.

Wade was embarrassed. He tried to turn attention away from himself by talking about the latest adventures of his cousin in Greenville, who rode a motorcycle and had fought in Korea. "That Johnny is really something," Wade said, pausing to take a long drink of beer. "He just took off last week riding his motorcycle out to California. Took that fine little girlfriend of his with him, too. He's a real cat, that Johnny..."

While Wade talked, Dicky White bought a beer at the bar. He stood alone in a far corner of the room, sipping it. Every once in a while, Wade interrupted himself to glance in Dicky's direction. After a while he excused himself to go to the bathroom. Wade was gone for a long time. When Tommy and Jack looked around for him, they saw him huddled in the corner with Dicky White, talking very seriously.

When Wade came back to the booth, Jack asked, "What's the deal here? First this guy comes over here giving you the bug eye. Then you're off in the corner with him. I don't get it. When did you get to be friends with Dicky White?"

Wade stammered, "Oh, we, we're not friends. It's just that he comes in the store sometimes. Once I got to telling him about my cousin Johnny and he said he'd like to meet him. So I was just telling him about Johnny going out of town for the summer, that's all. I swear."

"You swear?" Jack said.

While Wade was explaining, Mackey's front door slammed shut. Tommy looked toward the sound, and interrupted his friends. "Forget Dicky White," he said, "There's some real entertainment coming in." Wade and Jack looked to the door. Barry Kimbrough was walking in with two of his buddies following close behind. All three of them were sunburned and sweaty, and their work clothes were red with gravel dust from the county road crew. They were already drunk.

Barry walked up to the bar and ordered two six-packs to go. While waiting for the bartender to bring the beer, he surveyed the room and spotted Dicky White, still alone in the corner. Kimbrough's sunburned face turned a deeper shade of red and he said loudly, "Of all the fucking nerve!"

The room got quiet, but Kimbrough's voice got louder. "What is Dick-sucking White doing here?" he asked, addressing the crowd. Seeing that he had everyone's attention, Barry stood on a chair and pointed to Dicky across the room. "Everybody look real good. This is the little pussy whose daddy is defending that Farmer nigger. Ain't that right, Master Dicky?"

Dicky didn't say a word or move a muscle except to look down into his beer. Barry jumped down from the chair and walked toward him. Chairs scuffled as people cleared a path. Barry said, "You and your almighty daddy think that dead nigger is worth more than my innocent little cousin. Ain't that right?" He was right up in Dicky White's face, sneering, "Answer me, you yellowbelly!"

Dicky raised his eyes to Kimbrough and said, "I wouldn't talk about anybody's daddy if mine was a common thief, and God knows what else."

Kimbrough sputtered, "Son of a bitch." He grabbed the glass of beer from Dicky's hand. "Keep my daddy out of this, nigger lover," he said and poured the beer over Dicky's head.

Dicky White looked up with beer dripping from his hair and into his eyes. He stood absolutely still with his hands balled into fists at his sides. He raised his voice and said, "I'd rather be a nigra than a white trash jailbird."

Barry Kimbrough exploded. He brought his knee up into Dicky's belly. Dicky crumpled over at the middle. "Don't you know?" Kimbrough asked. "Don't you know any goddamn thing? The great Hayden White fired my daddy from his job last night. Claimed Daddy stole something from the house. But it was all because of that Farmer nigger. He's had the sheriff all over Daddy's ass all summer and now he's fired him. Put him out in the fucking street to starve. All over some dead piece of shit nigger."

Dicky was upright and Barry kneed him in the belly again. This time Dicky threw up on the floor. "Get him out of here!" Barry said to his two friends, "he's stinking up the joint."

The two boys took Dicky White by each shoulder, pulled him to the door, and pushed him down the stairs into the parking lot. Barry picked up his grocery sack full of beer from the bar and headed out the door himself.

A couple of minutes later, muffled thuds and grunts were heard from the parking lot. People started running to the door. "It ain't over," somebody yelled. "They're working him over with axe handles." There was a rush to the door. Tommy, Jack and Wade all joined it.

Outside Dicky was still trying to fight back. He was flailing his arms around wildly while the three boys circled him and landed body blows with the thick wooden handles. Finally one of the blows struck Dicky's head, and he fell to the ground with blood coming out of his mouth. Kimbrough's buddies ran to the old red pick-up truck and threw the axe handles in the back. Barry Kimbrough kept standing over Dicky, kicking him again and again in the head and belly. All the while he was yelling, "Niggerlover! Niggerlover! Go tell your daddy to leave our people alone!"

Finally Kimbrough was still and silent. He looked down at Dicky's unconscious body. He got scared at the sight of all that blood coming from Dicky White's mouth. He dropped his axe handle where he stood, walked to the truck, and drove away in a spray of gravel and dust.

Finally somebody in the crowd said, "Maybe we ought to take him inside or something?" But nobody did anything for Dicky White. They all just trickled back inside to their waiting beers. A few minutes later there were sirens. An ambulance and a police car pulled into the parking lot. While they loaded Dicky into the back of the ambulance, the cop came inside and asked the bartender what had happened. When the bartender had told it all, the cop asked to use the telephone in Mr. Mackey's office. He made his call and left without asking any more questions.

That Sunday morning, Hayden White didn't show up for his Sunday

School class. A baldheaded old man with brown spots on his hands came in to substitute. The old man told Tommy, Wade and the other boys that Mr. White's son, Dicky, had been in an accident. "Mr. White is with him at the hospital in Memphis," the man said, "Dicky is hurt pretty bad, but he's going to recover just fine." The old man told them to bow their heads and pray for Dicky's recovery.

Tommy bowed his head, but found that he couldn't pray anymore. All he could think was, "I did it. I might as well have beat him with a stick myself. If I told what I knew, this would all be over now."

Then he thought, of course it wouldn't all be over. Even if Billy Kimbrough was in jail, his son would still be on the street, madder than ever. Tommy wasn't making sense anymore, not even to himself, and he didn't care. He felt a horrible sense of responsibility and a weakness inside him that would not let him act.

When the old man finally said, "...in Jesus' name, amen," Tommy didn't hear him. He kept his head down and his eyes closed, wrestling with confusion and fear. The next thing he knew, Wade was poking him in the ribs and whispering, "Tommy! Wake up! He wants you to read!"

"I'm sorry, what was that, sir?" Tommy asked the teacher. The old man had a very long skinny neck. When he talked, his Adam's apple rode up and down his throat, like a bubble in a straw. "Matthew 5:14-16, son," the old man answered.

Tommy leafed through his Bible, found the verses, and started to read out loud, "Ye are the light of the world. A city that is set on a hill can not be hid. Neither do men light a candle, and put it under a bushel, but on a candlestick; and it giveth light unto all that are in the house. Let your light so shine before men, that they may see your good works, and glorify your Father which is in heaven."

When church was over and Sunday dinner at the Jackson house was finished, Tommy told his father that he wanted to go for a drive, maybe over to Jack's. He took the old green Chevy downtown and circled by the Zion Missionary Baptist Church. When he drove by it was time for the service to start, but the little churchyard was still full of people laughing and visiting. Tommy kept circling the block. After at least half a dozen passes, everyone was inside the church building. The sound of the church organ came through the open windows as Tommy pulled the car over to the curb and got out. The congregation was singing "Just a Closer Walk With Thee."

Tommy knew that song. They sang it at his church sometimes, and a lot of the white gospel groups, like the Blackwood Brothers and the Goodman Family, sang it, too. But Tommy had never heard the song like this before. It was starting to swing. The congregation clapped a mournful cadence that lagged just behind the backbeat. Tommy stood on the sidewalk below an open window and let the music take him.

The song went on and on, gaining substance and power as it went, like the rings of a tree. Individual voices floated in and out of the tune, soaring above it and grunting punctuation marks from below. The sound of the organ was the warm, damp soil from which the song took life. Through it all the clapping of the congregation never varied. The singing reached up toward heaven, but the song touched the earth twice in every measure, a little late, but right on time.

Tommy felt tears rising up behind his eyes. His legs were quivering and his fists were clenched. There was something sad in this sound, and it spoke to everything that was sad in Tommy Jackson. But there was something very strong here, too, and Tommy felt a strength he'd never known before. He felt lifted up and free. He felt that if he could have stayed there in that spot, his prayers would be answered. He would know what to do and how to do it.

After countless choruses, the singing inside the church faded out, but the organ kept right on playing. From the background music, the voice of the preacher rose. As the sermon started, Tommy looked around for a moment. He suddenly realized that a steady stream of cars was going by on the street where he stood.

It seemed that in every car someone turned to catch a glimpse of this strange white boy loitering outside the colored church. Suddenly Tommy's freedom and strength flew away. He was afraid again, and he ran to the car and headed for home.

- Seven -

Toward the end of summer came the news that Dicky White was dead. He didn't die from Barry Kimbrough's beating. The small notice in the newspaper said that he died when a hunting rifle he was cleaning accidentally went off. There was a lot of whispering around Calhoun about that. Dicky White was no sportsman. It seemed odd that he would spend an August afternoon cleaning guns.

People whispered about all this. But they didn't talk out loud. After all, the Whites were the Whites, and if they said it was an accident, it was.

Wade Suggs was laid up sick when Dicky White died. He wasn't showing up for work at the Piggly Wiggly, and when Tommy called, Wade's mother said that he was too sick to talk on the phone. Wade could be a big faker, but Tommy and Jack decided that he must really be sick to stay cooped up in the house through the hottest days of summer.

On Friday evening of the week after Dicky White died, Tommy got a call from Wade. "Mama told me you been calling," he said. "I had some kind of fever. Couldn't get out of bed for nothing. I had chills and nightmares and the works. I'm feeling better now, though, and all I want in the world is to go out and get snake-walking drunk."

Tommy called up Jack, and after supper, when the sun was down, they went to pick up Wade. When they arrived, the house was completely dark, and Wade was sitting on the edge of the front porch in the shadow of some bushes. He walked out into the streetlight, and Tommy and Jack gasped. Wade looked as if he'd gained 20 pounds in the past two weeks. His face was as round as a basketball and his belly hung out over the top of his pants. His eyes were red and swollen.

Wade opened the back door of the car and sank into the corner on the driver's side. Tommy started driving toward Mackey's. Jack looked back and asked, "So, how you feeling?"

Wade answered, "Oh, I'm OK now. Mainly I'm just sluggish from being in bed so long."

"What did you have?" Jack asked, "Malaria?"

"Naw," said Wade, "But it was some other rare something or other that you get from mosquito bites. Doctor told my mama the name, but she can't pronounce it."

"What was it like?" Tommy asked.

"Well, mostly I just laid in bed and slept."

"You're not contagious are you?" asked Jack.

"No, I'm not contagious, you moron," Wade said, "and I ain't talked about nothing but being sick for the last two weeks. Let's get off it."

This reticence puzzled Tommy. He thought a rare tropical disease would appeal to Wade's flair for drama. He had expected endless and increasingly elaborate retellings of Wade's symptoms and sufferings. "OK, we're off it," Tommy said, "and we're here." The gravel of Mackey's parking lot crunched beneath their wheels.

When the car stopped, Wade said, "I don't want to go in tonight, guys. Let's get a couple of six-packs and ride around."

"OK," Jack answered, "go get 'em."

Wade said, "Naw, you go in. Here's some money." He passed up a fifty cent piece, as Jack and Tommy were each producing dollar bills.

"Cheapskate," Tommy said.

"Aw, come on," Wade whined, "I don't have any more. You know I ain't been to work for two weeks." Tommy and Jack emptied the change from their pockets and Jack went inside and bought two six-packs and a quart.

When the car was moving again, Wade said, "Why don't you just let me have the quart to myself, Jack? Then you won't have to worry about me being contagious." Wade took the big, brown bottle and Jack opened two cans. Tommy drove out on the highway toward Johnson City for a few minutes. The radio was playing, and in the front they were talking about baseball. Wade was quiet except for the steady gurgle of beer going down and a partly stifled belch.

Suddenly there was a frightening "Whack!" The quart beer bottle flew out of a rear window and made a dead hit on a roadside speed-limit sign. Wade pulled back from the window and said, "Hit me again, barkeep."

Jack looked over at Tommy suspiciously, but opened a can of beer and handed it back to Wade. A few minutes later, there was a smaller "whack" as the empty can flew. Jack passed back another and then another. When Wade had drained the third can, he reached over to the front seat and grabbed the entire second six-pack. He dropped two cans on the seat for Jack and Tommy and took the rest for himself.

Wade sat in the back seat opening beers with his pocket knife and sucking them down one after the other. By the time Tommy and Jack had drunk three beers apiece, Wade had already put down a quart and six cans, and was starting to act crazy.

"Pull over," Wade commanded. "I got to piss." They stopped, and Wade jumped out and ran to the woods at the edge of the road. When he came walking back to the car, his shirt was all unbuttoned. He left the top of his pants loose to accommodate his beer-glutted belly. There were red splotches all over his skin.

"I got to have some more booze," Wade said. "I got to get good and loose. I'm going to howl at the moon tonight. Where can we get some more goddamn booze?" The car was moving and Wade babbled on. "Step on it, Mister Tommy, I'm bad thirsty. I'm starting to get the D.T.'s. There's pink elephants all over the road. I got to have strong drink. I need whiskey. Yeah, that's it. Old Charter. Straight up. No sissy stuff."

Jack said, "Fool, you done drank up all our money." But Wade kept going on like a wild man. He stuck his head out the window at every car that passed and yelled, "Whiskey, whiskey, give me whiskey, or I'll puke on you."

"OK," Jack said, "Maybe I can sneak into my house and grab a bottle of my daddy's whiskey. Would that shut you up?"

"Sounds good," said Wade.

"What the hell," Tommy added, "If he's going to get blind-pig drunk, we might as well, too. Who knows, there might not be another chance this summer."

"Hell!" Wade hollered, "there might not be another chance ever. We could all wake up dead tomorrow. Shot through the head, deader than shit."

Jack and Tommy looked at each other with question marks on their faces. Tommy kept driving and he turned the radio up loud. They made their way to Jack's house surrounded by Sonny Boy Williamson's "Eyesight to the Blind." The blues harmonica seemed to howl at the moon.

As they neared Jack's house, Tommy turned off the headlights and the radio. Jack got out, walked across his big, green front yard, and disappeared around the side of the brick house. Five minutes later he trotted back across the front yard, clutching the bottle high in his right hand like a torch.

"Got the goods," he said when he reached the car.

Wade said, "Give it here," and grabbed the fifth. "Mmmmm... Old Charter it is, and ten years old, too. This will do nicely." He ripped off the seal with his fingernail, opened the bottle and took a sip. "Yes, yes, very nice," he said, and pulled back to his corner of the car with the bottle held to his chest.

When they were rolling again, Jack said, "OK, don't be a hog." Wade passed the bottle up and Jack took a drink. He poured some into empty beer cans for Tommy and himself and passed the bottle back. Wade sat with his legs stretched across the backseat, nursing himself on the bottle and uttering contented groans.

After a while, Wade reached another, more profound, level of drunkenness. He stopped sucking at the bottle and raised himself up on the seat. Even in the darkened car, Wade's face looked dangerously red. He was short of breath, but between his gasps for air, he growled, "This is the life. Wouldn't it be great to be filthy rich and have somebody drive you around while you sit in the back and drink whiskey?"

"Yeah," Tommy said, "but maybe being rich ain't everything it's cracked up to be. Might make you crazy, too. Why else would old Dicky White kill himself? He was going to inherit half the county, and he just hauled off and blew himself away."

"Yeah," Jack said, "You'd have to be crazy to do that. But being rich don't explain it. Look at all those rich bastards in my mama's family. None of them ever shot themselves. Besides, you don't really know that Dicky White killed himself. It might have been an accident like they say."

"Yeah," Tommy answered loudly, feeling the whiskey thicken his tongue, "and shit might smell like roses. That boy shot himself and everybody knows it."

Wade leaned over the front seat, redder than ever. Veins were jumping out in his face. "Dicky White killed himself," Wade said with a slur, "I know it for a fact. It wasn't no hunting accident. That boy hated hunting. He took that rifle and went to the barn and shot himself. That's what he did. And he had to shoot twice."

Wade stopped for a moment and put his head down on the seat to rest. He reared back up and continued, "The first time he screwed up and hit himself in the neck. He was bleeding like a stuck pig. His clothes were soaked with blood all the way through when they found him. But the first shot didn't kill him. The second time he put the gun barrel in his mouth and his brains went all over the barn. When they found him, the dogs were licking up the blood and eating at his brains."

Wade fell into a deep silence. They were all quiet for a long time, then Wade took a drink from the whiskey bottle and started up again, wilder than ever, "He killed himself 'cause he was a coward. He was too scared to fucking live, and being rich didn't have nothing to do with it." Wade gulped twice, first for air and then whiskey, "Now he's dead and gone to hell, and to hell with him."

Wade sat back in his seat and was quiet. So were Tommy and Jack. The only sound in the car was the horrible rasp of Wade's breathing. They all drank. Jack passed around a pack of cigarettes and they all smoked, while the tall, green cotton fields rolled past their windows.

Tommy was scared. He wondered how Wade knew all those details about Dicky White's death, and why he was so worked up about it all. He wondered if this all had something to do with Darrell Farmer, since Barry Kimbrough was so mad at the Whites about that. Tommy's head was spinning. Nothing made any sense anymore.

Suddenly Tommy hit the brakes. There was somebody walking in the road. The car slowed to a crawl as they passed an old, grey-haired, black man who was weaving down the road with a bamboo walking stick. He was dressed in a Sunday suit and carrying a bottle. As they rolled past him, through the car's open windows they could hear him sing, "...mean things happening in this land, in this land. There are mean things happening in this land..." The song hung in the air for a moment, and disappeared when Tommy speeded up again.

Finally Jack broke the silence inside the car. Gesturing back toward the old man with his thumb, he said, "Now that is crazy."

Tommy tried to chuckle in response, then fell silent again. He lit another cigarette from the butt of the last one and looked at the sky outside the car window. The clouds blew rapidly across the face of a full, yellow moon. The radio played "Smokestack Lightning" by Howling Wolf.

After a while Jack spoke again. "Now I got to pee," he said. Tommy pulled off the road. The three friends got out and stood in a row, with the wind at their backs, and pissed into the cotton field. The moon was so bright that it cast their shadows across the field like giants. The noise of frogs and crickets was louder than the car engine.

Back in the car, Tommy drove aimlessly in silence until Wade roused himself and spoke again. "Go to town," he ordered. "Get ye to the Odd Fellows Cemetery."

"The graveyard?" Jack asked.

"Yeah," Wade answered, "the graveyard, you stupid shit. The one on Benson Avenue, where I'll bury your ass if you keep asking dumb questions."

"Take it easy, Wade," Tommy said, "we're on our way. We'll drink with the ghosts in ten minutes."

When they reached the cemetery, Wade commanded, "Go in and drive around until I tell you to stop." They passed the gate and started down a single lane road that went winding among the graves. The full moon was shining so bright between the clouds that it reflected off the marble headstones. The wind was blowing hard. It shook the trees and bushes with a ghostly rattle.

Jack looked at his watch and said, "Holy shit! Do you realize that we're out here under a full moon, right at the very stroke of midnight, on a Friday night? If I was sober I might be scared."

Wade croaked, "Stop the car and back up a little." Tommy obeyed. "OK," Wade said, "Park it right here. This must be the place."

Wade had directed them to a spot right in front of a new grave that was still surrounded by flowers and wreaths. Wade got out of the car and started walking toward the mound of dirt. He held the whiskey bottle in his hand like a drum major's baton. Jack and Tommy followed, through a wall of flowers, until all three of them stood at the graveside. They looked down at the marker that read, "Richard Delaney White. Born March 16, 1938. Died August 9, 1955."

As they stood with the wind blowing all around them, Tommy was filled with horror. Suddenly, looking down at the newly turned dirt, he could see Dicky White lying in that barn with the dogs chewing his brains. Then he saw him in the grave with worms crawling from the big bullet hole in his head. Tommy was shaking. He closed his eyes tight and tried to erase the picture from his mind, but it wouldn't go away.

"OK, Wade, this ain't funny," he said. "Let's get out of here."

But Wade was already sitting down on the graveside grass, drinking again. He said, "Sit down. We ain't going nowhere." Tommy and Jack took places on the grass with Wade between them. He passed the bottle, and they all sat and drank and listened to the wind, and Wade started talking. "He didn't really kill himself, you know."

"Oh Lord, is it story time again?" Jack said. "What happened to all that shit about the barn and the dogs?"

Wade tried to speak again but he began to cry. Tommy realized that this was no story. This must be real, and he wished to God he didn't have to hear it.

"That was the way it happened," Wade said between sobs. "Dicky shot himself. But that Billy Kimbrough, Barry Kimbrough's daddy, he was the one that killed him."

Tommy felt sick. This was starting to make sense in all the wrong ways. He put his hands over his ears to keep out the sound, but it didn't work. Tommy could still hear Wade's voice when he said, "It was all about Darrell Farmer."

"Oh shit," Tommy said. The words rose out of his mouth before he could catch them.

Wade didn't notice the interruption. "Billy Kimbrough worked on the Whites' place, you know. And Mr. White figured that he was one of the guys who killed that Farmer nigger. But he couldn't prove it, since there wasn't any witnesses."

Tommy felt as if every eye in the graveyard, living and dead, was staring at him. Wade didn't even pause. "He couldn't prove it, but he knew it just the same, Mr. White did. So he fired Kimbrough from his job, and he was leaning on the sheriff to go ahead and arrest him. Just like Barry said that night at Mackey's."

"But what does any of that shit have to do with Dicky?" Jack said. "He wouldn't kill himself because somebody had a beef with his daddy."

Wade took a long swig from the bottle. Some of it spilled on his chest and ran down his belly. He was extremely drunk. His eyes were closed and he was talking in a slow mumble, like a man talking in his sleep. Tommy edged over closer to Wade so he could make out the words through the noise of the wind.

"Finally," Wade continued, "the sheriff come to Billy Kimbrough and told him that unless something else turned up, he was going to have to arrest him and charge him with something on the Farmer killing. He told Billy that he'd wait another week, and then he'd have to do it. He gave him that week so he'd have a chance to get out of town, you see. That would get everybody off the hook.

"But Kimbrough didn't run for it like he was supposed to. He went straight back to see Mr. White instead, because he knew something that he could use for blackmail. It was something really awful about Dicky."

"What was it?" Jack demanded. Tommy was sitting with his knees pulled up and his head between them, barely breathing. He kept seeing Dicky with the dogs and the worms. When he managed to shut out those pictures, they were replaced by the image of the red pick-up truck by the river and the men dropping the body. He wanted to crawl down into the ground with Dicky White, down in the dirt where everything was safe and settled.

But Wade kept talking and Tommy couldn't block out the words. "It was terrible. One day, just before he got fired, Kimbrough was out fixing fences on the Whites' place and he saw Dicky out in the woods, fucking somebody."

"Big deal," Jack said. "I mean, you wouldn't want to go home and tell mama. But that ain't exactly life or death." Jack paused and thought, "Unless it was a nigger girl. It wasn't a nigger girl, was it?"

"No, it wasn't no nigger girl," Wade answered. He was crying again now. He sobbed and took a drink and blew his nose on his shirttail.

Jack wouldn't let up. "Then what the hell was it? Who, or what, could he be fucking that was so goddamn shameful? Was he doing the cows or something?"

Wade broke down completely. His face was covered with tears and sweat, and his sobs sounded like hiccups. For a long time he fought to control his breath. He said in a low, even voice, "He was fucking a boy."

"Oh, my God," Tommy breathed. He felt dizzy. The graveyard was starting to spin and the smell of the flowers was making him sick. The wind was getting stronger. It blew his hair into his face and sounded like a freight train in his ears. Tommy felt that it might blow him away. He gripped the graveside grass and closed his eyes.

Jack was more nonchalant. After a few seconds passed, he said, "Well, that sure explains it all." Jack stopped to think again. He looked hard at Wade and said, "How do you know so much about all this?"

Wade didn't answer. His head was down in his lap and he was crying uncontrollably. But Jack wouldn't back off. He kept saying, "Tell me, tell me, tell me, you sissy. How do you know? Did you make all this up?"

Wade whimpered, "No, I didn't make it up. It's all true. Now leave me alone."

But Jack was getting crazy. He stood up with his back to the grave and leaned down into Wade's face and screamed, "Tell me, tell me, tell me where you heard this shit."

Tommy jumped up and grabbed Jack by the shoulders. "Damn it, Jack, quiet down," he said. "You're going to wake up the dead folks."

The joke didn't work. Instead Jack started shaking Wade by the shoulders, screaming, "Tell me! Tell me!"

At last Wade stopped crying, and tried to yell an answer to Jack's demands, but he was so hoarse and out of breath that his voice just croaked something unintelligible. Jack quieted down and asked, "What was that?"

Wade answered quietly, "I said, 'It was me.'"

Tommy was dizzy. He sat back down on the ground and put his hands over his ears again.

Jack didn't get it. "What was you?" he asked.

"It was me in the woods with Dicky White," Wade said in a rush. "Now leave me alone." He dropped the whiskey bottle on the grass and reached out for the tombstone to pull himself upright.

"You mean it was you he was fucking?" Jack asked.

"Jack, that's enough," Tommy said, "just shut up."

Wade didn't say anything. He was leaning against the side of the waist-high tombstone, quivering. Then he lowered his head behind the stone and vomited. When the vomit was done he collapsed onto the grave, still gagging and heaving.

Jack couldn't let go. "He made you do it?" he demanded. "Did he have a gun? Did he give you money? How much? A hundred? A thousand? Hell, I might do it for a thousand."

Wade's face was buried in the fresh dirt on top of the grave. His sweat and tears and mucous turned the dirt into mud. His voice was small and distant, but clear. "No. He didn't pay me nothing. I did it because I wanted to. I liked him. He made me feel good. He was nice to me..."

"Aw, shit," Jack said and spat on the ground. "I can't listen to this." He started pacing in a circle around the grave. But Wade didn't stop talking.

"You don't understand," Wade said, still lying in the dirt talking as if he were far away. "Hell, I don't understand. I'm all messed up. Everything's backwards with me. I get hard like everybody else, and I look at pictures and jack off, just like y'all do. But it's always boys. Always has been. I'm backwards. I'm all messed up and backwards.

"One day Dicky White came up to me in the parking lot after school," Wade continued, "and it was like he knew. He didn't say nothing, he just put his hand on my shoulder and we went to his car and drove out in the country and... we messed around some... and then we talked for a long time. He talked about all kinds of stuff, about growing up, about the military school they sent him to. He said that's where he started doing it.

"I never felt so good in my life as I did that day. Nobody had ever been so nice to me. He really liked me. He was older and rich and smart. He was going to go to college up North. But he liked me.

"That first time was back the week before we saw Elvis. I seen him at least a couple of times a week after that. Sometimes we went over to Greenville. He had some buddies over there that were, different, like that, and they had parties and stuff. But mostly Dicky would just take me out to his daddy's farm, and we'd go to the woods by the river and do stuff..."

Wade started to cry again. He curled up in a fetal position on the grave and started to rock back and forth. "That's where Billy Kimbrough saw us," he said between gasps and sobs. "I don't know if he saw me. I don't know if he gave my name. But it's killing me just the same. Dicky's dead and I might as well be. I can't take it alone. It's killing me. It's killing me."

Wade kept saying those same words over and over, and rocking and crying, until finally he was quiet. Jack stopped pacing and looked down at him. Tommy sat on the ground beside him. They said nothing.

Tommy wanted to say something. He felt words rising up in his throat. But they wouldn't come out. He wanted to say, "It's all OK. It's going to be alright." But it wouldn't come out. He wanted to say what he knew. It seemed like it might help somehow. But he couldn't say it.

Wade started to breathe in deep, heavy sighs. His body uncoiled and he began to snore. He had passed out. He was stretched across Dicky White's grave dead asleep. As Tommy watched, he noticed the words at the bottom of Dicky White's gravestone. It was a verse from the Psalms. Tommy read it out loud, "Why do the heathen rage, and the people imagine a vain thing?"

"What?" Jack said.

"There, on the stone, the Bible verse at the bottom, under the name and dates. It says, 'Why do the heathen rage, and the people imagine a vain thing?'"

"What the hell does that mean?"

"Don't ask," Tommy said.

They sat for a while longer. The wind kept getting stronger. They heard a tree branch crack. The clouds covered the moon and the air felt damp, like a storm coming in. Finally Jack said, "Let's get the hell out of here."

Without speaking, they picked Wade up by his arms and legs and towed him into the back of the car. Tommy drove very slowly to Wade's house. It was sometime past 2:00 a.m. and they were all exhausted.

When they reached the house, they carried Wade out of the car and around the back. They laid him out quietly on the porch. Tommy found a torn and frayed blanket in a box of old rags, and he spread that over Wade's body. Then he and Jack went back to the car and to their homes without saying a word.

When Tommy woke up the next day, Saturday, it was almost noon. He was soaked with sweat and his bedsheets were twisted from violent tossing. He sat at the edge of the narrow bed and tried to figure out which of the horrors in his head were nightmares and which had really happened. He got up and looked out the door of his room. There seemed to be no one in the house. His daddy worked Saturday mornings, and his mama was probably at Josie's. Tommy went to the kitchen, grabbed a bottle of Coke from the refrigerator, and took it with him to the bathtub. He also took his transistor radio so he could listen while he bathed.

The radio announcer said that a cluster of tornadoes was rampaging across the Delta. One had already touched down in downtown Calhoun and severely damaged the courthouse. Tommy wondered how he had slept through the sirens and noise. He quickly got out of the tub and dressed and went outside.

He could tell something was wrong when he stepped onto the front porch. The air was clammy and stagnant, like a cold sweat. Weird sunlight glowed through the clouds and turned everything a pale, sickly yellow.

Tommy stepped off the porch and started walking. He headed toward the end of the street where the cotton fields started. As he walked, the sky turned black. The winds kicked up for a while, then the air was still again, but the sky stayed black.

Tommy reached the end of his street and stood at the edge of the fields, watching the sky. He felt the wind pushing hard against him. There was a funnel cloud way off on the horizon headed his way. He looked around for a ditch to lie in if the funnel got close, then he watched the tornado creep across the fields.

The cloud passed through an old barn and the barn exploded into a million pieces. The pieces flew around and around in the wind and then scattered. After that the tornado changed direction and began to veer away from town. Then it lifted off the ground and was out of sight.

Not long after the funnel cloud lifted, the rain started. Water fell in blinding sheets. It hit Tommy's face and chest like a fire hose. He couldn't see more than 20 feet in any direction. Tommy stood soaking up the water and waited for the storm to subside. When it did, he walked home and dried off and went back to bed.

- Eight -

Wade Suggs disappeared at the end of summer. The week after the tornadoes, he and his mother just moved, to parts unknown, with no forwarding address. At school no one noticed that Wade was gone. Tommy and Jack never talked about him.

Nothing happened about the killing of Darrell Farmer. The sheriff said the files on the case were all destroyed in the tornado. He called it an act of God. He also said that it didn't matter, because the investigation had reached a dead end anyway.

For a long time Tommy told himself he would talk. He told himself that he owed it to Wade. He didn't know who he would talk to. He would be going against the sheriff, the Klan and most of the other white people in town. He couldn't forget that fat, filthy rat nailed to the door of Hayden White's office, and the words in the Klan message about "rat-killing time." They must have meant it, because Hayden White got quiet after that. Coming out would even set Tommy against his own parents. Probably no one would believe him, anyway, and he would end up being sent away from town on his own, or worse.

The year passed in silence. There was the usual round of school and church and family. But at the center of it all was silence. Tommy was mostly alone. He still hung out with Jack Gerard at school, but he didn't go out with anybody. He stayed home in his room and listened to the radio and read books. He read *1984* and felt just like Winston Smith. He listened to the rhythm and blues and felt just like it sounded. He rode around town in the old Chevy at night, spinning the dial on the radio. For hours he listened to a Spanish station from somewhere in Mexico, without understanding a word. He tried to fill up his head with noise to block out what he knew.

Still, the pictures came at night. They were in a dream that kept coming back, not every night, but often enough. In this dream, Tommy always saw Darrell Farmer. It was the face from the school picture in the newspaper. Darrell Farmer never spoke, but he was clearly alive and present somehow. Later in the dream, Tommy saw his friend Wade asleep on the back porch the way he was on that last night. As Tommy got closer, things got jumbled. The body on the back porch became Darrell Farmer, and Tommy covered the black boy with an old blanket. When Tommy woke, that picture would hang in his head. It wouldn't go away for days at a time.

In 1956, when Tommy was in the eleventh grade, Elvis Presley appeared on *The Ed Sullivan Show*, and people all over America went crazy. It seemed that everyone in the country under the age of 21 was soaked with gasoline, and Elvis struck a spark. Jack Gerard was completely ablaze. To him rock and roll was about kids thumbing their noses at the adult world. Jack understood that, he liked it, and he went for it whole hog.

One Monday morning in early October, Jack arrived at Calhoun High School driving his mother's big, blue Plymouth. He parked at the front of the school lot, checked himself in the rear view mirror, and lit a cigarette. He got out of the car with the cigarette perched in the corner of his mouth. He left the radio turned on loud, with all the windows open. It was playing "I Walk the Line" by Johnny Cash as Jack took up his position, leaning against the hood of the car.

He had on dark glasses, though it was a partly cloudy day. He was wearing an open-necked black silk shirt with a huge collar spread over the lapels of a shocking pink sport coat. He had on tight and shiny black slacks and red shoes with buckles and pointed toes.

People noticed Jack and a wave of murmurs swept across the parking lot. Nearby Tommy was having a smoke with some other guys from his class. Seeing Jack, he threw down his cigarette and ran through the gawking crowd that was starting to form. When he reached Jack's side, Tommy grabbed the sleeve of the pink jacket. "What on earth are you doing?" he asked, "Trying to integrate the school?"

"Ain't nothing like that," Jack answered from behind his shades, "It's just time to shake things up. So I'm shaking."

"But ain't you afraid?" Tommy asked, "They might send you home."

The crowd around Jack continued to grow. Word passed quickly, and some teachers were coming out to see the sight.

"What's to be afraid of?" Jack said, "I read the dress code and I'm not breaking it. Besides, since when do you care what they think?"

"Well," Tommy said, "I don't, but..."

"So get with it, then," Jack replied.

While Tommy and Jack were talking, two girls came over to Jack's car. They were Brenda Haley and Patricia Stevens. Both of them were in the eleventh grade with Tommy and Jack, but the the boys had no idea that they were rock-and-rollers.

Brenda Haley had only been in Calhoun for about a year. Her father was the pastor of the First Methodist Church. She was a tall, thin girl. Her straight, dark brown hair was cut chin-length with bangs, like a frame around her narrow face. She wore a green sweater that was way too big for her and a brown plaid skirt.

Around school Brenda Haley always seemed quiet and lost in her thoughts. But in the parking lot she was the one who spoke first, saying, "Jack Gerard, I had no idea that you were such a gone cat! Where did you get those clothes?"

There was something strange about her eyes as she spoke. They seemed to jump from her face and grab everything before her, as if there were a fire in her brain that needed fuel immediately.

Jack said, "Up in Memphis. I was in Oxford with my cousins, for the Ole Miss homecoming. Early Saturday morning, while everybody was still hung over, I took off and drove to Beale Street..."

Brenda interrupted him and said to Patricia Stevens, "Oh, isn't it the wildes t?Beale Street! He's a real cat, honey. Right here in Calhoun."

Tommy was confused. "What do you mean?" he said, "A cat's just a guy, right?"

"No, I mean a *cat,* child," Brenda answered. "One of those white boys who hang out on Beale Street and places like that, and dress like the Negroes and go to juke joints and all. That's what Elvis was before he was famous. There were some of them where I used to live down on the Coast, too. I bet Beale Street is just full of them these days, isn't it Jack?"

"Oh, yeah," Jack said, "can't stir 'em with a stick."

Patricia Stevens asked, "When did you get with rock-and-roll, Jack? We had no idea."

"Oh, Tommy here was pushing it at me for years," Jack said, "We went to see Elvis over in Greenville about a year and a half ago, before he hit TV and all."

"Why, Tommy Jackson," Patricia said, looking at him for the first time, "Who'd have thought. You can't judge a book by the cover, can you?"

Tommy had been in school with Patricia Stevens since they were six years old in Robert E. Lee Elementary. He'd never really known her, but he watched her and heard a lot about her. She was a short, blonde girl with a broad, stocky body and a wide, open face. She was dressed simply in a plain blue blouse and a khaki skirt. She could have been ordinary-looking except she had large breasts. Ever since the breasts started growing back in the sixth grade, the boys had talked about Patricia Stevens. They talked about what she was like, about how they could get her, and about the things they imagined she was doing with older boys.

Tommy answered Patricia without looking at her. "Yeah," he said, "I've been a nut for rhythm and blues since I was a child. Listen to it all the time."

Tommy stopped and glanced at Patricia Stevens. She was waiting for him to say something else. In that glance, Tommy noticed something unusual about Patricia Stevens, above the neck. It was her eyes. They were small dots of pale blue, set deep in her face, like they always were, but suddenly Tommy saw that her eyes were laughing at something. Those laughing eyes stuck hard in his mind. Tommy wondered if they were laughing at him. He looked away quickly.

The electric school bell sounded from inside the building. It was time for Jack to face whatever was coming. As they parted, Tommy shook his hand and said, "Well, good luck in there, old buddy."

Brenda Haley touched his pink jacket sleeve and said, "Yeah, good luck, Jack. Let's talk some more sometime, OK?"

Jack didn't get sent home for wearing his cat clothes. The principal called him in for a talk, but Jack was right about the dress code. There was a lot in it about shirts without collars and the length of pants and dresses, but there was nothing about loud colors or shiny fabrics.

Brenda Haley and Patricia Stevens dropped by Jack's car at lunch that day to smoke cigarettes and listen to the radio. They came the next morning and the next lunch period, too. The meetings became routine, and the four became friends. They would turn on the radio, fill the car up with smoke, and try to tell each other things no one else could understand. Sometimes they joked about applying for recognition as a club, like the Future Farmers or the Christian Athletes. If they did, Brenda decided, they should call themselves The Rockers.

At one of their early morning meetings, a thunderstorm roared outside the car. The radio put out static, so they turned it off and watched the rain, and listened to it drum against the roof of the car. "It rained like this during hurricane time on the Coast," Brenda said.

A bolt of lightning shot over the top of the school building and a clap of thunder shook the windows of the car. "Did you like it down there?" Tommy asked.

"Yeah, I miss it," Brenda said. "Up here people think I'm just a preacher's kid. I was somebody else down there. I was an actress. I did Little Theater plays with the grown-ups and had some small parts over in New Orleans. Even got paid once."

"What's New Orleans like?" Jack asked, "My daddy's always going down there."

"It's great, not like anyplace else, especially the French Quarter," Brenda said. "You can do whatever you want. Everybody's mixed together, colored and white and foreigners, men dressed like women and the other way around. And the music is everywhere. I could never get enough of it. Last year I skipped school one day and took the bus over there and didn't come home till the next morning."

"Wow, what happened?" Jack asked.

"I had a lot of fun, got suspended from school for a week, grounded for a month," Brenda said.

"Why did y'all move up here?" Tommy asked.

"The bishop transferred Daddy away from the Coast. He was in too much hot water down there. He tried to organize a bi-racial committee on school integration, you know, after the big Supreme Court case. It didn't go over so good." Brenda stopped talking and stared out into the rain. "Don't tell anybody what I just said. Nobody up here knows, and Daddy's trying real hard to stay out of trouble."

Brenda was quiet, staring at the rain again. No one else said anything. Finally Brenda snapped her attention back into the car and said, "Of course,

I'm all in favor of the integration, too. Colored people in Mississippi are treated just like Hitler's Jews. We should be ashamed."

Tommy listened very carefully while Brenda said those things. He had never heard a white person talk that way. He wondered if she would get in trouble, but he was relieved to know that somebody else's conscience was bothered. He said nothing.

"What do you think about all that, Jack?" Brenda said after a long pause.

"Oh, I don't know, I guess I can see both sides of it."

"Both sides? That's a joke," Patricia said. "You just think whatever you're told." Patricia Stevens agreed with Brenda. She was used to thinking her own thoughts, or she never would have picked Brenda out to be her friend. Patricia read stories and poems. She read all the collections in the library, and new things when she could find them in the magazines.

When the four friends huddled together in Jack Gerard's car, Tommy felt human again for the first time in more than a year. He still couldn't tell what he knew, but he could now tell who he was. Besides, he had another new secret that was burning him up. He was in love with Patricia Stevens.

Tommy had never been in love before, but he knew this was it. He felt all tingly and hot around her. He said stupid things and felt like his arms and legs were made of cement. When he was alone, he couldn't think of anything but what she looked like and how he could be with her. But Tommy was too frightened to ever say anything to Patricia. Everyone knew she had lots of guys, anyway.

Brenda was really interested in Jack. She always looked at him when she talked, and Jack looked back. He kept dressing up cool every day, and he talked about taking a drama class in the spring. Jack kept driving the blue Plymouth to school, and soon his mother was out shopping for a new car. He picked Tommy up every morning and dropped him off after school. Brenda tagged along in the afternoon. She sat in the front with Jack and they would drive away from Tommy's house together. Patricia Stevens was never around after school. She was always either going to the library, or going to meet people. She never said who the people were, and Brenda said she had sworn not to tell.

At home one afternoon, Tommy read in the newspaper that Elvis Presley's first movie, *Love Me Tender,* was coming to the Paramount. He decided this would make a perfect group outing for The Rockers, and he couldn't wait to make the announcement.

The next morning was chilly. It was the week of Halloween, and fall was arriving in the Delta. There was frost on the grass, and steam rose from it as the morning sun began to shine. There was more steam inside Jack's car as warm breath collided with autumn chill. The steam mingled with the cigarette smoke and made the car look like a sauna or an opium den.

Tommy was sitting in the front seat beside Jack, and the two girls were in the back. He turned to address them all, "Hey, everybody, I've got a great idea! It said in the paper that *Love Me Tender* is starting Friday, and I think we should all go see it together. Maybe Saturday afternoon or something."

There was a long silence. The air in the car got clearer, as if everyone had stopped breathing. The radio was playing "In the Still of the Night." Jack looked down at the dashboard with his arms draped over the top of the steering wheel. When the song ended and a commercial came on, Jack spoke without looking up, "Yeah, I heard about the movie." The words fogged out of his mouth. He paused long enough for them to evaporate before he breathed the rest of the sentence, "I'm already going Friday night... with Brenda." Jack took a puff on his cigarette. The smoke stuck to the cloud of his words and made them hang in the air around his head.

Tommy was suddenly very cold. He held his hands to his mouth and blew on them, then put them in his jacket pockets. "Oh. That's OK," he said. "I can always go by myself." He looked back at Patricia. He hoped that she would rescue him, or make some sort of gesture toward him. She avoided his eyes and looked at Brenda.

Brenda cleared her throat. "Maybe we can all go together sometime, too. I'm sure it's worth seeing more than once."

"Yeah, maybe," Tommy said.

Things were awkward for a couple of days after that. Jack and Tommy rode to school in silence, and Brenda and Patricia stayed away. But in another week The Rockers regrouped. The movie was really bad and they had to get together to talk about it.

Two Mondays later, Brenda showed up with a newspaper clipping from the Sunday edition of the Memphis paper. It said that Allan Freed's Rock and Roll Caravan was coming to the Memphis City Auditorium on the Friday before Thanksgiving.

"Of course," Brenda explained, "Allan Freed just organizes these things. He doesn't actually go around on the bus. But listen to who all will be there." She read the names of the performers, with a dramatic pause between each, "Carl Perkins... Gene Vincent... Lavern Baker..." Brenda's voice grew more excited as she went down the bill. "Little Richard..." The Rockers squealed in unison a falsetto, "Oooooh!"

"...and the one and only Bo Diddley!" she concluded. The car rocked from the bodies shaking and the fists thumping to Bo Diddley's hambone beat.

"We just got to go to this thing!" Brenda shouted above the clamor.

"Yeah, and make it a big deal, too," said Jack. "Get everybody we know to go, and fill up as many cars as we can. We'll call it The Rockers Caravan to the Caravan."

- Nine -

The Rockers solicited all their friends for the trip to Memphis, but when the deadline for ticket orders came, there were only ten. That included the original four and Brenda's 13-year-old brother, Keith. They planned to travel in two cars and one pick-up truck. The caravan grew to four vehicles when, on the day of the show, Patricia announced that her friend would be driving his own car.

They gathered in Mackey's parking lot at 5:00 that evening. It was almost dark and already cold. Tommy sat in the backseat of Jack's car, with Brenda's little brother. It was either that or ride with another couple he barely knew.

Patricia arrived with her friend in a big, red Buick. They got out, and Patricia introduced the guy. His name was Terry Warner. He was a little older than any of them. He was 6' 2" and looked like a lifeguard, with blonde hair that was almost white and a fresh tan in late November. He was wearing a dark blue sport coat and a necktie. The others were wearing jeans or cat clothes. Terry Warner seemed embarrassed. Patricia didn't say anything about him except his name. They got back in his car, and in a cloud of gravel and dust, the caravan was underway. "What do you know about Terry Warner?" Tommy asked when they were on the road.

"Not much," Brenda said. "He's 22. He went to Yazoo State College over in Wellsburg. He works for State Farm Insurance, and their office is in the same building where Patricia's daddy works. That's where she met him. They've been seeing each other on the sly for a while. I don't think he knows what he's getting into tonight."

"Yeah," Tommy said, "I saw the tie."

They drove under the cover of the tall, barren oak trees that stood on the roadside. The radio played WDIA from Memphis. Tommy tried to tell his friends everything he knew about the performers they'd be seeing. "Carl Perkins is from Jackson, Tennessee, and his brother plays guitar for Johnny Cash. Bo Diddley is from Belzoni, here in the Delta, and his real name is Ellis McDaniel. Little Richard's real name is Richard Penniman..."

"OK, Professor," Brenda interrupted, "did you know that Little Richard Penniman is a homosexual?"

"Naw," Jack groaned and hit the steering wheel, "don't give me that shit."

"No, he's not," Tommy said, "That's just something people say to put down rock and roll."

"What are you talking about?" Brenda's little brother asked.

"Yes, he is," Brenda said. "He's a homosexual. It's not a put-down, it's just what he is."

Jack turned up the radio and leaned as far over the steering wheel as he could.

"How do you know that?" Tommy asked.

"From New Orleans," Brenda said. "It was common knowledge in the French Quarter. All the theater people knew about him. Called him the Queen of Rock and Roll. When he was in town he would go to those nightclubs they have, dressed as a woman, and get up and sing. Even after he started getting famous."

"Well," Tommy said, "He did make all his early records in New Orleans..."

"You watch him tonight," Brenda said, "how he acts and everything. You can tell."

"Not always..." Tommy stopped himself in mid-thought. Jack glared back over his shoulder.

"What are you people talking about?" Keith Haley asked again.

"Nothing," Brenda answered, "Nothing at all."

The miles disappeared in darkness, and the signal from the Memphis radio station got stronger. It was like radar guiding the caravan through a wilderness of naked cotton fields and closed-up little towns. The traffic on the highway increased, and subdivisions appeared in the woods and fields along the side roads. On the right side of the road loomed a huge billboard that showed a map of Tennessee broken into its western, central and eastern parts. Across the map were printed the words, "The Three States of Tennessee Welcome You." They were in Memphis.

The City Auditorium was downtown, near the riverfront. It was 20 minutes before show time when the caravan arrived. They parked the cars on a deserted side street and walked quickly through the chilly night, all ten of them parading in a line. The downtown streets were empty until they reached the auditorium. At the front of the building was a broad flight of concrete stairs. These were filled with two lines of people, about equal in size, entering the auditorium through two separate doors. The lines were separated by a rope that ran the length of the stairs. One line was for "white" and the other was for "colored."

Tommy was startled. He had not considered who might be in the audience at a show where three of the five performers were black.

"I guess they're going to put them in the balcony," Jack said.

"Better be a big balcony," Tommy answered. "Looks like there's as many of them as there is us."

The group from Calhoun got their tickets out and took their place in line. Ten minutes passed. It was almost show time, and the crowd was getting restless. People in both lines clapped in unison as a show of impatience. A policeman stood at the top of the stairs and spoke through a bullhorn, "Attention, please. Everyone please be patient. There was a problem with the arrangements, but it's fixed now. The show won't start until everybody's inside."

The lines moved more quickly after that. Tommy, Jack, Brenda and Keith were separated from the rest of their group as the crowd of white bodies bottlenecked into the single door. A man tore their tickets at the door, and they creeped inside.

The cavernous lobby also had a rope strung down the middle separating the "white" and "colored" sides. A cloud of cigarette smoke hung near the ceiling, and a clatter of voices bounced around walls of stone. There were three sets of double doors leading from the lobby to the performance hall, but the middle one was closed, and there was another bottleneck as the lobby full of people made their way through the two separate entrances. The people were packed in too tightly for whites and coloreds to see each other except right along the boundary.

On each side of the lobby was a stairway leading to the balcony seats. The group from Calhoun held tickets on the lower level, so they followed the herd across the lobby. Jack was the first to make it in. From a few feet back, Tommy heard him exclaim, "Holy shit!"

When Tommy entered he understood. He expected the auditorium to be a bigger version of a school assembly hall, but this was a plush and ornate opera house from the turn of the century. The aisles were covered with thick red carpet. The seats had black steel frames and thick cushions that matched the carpet. The ceiling was plaster, with lots of swirling scroll work. A huge glass chandelier hung over the center of the hall.

People took their seats with difficulty. The makeshift rope barrier between the races ran right down the center aisle and all the way up to the edge of the stage. People could only get down the aisle single file. Black and white teenagers bumped hips and elbows as they navigated the divide. On either side of the aisle, they were seated as little as four feet apart with only a twine barrier between. The rope was thick, but it was just a rope.

Slowly members of the Calhoun group found their places about ten feet in from the center aisle. Tommy sat with the couple he didn't know on one side of him and little Keith Haley on the other. Jack and Brenda were right in front. Patricia Stevens and friend were in that same row a couple of seats in toward the center.

Tommy tapped Jack on the shoulder, pointed to the rope, and said, "That must be the 'arrangements' they were talking about."

"Yeah," Jack said, "I hope this don't get out of hand."

"Don't be ridiculous," Brenda said, "It just shows how stupid and petty the whole thing is."

Tommy twisted his body and craned his neck to get a view of the black teenagers on the other side of the rope. They were yelling greetings to one another and flirting and making jokes about each other's clothes. They didn't seem dangerous, Tommy thought, and they didn't seem unnaturally cool, either.

As he looked across the rope, something on the far side of the hall caught Tommy's eye. He rose in his seat and looked harder, but he couldn't find it. He stood and looked a little closer to the front of the room. As he scanned the rows, the face appeared. Tommy saw it in a flash before it dissolved back into the crowd. It was the face of Darrell Farmer. Tommy tried to refocus his eyes and get it back, but he couldn't. The face was gone, except in his memory.

Slowly Tommy lowered himself into the cushioned seat. This was the strange moment from the dream, when Darrell Farmer was with him and alive. It was the same face and the same feeling and it was real. The noise in the hall was deafening, but to Tommy it was all distant and indistinct. He closed his eyes and saw that face again. He opened them and there was only darkness, and howls of terror.

Tommy shivered and grabbed the cold steel arm of his seat. With a jolt he remembered where he was. The house lights were down for the start of the show. The howls were just kids joking in the dark. Tommy rubbed his eyes and tried to focus on the darkened stage. A spotlight hit front and center where the master of ceremonies was already standing at a microphone stand. It was a local white disk jockey who called himself Rocking Russ Randolph.

Randolph was middle-aged, overweight and dressed in a wrinkled blue suit. His hair was greased and combed over a bald spot on the top of his head. "I've been playing rock and roll on the air since before it had a name," he said. "I've heard all about its bad influence. They say it makes you kids wild and disobedient..."

A cheer went up. Randolph stepped back from the microphone with a baffled look. At a lull in the cheering, he stepped up and tried a harsher tack. "They say it is Satanic and subversive," he growled. The cheers turned to boos and hisses. Randolph started to smile. "You and I know that's a bunch of baloney, and I want all 3,000 of you to prove it tonight. Everybody stay in your seats, follow the rules, and we'll all have a nice, safe evening of rock and roll."

The cheers returned when Randolph introduced Carl Perkins, and the show was underway. Perkins drew wild cheers from the white side of the hall, and his guitar solos got a rise from the other side, too. By the time he played "Blue Suede Shoes," everybody was clapping in time.

Things got really hot during Lavern Baker's set. When she did "Jim Dandy (To the Rescue)," couples on the black side of the auditorium were on their feet, dancing in the narrow seat rows. A few white kids stood up, too, but most of them clapped and swayed in their seats.

When Little Richard hit the stage, Tommy stood to get a good look at him. From 11 rows back, Tommy was shocked at what he saw. Richard was wearing a shiny suit. His hair was shiny, too. It was piled high on his head and held in place with some kind of ointment that glistened under the spotlight. He was also wearing make-up. Not normal stage make-up, but a thick mask of tan powder, and gobs of white lipstick and rouge, with silver eyeliner and thick penciled-on eyebrows that made him look surprised. Tommy couldn't take his eyes off of the man.

Richard greeted the crowd with a limp-wristed wave and went to the piano. He bent over the keyboard, and the spotlight picked up the glint of a single ruby earring in his right earlobe. He counted four and began to pump out a hot lava flow of power and desire. The song was "Tutti Frutti." The tunes poured out one after another without interruption, each one faster and wilder than the last.

Tommy was still standing, and his feet and hips had started to move in a way they never had before. He caught himself and stilled his lower body. He looked around. All of his group were standing now, except Terry. Across the rope the center aisle was still clear, but the side aisles had filled with dancers, and some people were standing on their seats. There was wildness in the air.

Tommy looked again at Little Richard on the stage. He was a blur of light and heat, flinging rainbow drops of sweat into the spotlight, and howling and trilling in ecstasy, over and over, "You keep a' knocking but you can't come in..."

Tommy thought about Wade Suggs. He wondered where Wade was now. Maybe he was in this crowd. It was possible, not likely, but possible. Tommy wished that he were. He wished that Wade were there with his friends, with Tommy and Jack, and with the new friends he might have. He wished Wade could see this thing that was happening on stage and somehow know that he was alright, that there was a place for someone like him. That he didn't have to be afraid.

The music stopped, and Tommy was still standing. His eyes were wet, and he could barely see Little Richard leaving the stage. His throat was clenched and he was burning hot. He shuddered and rubbed his eyes and gained control of himself. He looked around. Everyone else was still standing. Little Richard came back for an encore. Tommy barely noticed the music. It blended in with the roar of the crowd and the roar of blood rushing in his head.

The music ended, the cheering faded away, and they all sat down. Brenda turned back to face Tommy, "So what do you think?"

Tommy barely heard the question. "It's incredible," he said.

"I mean what we were talking about before. What do you think?"

"Oh, that," Tommy said. "Yeah. I guess so. Who knows? Who cares?"

There was a long break before Bo Diddley. All the house lights came back on to let everybody go to the drink stand and the segregated restrooms. Then it was dark again, and Russ Randolph made the introduction. Bo Diddley walked into the spotlight carrying an electric guitar with a rectangular body. He planted himself in front of the microphone, his legs slightly apart, and stood, like a great black mountain rising from the mud flat banks of the Mississippi.

The band started the slow, two-chord vamp of "I'm a Man." Bo seized his guitar by the neck and banged a wrenching staccato phrase into the empty place in the riff. The crowd gasped. He began to sing some hoodoo stuff about being a seventh son, born on the seventh day, of the seventh month. Most of the crowd rose and began to dance in place. The music went on for ten minutes. It built up volume and intensity, then paused with a promise of release that was only a tease before it built back to an even higher peak.

Tommy was on his feet from the start, dancing in spite of himself. Everyone around him was up, too, even Terry, although he wasn't moving. Patricia was shaking wildly, flinging her hair and rotating her hips with the slow grind of the music. Her breasts flew back and forth under a thin jersey top. Tommy began to stiffen and sweat.

He forced himself to look away from Patricia. He surveyed the scene across the rope. It was pandemonium. All of the aisles, including the center one, were jammed with black dancers. The people who couldn't reach an aisle were dancing on the seats. The ushers started to walk the edges of the crowd along the rope, tapping people on the back and asking them to clear the aisle. They were ignored. Tommy looked toward the part of the hall where he'd seen the face, but he couldn't recognize anyone in the dark.

"I'm a Man" ended, but there was no relief. Bo Diddley paused for the length of a breath and fooled with the knobs on his strange guitar. Then he hammered a full-throttle version of his famous beat. The tom-toms came in behind him, then the bass. He sang, "Bo Diddley, Bo Diddley, have you heard..."

All decorum broke down, even on the white side of the rope. Everyone was dancing madly. The center aisle was full of dancing white and black teenagers, shoulder to shoulder and hip to hip, with only the rope between them. People were climbing over seats, rushing toward the stage.

The song reached the refrain. "Hey, Bo Diddley," the singer called, and 3,000 voices answered back, "Hey, Bo Diddley." Somewhere near the front of the stage, the rope disappeared under a two-toned sea of bodies. Then it disappeared entirely, trampled underfoot, the whole length of the center aisle. On both sides people began to edge across the border for elbow room or a better look at the stage.

Tommy was standing on his seat. He saw a few people on each side deliberately dash across the aisle. One of them was Brenda Haley. Patricia followed. They were both on the "colored" side of the auditorium, six rows back from the stage, dancing together. Tommy jumped down and ran to join them. Jack stayed behind. So did the rest of their group.

The middle region of the auditorium was a solid, heaving mass of kids, of both colors, all chanting and bouncing and sweating like one body. When Tommy was on the other side, as close as he could get to where Brenda and Patricia were, he began to jump up and down, a little higher with each bounce. He yelled at the top of his lungs, "God, this is great!" But the electric guitar, and the drumbeat, and the "Bo Diddley" chant were so loud that he could barely hear himself.

A harmonica played a solo chorus and Tommy stood on a seat to take in the scene. Near the front a group of black kids were on the white side doing a line dance. His eyes tracked a little further toward the edge of the crowd. He saw the face again. It was a boy in a brown suit and tie dancing with a young girl. He smiled like the face in the school picture. He did look a little like Darrell Farmer, but he was just himself now.

Tommy climbed down and began to dance. Bo Diddley played his guitar with a trebly, double-time frenzy. People started pouring down from the balconies and toward the stage. The glass chandelier at the top of the hall trembled. Beneath the carpet the old wooden floor bounced from the force of bodies leaping and shaking.

Then the music stopped. The guitar and bass dropped out, and after one last drum beat the hall grew so quiet that you could hear the glass on the chandelier tinkle. The house lights came on. Russ Randolph was on the stage. He motioned Bo Diddley away from the microphone and took it himself. "Everyone back in your seats," he shouted. "The show is over till y'all are back in your seats."

While Randolph was talking, Bo Diddley walked to the side of the stage. His guitar was slung across his back like a rifle, and he was laughing so loudly that the microphone picked it up from ten feet away. He looked out over the crowd with a contented smile.

Randolph repeated his order and added, "The police are entering the auditorium. Anyone not in their proper seat will be removed." Uniformed cops began to file in from the fire exit doors at either side of the stage. They held their billy clubs sideways in front of them and marched up the center aisle as the last stragglers fled. Bo Diddley and his band left the stage.

When the aisle was cleared, the cops raised the rope. Russ Randolph came back out with a cop at his side. "Due to the late hour, the rest of the show is cancelled," he said. Policemen stood posted all around the building as 3,000 young people slowly and quietly filed out into the night through two separate exits.

Outside the Calhoun caravan regrouped and walked toward their cars. It was bone-chilling cold, but that served to revive their spirits. They were hot and sweaty from the crowd and the dancing. In the cold night air, steam rose from their damp heads and came out of their mouths and noses with each breath. They all lit cigarettes.

"I can't wait to tell Daddy about this," Brenda said, "He's always saying how 'vulgar and destructive' rock and roll is," she said, taking on a stern voice meant to imitate her father. "Now I can tell him that rock and roll has done what all his sermons and meetings will never do."

"Thank you, Jesus, and amen!" Patricia shouted and spun down the street. She stopped and turned back to Brenda. "But don't you dare tell your daddy, 'cause if you do, sooner or later Big Bob Stevens will hear about his little girl wiggling her ass in the colored section... Aw, hell, go ahead and tell." She leapt and spun again. "'cause, you know, it felt so good that I just don't give a shit."

She cocked back her head and poured steaming laughter into the night. Tommy watched her in wonder. He watched so hard that he forgot to keep walking. He felt warm watching her, like she was sunshine on these pitch-black Memphis streets.

Terry trailed behind, with Jack. They reached their cars, and Terry glared as he corralled Patricia into his Buick. "See y'all around," he said, "I guess." He slammed his door, gunned the engine, and was gone.

Everyone else said goodnights, and Tommy climbed into the backseat of Jack's car with Keith Haley. The lights of Memphis disappeared quickly behind them. In the hills of DeSoto County, spots of fog hung over the road like ghosts. The car heater was starting to work, and Keith was asleep. All was silent.

Tommy leaned over the front seat, "Well, that was sure worth the trip, huh?"

"Yeah, I guess," Jack said. "Got kind of scary for a while, though, when the coloreds started charging."

"Jack Gerard, cut the crap," Brenda said. "Didn't nobody charge nothing, and you know it."

"Yeah," Tommy said, "besides, I thought that was the best part of the whole thing."

"Well, I didn't," Jack said. "It's nothing but bad trouble mixing up what's not supposed to be mixed. Maybe y'all are looking for that, but I ain't."

Jack and Brenda looked hard at each other. Tommy felt uncomfortable with his head stuck between them. He pulled back to his corner of the back seat and stayed there for the rest of the trip. He looked out the window and pictured Patricia Stevens in his mind, dancing and laughing.

Tommy Jackson woke the next morning with ringing ears and a head fogged with dreams. He jumped out of bed and dressed and walked downtown. He wanted to know what the Memphis paper said about the Rock and Roll Caravan.

The day was cool and clear, and as Tommy walked, one of the dreams in his head came back into focus. The dream was filled with black people. Darrell Farmer wasn't in it, neither was Bo Diddley or Little Richard or Lavern Baker. The people in the dream were just regular black people. He recognized some of them. There was Edward Banks and some other guys he worked with in the summer, and the woman who cleaned house for the old people next door.

In the dream Tommy was in a strange town, and all of these familiar black people were on the street. He was trying to get somewhere and couldn't find his way. He kept asking the black people for directions, but they couldn't hear him.

The dream was so real in his mind that Tommy had to stop walking for a second and remind himself that he was in his hometown, going to the drugstore. He bought the paper, walked to the courthouse, and sat on the steps to read. Across the lawn some Daughters of the Confederacy were tending the flower bed around the memorial statue.

There was nothing on the front page about the show. Tommy tore through the paper looking for the story. He found it way back on page 19 with the movie advertisements. It was a small item, four inches long. It just said that the show happened, who played, Russ Randolph emceed, and it was a sellout. That was all. There was nothing about the race rope falling, or about the cops moving in and shutting down the show. Nothing at all.

A month later it was Christmas. Christmas was a big deal at Tommy's house that year. Josie and Robbie were there with their baby, a little girl named Jenny. Together on Christmas Eve night, they all pulled the wrappings off the Jackson family's first television set.

One day after Christmas, when Tommy's parents had gone back to work, Tommy sat around the house all morning in his pajamas, watching the new TV. At noon the news came on, and the announcer said that the bus boycott over in Montgomery, Alabama was over. The Negroes had won. They would never have to sit in the back of the bus again. They showed pictures from Montgomery. The film was of Martin Luther King making a speech and a church full of black people singing and clapping.

Tommy J. Jackson sat in the empty living room, with an empty cereal bowl on his lap, and watched Reverend King. When the report was over, Tommy said to himself right out loud, "It's here." He trembled, took a deep breath, and said it again, a little louder.

- Ten -

In the spring of 1961, Tommy Jackson was finishing his third year at Stillwater College. It was a small Baptist school on the outskirts of Jackson, Mississippi. Tommy wasn't sure why he was there. He studied philosophy and liked it well enough, but it didn't seem to be leading anywhere.

In some of his classes he wrestled with the rights and wrongs of his life and the world around him and the things he had seen. Most of his teachers thought the situation in Mississippi was morally wrong, but none of them knew what to do about it.

Tommy knew that going to college was better than the Army or unloading boxcars. His parents and his preacher had told him that Stillwater was the place for him. Tommy didn't argue because the school was near Jackson. Jackson was a bigger town, and he thought it would show him a bigger world.

Jack Gerard and Brenda Haley had planned to go to Brooks College, which was also in Jackson. Brooks was run by the Methodists and had the highest academic standing in the state. It was suspected of harboring atheists and race-mixers. It was also expensive, but Brenda could go free as a preacher's kid, and Jack's mother had some college money set aside from somewhere.

The three of them had it all planned. They would meet in Jackson and continue their adventures together on a larger scale. Jack even studied during his last year of high school so his grades would get him into Brooks.

The summer after graduation, Brenda got pregnant, and that was that. They got married and Jack went to work in Calhoun. Next spring they had a baby girl named Zelda. When Zelda was two, the three of them moved 20 miles up the road to Wellsburg, and Jack started going to Yazoo State. Brenda and he were both working part-time. Brenda was supposed to start college when Zelda went to school.

Patricia Stevens went to Ole Miss. She was studying American literature and, according to Brenda, having a secret affair with a young professor. Tommy kept up with his Calhoun friends. They got together at Brenda and Jack's house during holiday breaks, and a few times each summer. In one of his classes Tommy learned that there were different kinds of families in different societies, and he decided that his Calhoun friends were his real family.

He had some friends at Stillwater. All the Baptist preacher kids were sent there, so there were bound to be some misfits. That went double for the foreign missionary kids. They had grown up in places like Brazil and the Congo and Korea and didn't really belong anywhere. Most of Tommy's college friends were from this group. They were drinking buddies, but none of them knew the first thing about rock and roll. They had been on the other side of the world when it started, and that was all supposed to be over now, with Elvis in the army and Buddy Holly dead.

In the spring of 1961, Tommy didn't know where he belonged. His Calhoun friends were his family, but Jack and Brenda had a family of their own. He had never gotten over Patricia Stevens, but she was 200 miles away, going places without him. Sometimes he still had bad dreams about Darrell Farmer and Wade Suggs. He thought about them when he was drunk.

He read in a book that there was no statute of limitations on murder. That meant he could still tell what he knew for as long as Billy Kimbrough was alive. When Tommy lay alone in his dormitory room, after a long night drinking with his friends, he told himself that he would talk some day. The next morning he would remember for a little while, and he would wash his face and shake his head and force the memory from his mind.

Tommy was 21. He was supposed to be grown. He was headed for his last year of college. He was supposed to know what he would do. There was a new president in Washington, and the times were supposed to be changing. But Tommy couldn't see anything in front of him that made sense. The things he held on to were the things he'd heard and seen in high school. The things that happened out Moriah Road. What happened to Wade. What happened in Memphis. Those things were real. Those were the things his life was about. He couldn't let go of them, but he couldn't see where they led.

On Sunday, May 21, 1961, Tommy sat in the lobby of his college dormitory with twenty other guys and watched a TV news special about the Freedom Ride. The college boys filled all the orange vinyl couches and chairs in the room and all the available space on the cold tile floor. Tommy sat cross-legged on the floor, at the front of the room, just inches from the TV screen. The sound was turned up high and echoed harshly off the green cinderblock walls.

At first they all watched quietly as the TV announcer filled in the background on the Freedom Ride. It was a rolling civil rights demonstration that had left Washington, DC on May 4 bound for New Orleans. The 13 Freedom Riders, six whites and seven blacks, were taking public Greyhound and Trailways buses across the Southern states and defying all local segregation laws along the way. The Ride was intended to force the new Kennedy administration to act against Southern segregation.

The announcer said that the Freedom Riders had expected to be jailed and beaten somewhere along the way. At that point the screen showed a white-haired, middle-aged black man saying that the Freedom Ride was an exercise in Gandhian nonviolent resistance, and the Riders were trained to take all kinds of harassment without striking back.

In Rock Hill, South Carolina, one of the white Freedom Riders was beaten by a group of young white men dressed in black leather jackets and blue jeans, with ducktail haircuts. The boys in Tommy's dormitory lobby laughed at that description.

The room grew quiet again as the announcer reported the events of the past Sunday, May 14, 1961, which had also been Mother's Day. On that day a Greyhound bus carrying several Freedom Riders pulled into the station at Anniston, Alabama. There a mob of 30 or 40 angry white people was waiting armed with chains, boards and iron construction bars. They pulled some of the Freedom Riders off their bus and beat them bloody. Local police stood by for several minutes and made no move to stop the attack.

Finally the police intervened and allowed the bus to proceed, but members of the mob followed the bus onto the highway. They blocked the road with their cars and slashed the tires on the bus. Someone tossed a firebomb into the bus, and the inside filled with flames and smoke. The Freedom Riders fled on the roadside and were attacked again.

The TV screen showed a picture of the burned-out Greyhound, sitting on its flattened tires, at the edge of a rural two-lane highway.

A couple of hours later, a Trailways bus carrying the rest of the Freedom Riders arrived in Birmingham. There was a TV camera at the Birmingham station, and the whole world saw what happened. The first Freedom Rider to step from the bus was a tall, thin white man in his mid-30s. He was immediately jumped by a crowd of local whites with sticks and pipes. He fell to the ground, but the white men kept beating him. They beat him until he was lying unconscious in a puddle of blood.

Some of the boys in Tommy's dormitory groaned and muttered at those pictures. Tommy felt light-headed and sick. He tried to close his eyes but they wouldn't shut. He kept watching the screen as it showed men and women, black and white, being beaten to the ground. None of them offered any resistance. After the Mother's Day attacks, all of the original Freedom Riders were too seriously injured to continue.

There had been no police officers at the Birmingham station. The TV news man quoted Police Chief Bull Connor as saying that his officers were all busy visiting their mothers on Mother's Day. On that line, the show stopped for a commercial break.

"Nigger propaganda!" somebody said from the back of the room.

"I'm going to call the station and complain," another guy said. He stood and walked to the pay phone in the hall. "Line's busy," he called back. "I bet half the state is calling about this."

Tommy sat dead still on the floor and pretended to watch the ads for Winston cigarettes and Schlitz beer. The program returned, and the pictures on the screen showed 21 new Freedom Riders filing onto a bus out of Birmingham on Saturday, May 20. They all looked like students, and only a few of them were white.

Their first stop was Montgomery. Again there were no police, but once again the cameras caught the full fury of the mob. The pictures showed people curled up on the ground, bleeding and sobbing, while angry white people stood over them spitting and kicking and beating them with axe handles.

The Freedom Ride was stalled in Montgomery. That very night, the news man said, a protest meeting was going on at the First Baptist Church. Rev. Martin Luther King, Jr. was there, but the church was under siege, surrounded by a crowd of about 1,000 white people who were throwing rocks and stink bombs.

The reporter ended the show saying that if the Freedom Riders ever did get out of Montgomery, their next stop would be Jackson, Mississippi.

"No way!" one of the Stillwater guys yelled. A shower of paper cups and wadded napkins flew toward the front of the room and bounced off the

TV screen as the closing credits rolled.

"They'll wish they were back in Alabama," another guy huffed, as he turned off the set. Most of the students filed into the hall and back to their rooms without speaking.

Tommy hardly noticed any of this. He sat glued in the same spot on the floor, staring at the TV screen, even after it went blank. He was consumed by what he had seen. He felt excitement and dread stir inside him. When the lobby was empty, Tommy stood and returned to his room. He lay on his bed in the dark and let the TV images roll over and over in his mind. It was as if the conflict inside him had escaped into the world. It was war out there. Tommy was afraid that he would be drawn into the battle, and he was afraid that he would not. He resolved that if those Freedom Riders made it to Jackson, he would be there.

On Wednesday, May 24, 1961, 27 Freedom Riders left Montgomery, Alabama. Their bus was escorted to the Mississippi line by the Alabama National Guard.

On that same Wednesday morning at Stillwater College, Tommy got into his car. It was the green 1948 family Chevy that he had driven off to college as his own. Tommy was skipping his morning classes and had not told anyone what he was doing. He just got into the car and drove, alone, down the road to Jackson. He didn't know what he would find there or what he would do. He just went.

As Tommy pulled out of the Stillwater campus he turned on the car radio to get the news. They were talking about the Freedom Rides. The bus had left Montgomery that morning before sunrise. It was expected in Jackson at 11:00 a.m. All the other Jackson buses were cancelled and the terminal was closed. The radio news started playing a tape of Governor Ross Barnett talking about agitators and deviants. Tommy turned him off.

He was in Jackson. He drove past the city park on Ellis Avenue, and the

Jackson Zoo, and kept going on West Capitol Street to the downtown area. There was nowhere to park around the bus station because the police had closed the streets. Tommy parked on Pearl Street, by the railroad tracks, five blocks from the bus terminal. The day was sunny and warm, just on the edge of summer.

The Jackson bus terminal was on an old, neglected downtown block. The station fronted on Swann Street between Lamar and Farish. It was surrounded by cheap bars, diners and hotels that catered to people on the buses. Tommy had heard that evening ladies also worked these streets.

But all that trade was shut down when the Freedom Ride came in. The stores and cafes were closed, with blinds pulled shut on the windows and doors. As Tommy walked on Lamar Street toward the terminal, all that he saw were police officers at the intersections blocking off the traffic.

He rounded the corner at Ethridge and Lamar, at the back of the bus station. On the streets outside the terminal were a few hundred angry white people. Many were waving Confederate flags, or the Mississippi state flag with the stars and bars in it. They sang a medley of "Dixie" and the state song, "Go, Mississippi!" and chanted, "Niggers go home!" Some people were carrying banners with that same message, in enormous block letters. The banners were held high on long poles so they could be seen from the window of a Greyhound bus. There were TV cameras and men with notebooks and microphones running around to record the scene.

Tommy looked as closely as he could and didn't see any axe handles or other weapons. There didn't seem to be a chance that the mob would get inside the station. The place was sealed by a wall of police officers. They were stationed shoulder to shoulder around the entire city block, and stacked three deep at the entrances.

Tommy walked on the far side of the street away from the terminal, where there were fewer people. From that vantage point, he walked a full circle around the station and saw it from every angle. The mob was concentrated around the main entrance. The crowd was much thinner on the side streets.

Tommy poked his head around a corner onto a one-block street with no name. It wasn't much more than an alley. There was a cluster of uniformed men down that little street and he walked in their direction. Down by the uniforms, there was another door. It was the "colored" entrance to the bus station. Tommy walked closer. The uniformed men were Highway Patrol. There was a double line of them around this doorway. Behind them was another line, made up entirely of soldiers. Real U.S. Army soldiers, in fatigues, with rifles and bayonets.

The troops and officers blocked the entire sidewalk and part of the street around this back entrance. Tommy stayed on the opposite side of the street and walked closer. Behind the rows of armed men, about a dozen pro-Freedom Ride demonstrators walked a silent picket line.

Tommy found a place to stand across the street, on the stairs to a loading dock. From this perch he could see the demonstrators clearly. Most were college age, and all but two were black. A few wore sweatshirts that said "Tucumbee Tigers." Tucumbee was a black college on the northern outskirts of Jackson. The signs they were carrying said "Freedom Now," "Jim Crow Must Go," "We Are All God's Children," and "None Are Free Until All Are Free." They walked slowly in a small circle.

Tommy stood on the steps watching the picket line and felt something grab him in the chest. His breath got short and hard. His legs were shaky and his face was hot. He held on to the handrail to steady himself. He said quietly, under his breath, "Goddamn it, this is it."

He stood for a few minutes transfixed by what he saw. Slowly other white people passed by, noticed the Highway Patrols, and drifted down to see what was happening. Some of them threw Coke bottles at the picket line. The bottles bounced off the Highway Patrols' helmets and sticks. One of the bottles shattered on the sidewalk, and a group of Jackson City Police came around to reinforce the area.

Tommy stayed at his spot on the loading dock most of the morning. He was safely on the far side of the street with the white folks, but he now knew for certain that he belonged with the people who carried the signs. He wanted to carry the one that said "None Are Free Until All Are Free."

After an hour passed, there was a commotion on the other side of the station. The chanting and screaming from the mob grew louder, and bullhorn voices shouted orders. Somebody on the street said, "The bus pulled in."

On the little street where Tommy watched, a grey-painted, old school bus pulled up and parked right in front of the "colored" door. The army soldiers herded the picketers away from the entrance, and the Highway Patrol formed a corridor between the door and the school bus. Some people passed behind the wall of patrolmen and soldiers and into the grey school bus. Most of these people were black, and they walked very quickly, with Jackson police pushing them from behind.

These were the Freedom Riders, already under arrest. They boarded the grey bus and it moved away before they even took their seats. The bus disappeared around the corner and, before anyone on the street had time to react, the Freedom Riders were gone.

At noon the show was over. The news crews were packing up, and the police were opening the streets. Tommy stayed at his post and watched people leave. When most of the onlookers were gone, the demonstrators came from behind the wall of soldiers. A navy blue Tucumbee College van pulled into the space where the grey school bus had been. The demonstrators loaded their picket signs and water jugs into it.

Tommy saw one white boy put his sign in the van and come from behind the police line. He was a skinny guy with his shirttail hanging out. Separated from the demonstrators, he looked no different from any other white boy on the Jackson streets. He ran to a pay phone at the nearest corner, made a short call, and walked at a quick pace back toward the blue van. Tommy impulsively leaped from his place on the steps and hurried to intercept the skinny white boy before he rejoined the group.

As Tommy approached, he nodded in greeting, tried to put on a smile and said, "Hey, where y'all from?"

The skinny guy looked at Tommy suspiciously. He looked around to see if he was being watched and said, "Oh, different places. I go to Brooks College."

Tommy was shocked to hear a familiar accent. "Right here in Jackson?" he said. "Well, I go to Stillwater."

"Hey, y'all beat us pretty good at basketball this year," the skinny guy said.

"Yeah," Tommy answered. "But y'all got us beat to hell at demonstrating."

"Oh, there's really just a few of us," the white boy said. He stood on his tiptoes to see what was happening at the van. There was a silence. Tommy stuck out his hand and said, "Oh, I'm Tommy Jackson."

"Will Richards." As they shook hands, Will looked over Tommy's shoulder at the van. "Look, I got to go, Tommy. But if you're interested in this stuff, there's a meeting in the student center at Brooks tonight at 7:00, you ought to come."

"I might do that," Tommy said. Will was already halfway to the van.

- Eleven -

Back at Stillwater, Tommy had lunch and spent the rest of the day in the library trying to study. It was the week before final exams. At 5:00 he went back to the dorm. In the lobby a lot of guys were watching the TV news, but Tommy couldn't face that crowd again. He went to his room and listened to the radio.

The news said what he saw, that all 27 Freedom Riders were arrested within minutes of leaving the bus. The black ones walked into the white side of the empty terminal, and the white ones walked into the colored side. They were all charged with breaking state and city segregation laws. They refused to pay bail and were locked up, waiting for a court date. After the report, the mayor of Jackson talked. He said he was glad there was no violence, and he hoped this mess was over.

"Fat chance," Tommy said out loud to the radio. He switched it off and ran to the cafeteria. They were just opening for supper, and he didn't want to be late for that meeting.

Tommy arrived at the Brooks College gate a half-hour before the meeting time. He had never actually set foot on the Brooks College campus. Just driving by the place always reminded him of the plans he'd made with Jack and Brenda. The campus was near downtown Jackson, but couldn't be seen from the city streets. It was walled off by several acres of woods. Tommy drove through the gate and up a narrow, winding road. The sun was getting low and it was dark under the trees. At the top of a hill, red rays of sunlight broke through as the woods cleared and ivy-covered, red brick buildings appeared along the road.

Tommy drove a loop around the cluster of buildings and parked in a space marked "Visitor." He walked around the campus and smoked a cigarette. From the hilltop could be seen all of downtown Jackson. On one side, the Lamar Life Insurance building loomed over the business district. In the other direction were the state capitol and the steeple of the First Baptist Church. The gold-plated capitol dome glowed orange in the distance, reflecting the setting sun.

Tommy found the student center. It was a newer building, two-stories, long and rectangular, with glass all around the first floor. It was made from red brick that matched the old buildings. Tommy walked inside. In the lobby a wall clock said ten till seven. Below it a poster board sign said "Meeting Tonight-- The Freedom Rides: What Are They Saying and Where Are They Going?-- McCarty Lounge-- 7 p.m.-- Sponsored by the Brooks Human Relations Committee and the YWCA."

Around the corner was a door with "McCarty Lounge" above it. The door was propped open, and he could hear people inside. Tommy took a deep breath, balled his hands into fists at his side, and walked through the door. The lounge was a long, windowless room with brick walls and exposed wooden beams. At one end it was carpeted and furnished with sofas and easy chairs. The meeting was set up at other end, which had a shiny tile floor with a mosaic of the Brooks College seal worked into it.

There were about 50 people in the room already sitting on wooden folding chairs arranged in two horseshoe rows. The school seal was in the middle of the horseshoe. At the opening was a table where three people sat. On the left was a grey-haired white man who looked like a professor. In the center was a much younger black man who wore horn-rimmed glasses, grey slacks and a blue plaid sport shirt. The other person was a young white woman. She and the black man both looked about 25 years old. The white woman was wearing a short-sleeved brown dress, tan stockings and penny loafers.

The crowd seemed to be mostly Brooks College students. There were young people in button-down shirts and chinos, or neatly pressed cotton dresses, and a few with beatnik T-shirts and jeans. A young black woman sat in the last seat of the front row, next to the table. She wore a baggy Tucumbee College sweatshirt over her dress and held a large textbook on her lap. In the front on the other side was a middle-aged black couple dressed in their church clothes.

It sunk in on Tommy slowly. Those four black people made this one of those "interracial gatherings" he'd heard about. It didn't seem like a big deal, but in that room at that very moment, they were violating segregation laws. Tommy realized that he had been in rooms full of black people all his life, but had never sat down with them, eye-to-eye. It was time for that, he decided. He took a seat in the back row near the door and waited for something to happen.

Will Richards walked through the door in a big hurry, with a girl walking behind him. When he caught sight of Tommy, Will and the girl came over. Tommy got up from his chair.

"Glad you made it," Will said. "You're in luck. That's Joshua Robinson up there." He pointed to the young black man at the table. "We didn't know he was coming until this afternoon."

"Oh," Tommy said. "That's great." He'd never heard of Joshua Robinson.

Will turned to the girl. "Sheila, this is the guy I met at the bus station this morning, from Stillwater. Tommy..."

"Jackson," Tommy said.

"Yeah, Jackson... Tommy, this is Sheila Bissell."

Sheila Bissell had straight dark blonde hair pulled back in a ponytail. She was wearing a man's white dress shirt with the tail out, green plaid

Bermuda shorts, and dirty white sneakers with no socks. Her nose was long and blunt and her lips were thin. She wore no make-up. Nobody would have called her "pretty," that was too simple a word. But Sheila looked as if she didn't care what anybody thought. She was very quiet and still, as if she were someplace else in her mind. She had green eyes behind oval-shaped plastic-framed glasses.

Sheila slowly stuck out her hand to Tommy, and he took it. "Pleased to meet you," she said.

Will held up a piece of paper in his right hand. "Excuse me, they need this to start the meeting, and it's past time. I'll talk to you after, OK?" He dashed around the circle of chairs toward the table at the front of the room.

Tommy turned to Sheila. "Are you a student here, too?"

"Yes," she said. There was an awkward silence. They watched Will hand the piece of paper to the white woman at the front table. She stood up. "I better find a seat," Sheila said, "they're starting."

"Talk to you later," Tommy said. He watched her walk around the room and take the last empty seat in the front row. The woman at the table had been talking for a full minute when Tommy realized that he was still watching Sheila Bissell. He cleared his throat and tried to pay attention to the meeting.

The young white woman in the brown dress was from up North, and she didn't have much to say. She was mainly introducing the professor whose name was Dallas. Tommy had heard of him. Dallas was a historian at Brooks, and he wrote a book about the Reconstruction that they used in one of Tommy's history classes.

Professor Dallas was wearing a tweed jacket with leather elbow patches, a yellow shirt and a brown tie. He stood at the table and looked very uncomfortable. As people were applauding him, he kept looking at the door. Finally Dallas coughed loudly to clear his throat, the applause died, and he began to talk.

Dallas had a note card in his hand, but he looked out at the crowd and said, "Today marks the beginning of a new chapter in Southern history-- a Second Reconstruction. This one will succeed because it does not come at the command of an outside army. It arises from the native initiative of the Southern Negro."

Dallas paused and looked down at his note card. "Inevitable changes are coming." He stopped and looked into the distance for a moment. He looked down again and read from his card. He seemed to be speaking to the piece of paper, or to the floor. He said his words quickly and mechanically, but they came through clearly. "I support any of you and your generation who are ready to help bring these changes about."

Half the audience applauded when he said that. The rest whispered to each other. When the noises died down, Dallas said, "Now I want to introduce a young man from New York City whose reputation precedes him. Please welcome to Mississippi, and to Brooks College, one of the most articulate young leaders of the Freedom Movement, Joshua Robinson."

Robinson rose, and in a soft voice thanked the crowd for coming to hear the ideas of someone like him. For the next 20 minutes he gave the audience a sweeping picture of American Negro life, from near-starvation in the Mississippi Delta to rank dehumanization in the Northern ghettoes. "Contrast this," he said, "with the shining vision of American democracy-- of Jefferson, who said all men are created equal; of Lincoln, and his government of, by and for the people; of FDR and the Four Freedoms."

"It is," Robinson said, "in those very sharecropper shacks and ghetto flats that the American democratic promise is about to be fulfilled." It was strong stuff. As Robinson spoke the room was silent except for the rise and fall of his voice. Finally he came to a rest, and stood with his head down.

The room exploded in applause. When it subsided, Robinson spoke again. "Now let's get down to the nitty-gritty," he said. He described what happened to the Freedom Riders that day.

"All 27 refused to pay bail or fines," he said, "They'll stay in jail. They'll be convicted, and then they'll appeal. They'll stay in jail until the case reaches the federal courts.

"And there will be more of them," Robinson continued. "A group will leave New York City later this week. Another is gathering in Washington, and one in Chicago. All bound for Jackson. They will all go to jail and stay there. They will create pressure on the state simply by the burden of their incarcerated bodies. Meanwhile, white supremacy in Mississippi will be exposed before the whole world."

A fraction of the crowd, maybe a quarter, applauded this statement, but they were loud enough to make it sound like an ovation. Tommy kept quiet and still.

"The movement welcomes any of you who can step forward to help," Robinson said. "If you can't do that, I hope you'll at least help people understand what we're doing, especially back in your hometowns."

Robinson paused for a moment. "Thanks for listening," he said abruptly, and sat down. He looked out from the table with a blank expression as the room filled with applause. Some applauded out of politeness and a few out of fervent support. Both groups were clapping their hands, but the supporters were standing while they did it.

Tommy looked around the room to measure the standers and sitters and decide which one he was. It was like the altar call at a revival meeting. Will Richards was standing. Sheila Bissell was standing. A very nervous-looking Professor Dallas was standing. Tommy Jackson stood, too.

There were questions from the audience, mostly directed at Robinson. One of the button-down shirts asked, "Why can't you go through the official channels and let the system work?" Some groaned at the question, but Robinson answered patiently, "In Mississippi, the system is working exactly the way it's supposed to, and that's the problem." After some more of the same, it was 9:00 p.m. and the young white woman from up North closed the meeting.

As chairs bumped and people shuffled, Tommy walked around the room and found Will Richards, standing with Sheila, near the front table. "What did you think?" Will asked.

"Very impressive. Got some questions, though," Tommy said.

"Great," Will replied. "You drink beer?"

"Oh yeah," Tommy said.

"Then we'll all head for the local saloon," Will said.

"My car's right outside," Tommy said, as the three of them stepped into the hall.

"Good," Will said. "We'll go to J.W.'s. It's not far. It's almost an extension of the Brooks campus."

Sheila sat in the back of Tommy's car and Will took the front. He directed Tommy out of the campus and down a series of residential streets, each a little seedier than the last. They came to a boarded-up house on a double-lot covered with gravel and filled with cars. "That's J.W.'s," Will said.

The house had no front porch and no front door. The only entrance was in the back, up a flight of exterior stairs. Above the back door was a white sheet metal sign with red letters that said "J.W.'s Cafe." They entered beneath it and walked through a dark, smoky room with several pool tables and a jukebox. They continued into another, larger room that had tables and chairs in the middle, booths around three walls, and a bar along the fourth.

They staked out a corner booth, and Will went to the bar for a pitcher of beer, leaving Tommy with Sheila. They sat across the table from each other. "What year are you at Brooks?" he asked.

"Sophomore. Art major," she said.

"Junior in philosophy myself," Tommy said, to no response. He tried to start the conversation again. "Where you from? You don't have much accent."

"I grew up in California," she said. "But my parents were from down here, and all my relatives are here." She looked down at the table as she spoke.

"You go back there in the summer?" Tommy asked.

"Not this year," she said, and looked Tommy in the eye. "I'm staying here to do movement work."

Will returned from the bar with a pitcher in one hand and three glasses stacked in the other. He sat beside Sheila on the other side of the table. Tommy was disappointed. But he saw that she was ignoring Will and looking at him in a way that made him wonder.

They drank the pitcher, and another, and talked about the day. Tommy learned that the Northern white woman at the meeting was named Sally Keaton. The YWCA paid her to do human relations work on black and white campuses in the South.

"Human relations," Will said, "is a euphemism. What she does is organize student groups for the movement, and set up links between Negro and white students, since the colleges are segregated." The Brooks Human Relations Committee was one of her groups. Will and Sheila were both members, and Will would be president next year. There was another group at Tucumbee College. They worked together when they could.

Joshua Robinson was a leader in the student wing of the movement up North. He had just come down to organize in Mississippi, and had been working secretly in the Delta. He decided to go public when the Freedom Ride came along. Will explained that Sally and Josh were a little angry about the Freedom Riders blowing in uninvited and starting this crisis.

"But now that it's here," Will said, "they're going to make the most of it. It'll be one wild summer, that's for sure."

"How so?" Tommy asked.

"Like Josh said tonight, more Freedom Rides, dozens of them. We'll set up an organization here in town. Volunteer workers will come from around the country. Jackson's the center of the civil rights universe now," Will said.

"Unless Governor Barnett gets religion. Then I guess we'll all go to Gulf Shores."

"Is that what you're doing this summer?" Tommy asked, looking at Sheila.

"Yeah," she said, "Will, too. And there's a girl from Tucumbee, Rebecca Carter. She was there tonight. We're the beginnings of the volunteer committee. We don't know exactly what we'll be doing yet."

For a minute they drank without speaking and listened to the rattle of pool balls from the next room. "How did y'all start into this?" Tommy asked.

"I guess I come by it naturally," Will said. "My daddy's a Methodist preacher in Corinth, up in the hills, but he went to seminary up North. My mama's from New Jersey, and she hates the South in general. They've never agreed with the way things are down here, and they always taught me that."

"What's your major?" Tommy asked.

"Political science," Will answered. "Planning on law school, but I've got another year before that."

They both looked at Sheila. She looked into her beer glass and thought for a long time before speaking. "At home, in California, all my friends were interested in folk music and art and beatnik stuff, and we all believed in civil rights. It seemed normal until I got here. My daddy didn't like it, but he didn't like my friends, either. He's military."

Sheila looked across the table, directly at Tommy, "Why are you interested in this?"

Tommy lit a cigarette and looked around the room. It was getting late and most of the tables were empty. The bartender was sweeping the floor. It was quiet, except for the jukebox that played "Spanish Harlem." Tommy was a little drunk, and the marimba sound of the music rang in his ears like church bells.

He tried to concentrate on what he was about to say. He looked back at Sheila, right in her eyes for a moment, then he looked down at his beer. He talked about Elvis and Bo Diddley and what happened at Memphis. He took a deep breath and wondered what would come out next.

"Even before all that," he said, "back in 1955, when I was 15, there was a case in my hometown, you might've heard of it. Black kid named Darrell Farmer got killed by some white men. They found him in the river all beat up."

"Yeah, I heard of it," Will said.

"Well, most everybody in town knew who did it, but nobody did anything." Tommy's voice started to shake. He took a drag from his cigarette and waited for his insides to quiet down. "They got away with it," he continued, looking off into the distance. "Even back then I knew it wasn't right. That boy didn't hurt anybody. They just killed him 'cause he was black, and they got away with it."

Tommy stopped talking again. He put out his cigarette, took a drink from his beer, and lit another. "It's hard to live with that stuff," he said at last. "If I can change it, I want to."

No one spoke for a long time. The song on the jukebox ended. "Time to call it a night?" Will said, standing.

On the ride back, they all sat together in Tommy's front seat, with Sheila in the middle. As she got out at the campus, she touched Tommy's shoulder. "Take care," she said. "I hope we'll be seeing you."

"You'll see me alright," Tommy said.

Will stood on the sidewalk and leaned his head back into the car window. "You got a phone number?" he asked.

Tommy gave him the number of his dormitory floor, and they all said goodnight.

As Tommy drove back toward Stillwater, he turned on the car radio and heard "Hit the Road, Jack" by Ray Charles. It seemed like a sign. He felt like there was a new road opening before him that might lead somewhere. The music filled the car, and Tommy pounded his hand on the steering wheel with the beat. Everything seemed exactly right. He was also drunk, and he didn't feel like going home just yet. When he reached the Stillwater campus, Tommy kept on driving. He stopped at a late night honky tonk on the edge of town, bought a quart of beer to go, and drove west on Highway 80 toward Vicksburg.

Vicksburg was important in the Civil War. It was the last Confederate outpost on the Mississippi. The North besieged it for months. Every white child in Mississippi grew up with stories of the starvation and suffering inflicted on Vicksburg before it fell, July 4, 1863. There was a national park on the battle site and a military graveyard next door. Tommy and his college friends often went there late at night to sit and drink beer on the bluffs overlooking the river.

Twenty minutes after the beer stop, Tommy drove through the Vicksburg battlefield gates. The narrow, twisting road was lined with monuments to military units from Ohio, Indiana, Illinois and other Northern states. Some of them were statues of men on horses or soldiers with rifles. Others were large stone or marble obelisks. In the dark, the monuments were a looming, indistinct presence that cast large shadows over the roadway.

Tommy drove to his favorite spot on the bluffs and parked the car. He walked out to the edge until he could see the point where the Yazoo River joined the Mississippi. That was the end of the Delta. Looking north, up the Yazoo, Tommy could imagine the place where the Little Muddy emptied into it. He sat on the dirt at the edge of the bluff and opened his quart. There Tommy sat and drank and watched, as the waters rolled down from his homeland.

- Twelve -

A few days after the meeting, Will Richards called. He wanted help looking for a house to rent for the movement. They needed someone with a car. Tommy and Will met at the Brooks College cafeteria. Will was at the end of a long, empty table, drinking iced tea with a red-headed white man about 30 years old. It was the tail end of the lunch period, and only a few students were still eating. The black women who worked in the cafeteria were wiping down the empty tables.

"Tommy Jackson, meet Phil O'Toole," Will said. "Phil's a philosophy prof at Tucumbee, and he's in charge of volunteers for the summer project."

O'Toole was short and stocky. His skin was pale and freckled and his hair grew straight out in thick curls. He wore a white short-sleeved shirt and a blue and red tie. His arms were thick with red hair.

"Pleased to meet you," O'Toole said, and stuck out his hand. "You're the first member we've had from Stillwater."

Tommy didn't know he had joined anything, but he accepted the handshake. "I imagine," he said.

"Will tells me you're a philosopher," O'Toole said.

"That's my major." Tommy didn't remember telling that to Will.

"What do they teach out there?" O'Toole asked.

Tommy wondered if this was professional curiosity or an investigation. "Oh, we get the usual Plato to Kant, then some Kierkegaard, Marcel,

Whitehead, little Tillich and Niebuhr..." He wasn't sure if he sounded smart or obnoxious.

"The Christian Existentialist bag?" O'Toole said.

"Yeah, something like that," Tommy answered.

"Ever hear of Maritain? French guy?"

Tommy shook his head.

"Check him out, has a Catholic spin on the same stuff. I did my dissertation on him."

The conversation trailed off. "So, you're going to stick around this summer?" O'Toole asked.

"Hadn't decided. Is there anything I could do?" Tommy said.

"Oh, Will said you might work full-time and live at the house," O'Toole answered.

"Maybe, I'm not sure yet," Tommy said.

Phil banged the table with his hand. "Let's get to the business at hand." As Phil explained it, they were to look at available houses in parts of Jackson that were racial border zones. They needed something with at least four bedrooms, more if possible. But it had to be in an area where either black or white people could be seen on the street, even at night.

The house would be used by volunteers over the summer. There would be black and white living at the house together. That was a crime in Mississippi, and a serious one. Will and Tommy were to say they were with a group of Brooks students working as summer interns at the University Hospital. O'Toole gave them the name and number of a white Methodist chaplain who would vouch for them. Will had $50 in cash for a deposit if they found a suitable place.

Will and Tommy started their rounds in the neighborhood below Brooks College. They drove to J.W.'s and worked their way down from there. This was an area of old two-story wood houses with large front porches. They once were the homes of prosperous white merchants, but lately had changed hands and run down as the merchants and their children moved to new houses on the eastern edge of town.

Past J.W.'s the neighborhood continued down a long hill until it ended at a large, grassy drainage ditch. On the other side of the ditch was Jackson's traditional "colored section" of tar-papered shotgun houses. In some places the black population had spread across the ditch into the big, old houses, and that was where Will and Tommy concentrated their search.

As they drove, the two talked idly, getting-acquainted talk about their hometowns and their studies and their final exams. When they saw a "For Rent" sign, they stopped long enough to write down the address and phone number.

After about an hour of driving, when they were getting comfortable together, Will asked Tommy if he had a girlfriend. Tommy was embarrassed to answer "No." But it gave him an opening. "So how serious are you and Sheila Bissell?"

"Serious?" Will chuckled, "Oh, Sheila's very serious, but not about any guys. We're friends because we have the same commitments and there aren't many of us, but there's no boy-girl thing. I'm engaged to a girl from my hometown. She goes to the State College for Women in Columbus. We started going together in high school and we've visited back and forth every weekend the whole time we've been in college. She's going to Europe for the summer with her mother. That's why I'm doing this."

This news made Tommy think again about the summer and what it could hold, but he tried to put those thoughts out of his mind. If she wasn't interested in any of the guys at Brooks, she wouldn't be interested in him, he thought. And besides, Tommy was a little scared of Sheila and the way she looked at him so intensely.

They passed two more houses for rent. "That's enough," Will said, "pull over at that gas station and we'll make some calls." Tommy waited in the car and listened to the radio, while Will stood at a pay phone pouring in dimes.

He returned with two appointments for that afternoon and two more for the next.

The house they ended up renting was the biggest one they found. It was also the shabbiest. It was near the big ditch on a block that had gone mostly black, but still had two houses of white people. One held three generations of a family that most people would call drunken white trash. The other was rented by three middle-aged white ladies. From the number of male visitors that came and went, Tommy and Will guessed that they were prostitutes.

The house was set way back from the street, almost hidden behind oak and magnolia trees. It had five bedrooms upstairs and a living room, dining room, parlor and kitchen below. The house was partly furnished. There was a couch in the living room and a dining room table with several chairs. Each bedroom had a chest of drawers or a wardrobe, but there were no beds.

The paint on the outside of the house had been white but was grey and peeling. The front porch had holes in the boards and the swing had fallen down. The walls inside were cracked, and there were a few spots where wooden lath showed through holes in the plaster ceilings. But the house was big enough, the location was right, and the plumbing worked, so they took it.

When the papers were signed, Will and Tommy met Phil O'Toole at the house for a tour. Phil was enthusiastic. He stood in the dingy parlor, claimed it as the office, and said, "This is great. This is the place where you guys are going to make history. We'll call it Freedom House."

Tommy's exams were over that day. His dorm was about to close. It was time for him to declare himself about the summer. So, as they stood in front of the house about to get back in their cars, Tommy walked up to O'Toole. "I think I'm in, if you'll take me," he said.

"Great," Phil said. "Let me get something out of the car." He fished around in a briefcase that was on the passenger seat of his bright red Oldsmobile. He came out with two pieces of paper. "Just fill out this questionnaire," he said, "It's no big deal. Just who to contact in an emergency, do you have any health problems, stuff like that. Then you write a little statement about why you want to work for the movement."

"I'm going to Calhoun tomorrow for at least a week or so," Tommy said.

"That's OK. Just fill it out sometime, and when you get back, report here and give it to me. I'll take it from there."

That night at the empty dorm, Tommy packed his clothes in a suitcase and put his books and papers into cardboard boxes. The only things left out in the room were his radio, one sheet on the bed and the questionnaire on his desk. He lay in bed for a long time listening to music, smoking cigarettes, and staring at the two pieces of paper. The music echoed harshly on the bare concrete walls and the cold ceramic tile floor.

Tommy woke up in the morning and the questionnaire was still untouched. He found a manila envelope in one of his boxes and put the papers inside. He folded the envelope and stuck it deep into the bottom of his suitcase, beneath the socks and underwear. Tommy hauled his boxes outside and loaded them in the trunk of his car. He threw the suitcase onto the seat beside him and set out driving north on Highway 49, back to Calhoun.

- Thirteen -

On the evening Tommy returned to Calhoun, his mother fixed fried chicken and mashed potatoes. His father came home from work, and the three of them sat around the dining room table for the first time since Easter. The sun was low outside, but the lights weren't on yet. An electric fan hummed in the window to blow off the last heat of the day. Tommy's mother sat wearing her apron. His father bowed his head. Tommy watched him as he said the blessing. He looked tired, and his brown hair had more gray in it than Tommy remembered.

His daddy said, "Amen," and Tommy picked up a crusty chicken thigh using both hands to hold it by the ends. He took a bite and felt the hot grease and chicken juice pop in his mouth. He put down the thigh and scooped up some mashed potatoes. The brown gravy warmed his whole upper body as it slid down his throat. He turned to the string beans.

"How'd it go at school, son?" his daddy asked.

"Same as always," Tommy said. "Think I did OK. You'll get my grades in a week."

"You going to work with us this summer?" his daddy asked. "I talked to Mr. Rogers the other day, and he said they might put you inside."

Tommy set down his fork and swallowed a mouthful of half-chewed food. "I need to talk to y'all about that," he said. "I think I might stay at school this summer."

"Summer school?" his mama said. "Did you fail something?"

"Naw, Mama," he said, "Just thought I'd take a couple of courses this summer so I'd have a lighter load my last year, while I'm figuring out what to do and looking for a job."

"That's well and good," his daddy said, "but who's going to pay your keep?"

"It's OK, Daddy, I've already got a part-time job," Tommy said, "at the University Hospital, working for the chaplain."

There was a deep silence. Tommy's mother and father looked at each other with wide eyes, confirming that they heard an expression of interest in the ministry. Tommy knew what they were thinking. No one said a word, and they all turned back to their food.

"But where will you live, son?" his mama asked after a while. "Why'd you bring all your things home if you're going right back?"

Tommy hadn't thought about that. He cleared his throat and wiped his mouth. "Well, my dorm's closed for the summer," he said, "they're doing repairs, so I have to move down to the freshman dorm, then back up in the fall."

His mother didn't seem convinced. She put down her chicken leg, and looked straight into his eyes. "Tommy, is there anything else you need to tell us?"

Tommy looked straight back at her. "No, ma'am, that's all. Just what I said."

There was another long silence. The evening chorus of tree frogs had started outside the open windows. It was getting dark in the dining room. They sat in the twilight chewing their food. Tommy felt chicken hanging in his throat and took gulps of iced tea to force it down.

His daddy got up and turned on the lights. "By the way," he said, "did Mama tell you Josie's expecting again?"

That night Tommy went out to ride the streets of his hometown. It was a week night, and the place was all but dead. He drove past Jack Gerard's old house and by the house where Wade Suggs used to live. He drove past the high school and out Moriah Road to the spot where everything happened. He didn't stop, but drove on to Moriah. In front of the Moriah store, he turned around and drove back to Calhoun.

It was 10:00 when Tommy got back to town. He turned off The Boulevard to pass by Mackey's before going home. As he drove by, he slowed to see if there were any familiar cars. There weren't, but there was a familiar face. Four girls were sitting and drinking in a blue convertible, and one of them, on the back seat, was Patricia Stevens.

Tommy turned in the middle of the street and parked in a dark corner of Mackey's lot. He watched Patricia and her friends from a distance and listened to the sound of their laughter. He recognized the other girls as high school classmates but he didn't know them.

He saw Patricia get out of the car and go inside. He got out and stood in the lot to meet her when she came out. Ten minutes later, Tommy said from the darkness, "Hey, long time no see."

Patricia stood in the light by the door and shaded her eyes. "Who is that?" She began to walk toward the voice. "Why, Tommy Jackson!" She ran to him. "Hey, boy. When did you get back in town?"

"Just this evening," Tommy said. Patricia was drunk. She wasn't staggering or slurring, but she was loud and boisterous and shiny with sweat.

"Haven't seen you since Christmas," she said. "You looking well. Did you lose some weight?"

Tommy's head went light. Patricia had never noted his appearance before, hardly anyone had. "Maybe, been real busy," he said.

"Whatever you're doing agrees with you," she said.

"You're looking good yourself," Tommy said, "and feeling good, too."

"Oh, hush. You'd be drunk, too, if you had to put up with those ninnies." She waved her hand toward the convertible. "Silly 'girls' night out.' They set it up with my mama before I got home. They all go to the College for Women, and they're all boring. I'd love to ditch them." She grabbed Tommy by the arm. "Why don't we take off in your car, right now?"

"Sure," Tommy said. Patricia gripped his upper arm hard, and he tightened his muscle in response. She had never touched him before, not even to shake hands. He had dreamed of her flesh for six years, and now there was a small piece of it wrapped around his arm. Tommy felt like he would float away. He thought that her hand on him was the only thing keeping him moored to the ground.

"Go back to your car," she said, "and I'll go tell them something." She released her hold.

Tommy combed his hair and tried to stay calm. In all the years they'd known each other, he had never been alone with Patricia. They were always with Jack and Brenda. Patricia ran across the parking lot and bounded onto the seat beside him with a paper bag in her hand. "I stole their booze." She pulled out a bottle of something purple. "Vodka and grape juice, already mixed."

Patricia took two plastic cups out of the sack and poured. Tommy backed up the car, and when they were under the parking lot's light pole, he took a good look at her. She was wearing knee-length shorts and a white shirt with the tail tied around her waist. The top button of the shirt was open, and the vodka had raised red splotches on her throat and chest.

When they were driving, she leaned her head out the window and let her hair blow in the breeze. "Lord, I wish I had a car. My daddy says it's not right for a girl. We're not supposed to do anything for ourselves. It's ridiculous."

"I thought you were getting on pretty good up at Ole Miss," Tommy said.

"Well, I guess I am," she laughed. "But I have to connive all the time. Of course, most of the girls up there just love being helpless. They all think they're Miss Bo' Weevil of 1861 and some Confederate horseman is going to sweep them away."

Tommy watched Patricia as he drove. She had her back against the car door and her feet on the seat with her knees pulled up. One arm was stretched toward him on the back of the seat and the other was propped in the window. He was seized by heat and tension and said nothing.

"Did I tell you I'm going to law school?" she continued.

"No, I don't think so," Tommy said.

"Well, I am," she said, "Everybody says I'm crazy, but I'm going to do it. There are a few women lawyers, you know, even in Mississippi. Just a few. I figure that's all going to open up soon, though. Just like baseball, where at first it was just Jackie Robinson and now there's coloreds everywhere you look."

Tommy took a long burning swig of the vodka and juice. "Funny you should put it that way, about integration, I mean, 'cause, you know when the Freedom Ride came to Jackson a couple of weeks ago? Well, I was there."

"No," she said.

"Yep," he said. "And I went to a meeting about it and heard one of the ringleaders talk, and I'm going to work for 'em this summer and live in a house full of volunteers from all over."

"My goodness," she said, "How did all this happen?"

"It just happened. It seemed like the right thing to do," he said. "What do you think?"

"Oh, it's great, Tommy. I never would have thought, I mean, I'd be afraid," she said.

"I am, but I don't know what else to do," he said.

"Tommy, I do believe I'm proud of you," she said. She leaned over and kissed him on the cheek and her left breast brushed against his arm. Tommy swerved into the wrong lane of the empty street and spilled some purple drink on his pants.

Patricia settled back into her seat. "What'll you be doing?"

"Don't know. What I'm told, I guess. Except going to jail. I'm not up for that yet," he said.

"Well, of course not," she said. "What are these movement people like?"

"They're OK, mostly pretty regular. Smart. They're all real smart," he said.

"Well, you'll fit right in," she laughed.

"Oh, bullshit," he said.

There was silence. Tommy turned on the radio, but could find nothing good and turned it off again. Patricia looked at her wristwatch and said, "Hey, could you take me over to Jefferson Street? I want to check in with a friend of mine over there before the night's out."

"Sure," Tommy said. "There's a pay phone over there, you want to call first?"

"Naw, he... I mean, they don't have a phone," she said.

"Oh... OK." Tommy drove in silence.

"Alright, keep going to those new apartments down there," Patricia said as they reached Jefferson Street.

Tommy drove to a row of one-story concrete block buildings. The sign said River Garden Apartments, but they were a mile from the river and the yard was just dirt.

"OK, pull in here. I'll be right back," she said over her shoulder as she left the car. Patricia knocked on an apartment door, and a man in blue jeans and a sleeveless undershirt answered. It was Aubrey Miles. He'd been a Calhoun High football hero several years back, when Patricia and Tommy were ninth graders. He went to Yazoo State on a football scholarship and then up to Memphis to try and make it as a rock and roll singer. Now he ran a honky-tonk on the outskirts of town, and sang there on weekends.

Patricia and Aubrey Miles whispered to each other, and he went inside. She ran back to Tommy's car and leaned in his window. "It's OK," she said, "My friend's here. You can go ahead, I'll get a ride home." She put her hand on Tommy's shoulder. "I'm so glad I got to see you," she said. "I really am proud that I know you." She kissed Tommy on the cheek again and disappeared into the apartment.

Tommy backed his car into the street and drove away. He looked in the rear view mirror and saw the lights go out in Aubrey Miles's apartment. He drove to his parents' house, slipped into his old room, and slept, without dreams.

After two days of eating and sleeping and watching TV, Tommy called Jack Gerard in Wellsburg to set up a visit.

"Sure, man, come over and stay the weekend. We got serious catching up to do," Jack said. "We'll fill the fridge up with beer, chain the kid in the yard, and have a high old time."

Late Friday afternoon, Tommy drove into Wellsburg. He pulled up to a two-bedroom house with a green roof and white tile siding. The house was a block from the Yazoo State campus in one direction, and the railroad tracks in the other. Tommy stood in the yard and felt the whistle of a freight train rattle his ears.

Before Tommy could knock, the front door of the house opened. Zelda was the first one out. She ran around the yard pumping her arms and chanting, "Choo, choo, choo, choo-- whoo, whoo-- choo, choo..." Jack was behind her and greeted Tommy with a handshake and a bottle of beer. He herded Zelda back into the house.

Inside Brenda appeared from the kitchen wearing a red apron over a loose, sleeveless floral-print dress. She hugged Tommy. "Patricia called and told us about what you're doing. I've got to hear all about it once Zelda's asleep."

She went back to the kitchen, and Jack and Tommy sat down in the living room to drink their beers and watch Zelda draw with her crayons. The living room was crowded with toys and books and worn-out furniture. Jack looked tired. His wild red hair was cut short, and he was wearing blue slacks and a white shirt from his part-time job at the school library. A necktie was thrown over the back of a chair. "So you're a Freedom Rider, now," he said.

"Yeah, I'm on the team. Second string, though, hope to God they keep me on the bench."

"Well that's a damn fool thing to do," Jack said. "But you always were kind of bent, weren't you? Besides, I'm out-numbered here."

"Yes, you are," Brenda said loudly from the kitchen, "and y'all save that talk for when I can hear it."

"What's up with you?" Tommy asked.

"Same old stuff. Just wound up school for the year," Jack said, slumping deep in his armchair. "This was my last day at the library. This summer I'm driving to Calhoun every day to work for my uncle, Reed Glazier, the lawyer."

"Isn't he prosecutor now?" Tommy said.

"Yeah, I'm in what they call the criminal justice program," Jack said. "I get credit for working with Uncle Reed. It's good experience, too. If we can swing it, I may go to law school eventually."

"Patricia says she's going to law school," Tommy said.

"She's a fool," said Jack.

"I heard that, Jack Gerard," Brenda called out from the kitchen.

"She's got every right to do it," Jack continued, in a loud voice. "But the first year of law school is hell-- on guys. They'll kill her. I'd hate to see it happen, but it will."

Brenda answered with a clatter of pans and grumbling. Jack put on a Sam Cooke album. "What you listening to these days?" "This stuff is great," Tommy answered, "and Ray Charles. Some of the new Elvis stuff is OK.

Those movies just keep getting worse, don't they?"

"Tell me about it," Jack said. "We finally quit going to 'em. Just a waste of money."

Brenda walked in and announced supper. While "Chain Gang" played on the hi-fi they took seats around the table, with Zelda perched on an unabridged dictionary, and dug into corn bread and beef stew.

When Zelda was packed off to bed, the three old friends plopped down in the living room with fresh beers and turned the Sam Cooke record over. It was dark outside. A fogger truck passed on the street spraying DDT to kill the mosquitoes. The poison smelled horrible and Brenda got up and closed the front windows.

"So how'd this all happen?" she asked. Tommy told about going to the bus station, meeting Will Richards, and hearing Joshua Robinson.

"I've read about that Robinson," Brenda said. "He's been working up around here."

"She reads a lot of subversive literature," Jack said.

"*The New Republic, The Delta Democrat,* and the Methodist Social Action newsletter, to be exact," she said. "If you're going to turn me in to Senator Eastland, at least get the facts straight."

She turned back to Tommy. "So is it going to be dangerous this summer?"

"Could be, I haven't thought about it that much," Tommy said. "Just seems like the problems aren't going away, and this is the time I can do something. I'm not looking for trouble, though."

"Please be careful, Tommy," Brenda said.

"Yeah," Jack said, "things could be worse than you expect. Uncle Reed says the good old boys are getting restless, and they might be looking to make examples again. Whatever you do, don't let your name get out in the papers with this stuff. OK?"

Tommy slept on the couch. Brenda worked the next morning, and

Tommy sat with Zelda while Jack mowed the yard. That afternoon Jack drove him several miles into the country to a roadhouse that was his favorite getaway. The place was set in the middle of a cotton field and was bigger than most barns.

Tommy and Jack stepped in from the hot sun to the cool, dim-lit world of the roadhouse. The door opened onto a dance floor and a small bandstand, all empty that afternoon. The bar ran along the back wall. A few guys were drinking there, and an old white woman tended it. The rest of the place was mostly taken up with pool tables, a juke box and pinball machines. The two friends settled in for a long afternoon of drinking, shooting pool and playing rock and roll and hillbilly boogie on the box. In this dark world, the disagreements and different circumstances that lay between Tommy and Jack melted away. They were in perfect harmony on the subjects of beer, pool and jukeboxes.

At about a quarter to four a group of young men burst through the roadhouse door in a gale of laughter and curses. Above the clamor Tommy heard a familiar voice. He looked and saw a familiar fireplug form. He felt as if he had seen a ghost. Tommy tapped Jack on the shoulder. "Holy shit, is that Barry Kimbrough?"

Jack squinted across the dim barroom. "Yeah, it is. They must be fishing at Jawbone Lake; guys come in from there all the time."

"What's he doing now?" Tommy asked.

"Who knows?" Jack said. "Maybe following in his daddy's footsteps, unless he's too stupid to steal."

Kimbrough and his buddies took seats at the bar. Tommy wished he could leave, but he would have to walk past the bar to get to the door. It seemed safer to stay quiet at the pool table and hope for the best. The jukebox played "I'm So Lonesome I Could Cry," by Hank Williams, and Tommy and Jack returned to their game. After one more mournful verse, the record on the jukebox changed. The next one was "Good Golly Miss

Molly" by Little Richard, and that caught Kimbrough's attention. He turned on his barstool to see who was playing the box. Tommy started toward the bathroom to hide, but it was too late.

"Looky there, y'all," Kimbrough shouted. "If it ain't my old high school buddy, Tommy Jackson." He walked over and laid a stubby hand on tommy's shoulder, "Good to see you, son. You ain't been around much, have you?"

Jack stepped back from the table and stood against the wall alongside a rack of cue sticks. Kimbrough was red from the sun and sweaty and drunk. "I'm living in Jackson," Tommy answered.

"Doing what?" Kimbrough said.

"I'm in school."

"College boy, huh? That figures." Little Richard was shrieking and trilling madly. Kimbrough pointed toward the jukebox, "Son, did you play that shit?"

"I did," Tommy answered.

"Well, that figures, too. You always was partial to niggers and faggots, wasn't you?" he said with a laugh.

Tommy was silent. The hand lying on his shoulder gripped him hard. Kimbrough pulled him closer so that eye contact was unavoidable. "Wasn't you, you little son of a bitch?" he said through clenched teeth.

Tommy looked him in the eyes. They were redder and squintier than usual, but there was something sorrowful in them, too. Kimbrough acted as tough as he had in school, but that look in his eyes was like a whipped dog.

"Reckon there's worse things," Tommy said.

Kimbrough pushed him away with enough force to make him stumble. "Like what?" he asked.

"I ain't saying," replied Tommy.

"You ain't saying? Shit! Did y'all hear that?" Kimbrough said loudly, waving his arm toward his buddies at the bar. "Hell, only thing worse than niggers and faggots is nigger lovers." Kimbrough picked up a stick from the pool table and held it with both hands like a baseball bat.

"Get out of my face, Jackson," he said. "Just fucking leave. Now."

"We can do that," Tommy said, "You ready?" He looked toward Jack and Kimbrough looked with him.

"Oh, hey, Gerard," he said. "Didn't see you over there." Jack nodded. Tommy and he walked toward the door. Tommy's face burned and his heart raced but he made his legs walk slowly. He heard Kimbrough mimicking him from behind. "There's worse things," he said in a high-pitched lisp. His friends all laughed and he said it again.

Back in the car Tommy and Jack were quiet for a few miles down the road. "Tom boy," Jack said, breaking the silence, "you're my buddy, and you always will be, but that," he jerked his thumb in the direction of the roadhouse, "is what you're up against with this colored mess, and it's only going to get worse."

"I know what I'm up against," Tommy said. His heart was still pounding. "I know better than you think. That's why I got to do it."

"I don't see what that mess has to do with you," Jack said. "I just don't see it."

"I know you don't, Jack." Tommy lay his head back on the seat and stared out at the fields for the rest of the trip. The cotton plants were almost knee-high and thick with leaves.

When they got back to the house, Tommy decided to cut his visit short. He drove back to Calhoun and told his parents he'd leave for Jackson the next day, right after church and Sunday dinner.

Sunday afternoon Tommy was lazy about getting packed. It was past 3:00 p.m. when he had everything he would need for summer squeezed into a suitcase. He put the suitcase on the front seat and pulled away from his parents' house headed back to Highway 49. The day was still hazy and steaming hot. Tommy drove south down the highway with all four windows open for the breeze. He put his hand on the suitcase beside him. The questionnaire from Phil O'Toole was still crammed into the bottom of the bag.

After driving about a half-hour down the road toward Jackson, Tommy pulled off at a country store and bought a bottle of beer. He drove on to a roadside park near Bentonia and stopped, got out the questionnaire and a pen, and sat down at the picnic table. He planted the beer bottle on the corner of the paper to keep it from blowing away, and he began to write.

He wrote down who he was and where he was from, and put down Jack and Brenda Gerard of Wellsburg, Mississippi as his next of kin. He answered "no" to all the health questions. Where it asked why he wanted to volunteer in the movement, he wrote, as carefully as he could, "My first-hand observation of the 'Southern way of life' with regard to race has convinced me that it is not fit for human beings of any color. We must all change or we will all die."

He looked over his work and went back to underline both "alls" in the last sentence. He underlined so hard that it made a hole in the paper. He held the sheet up before him and read the statement again. "Goddamn, right," he said out loud to himself. He stood and drained the bottle of beer and pitched the empty into the woods.

The sun was going down as Tommy neared the city. On the right side of the road, across the cotton fields, the sky was dark blue with swirls of orange. To the left it was going black. Tommy smoked cigarettes and listened to the Sunday evening radio. It played mostly preachers and church services tape recorded that morning. Tommy drove with one hand on the tuning knob, roaming up and down the dial, trying to catch as much gospel music as he could without hearing a sermon.

He found a 6:00 p.m. news report from a station far away. He stopped turning the knob and listened. It said that the second wave of Freedom Riders had arrived in Jackson that afternoon.

- Fourteen -

Freedom House was hard to find in the dark. Tommy drove up and down the road along the drainage ditch for at least ten minutes before he found the right street. He knew he was getting close when he saw two white women sitting under a porch light in bathrobes waiting for visitors. Tommy slowed down and parked on the street in front of some familiar oak and magnolia trees.

Suitcase in hand, he walked across the yard under the trees. There were two cars in the gravel driveway and the porch light was on. As Tommy stepped onto the porch and set down his suitcase, another car came up the drive. It was a station wagon completely loaded with luggage.

Tommy walked toward the car. The driver was at the rear door loading his arms with suitcases. He was a lean, young black man wearing cuffed blue jeans and a t-shirt that said "Morgan State College." He had round, wire-rimmed eyeglasses and close-cropped hair. "Hey, need a hand?" Tommy asked.

The black man jerked his head back toward the station wagon. "Sure, it's all coming in," he said.

Tommy went to work. After several trips the job was done, and a pile of bags almost six feet high filled the front entry to Freedom House. Tommy stepped out on the porch and saw his co-worker already back in the station wagon. He hustled to the car and stuck his hand through the driver's window. "I'm Tommy Jackson," he said.

The driver gave Tommy a puzzled look as they shook hands. "Charley McGill," he said, "thanks for the help."

"That's what I'm here for," Tommy said, "Whose stuff is that, anyhow?"

"Freedom Riders, the new ones. They rode that bus all the way from New York, so they had baggage, and somebody had to pick it up," Charley McGill said. "Hope they can still use it when they get out."

"Yeah, it's tough, isn't it?" Tommy said.

"Never been different," Charley McGill replied, "I'll talk to you later. I was supposed to have this car back a half-hour ago."

The station wagon crunched out of the drive and the tires screeched on the street as it sped away. Tommy picked up his own bag off the porch and went inside Freedom House to look around. The dining room and the hallway to the kitchen were dark. The living room was empty but the lights were on. Tommy dropped his suitcase in there. The living room opened onto the parlor-office. Tommy stood in the doorway between the two rooms. The parlor was brightly lit and filled by three old desks and a card table that barely supported a manual typewriter. File folders and note cards were scattered amid a clutter of empty Coke bottles and potato chip bags.

A young dark-haired white woman was sitting at one of the desks, with her back to the door, talking on the telephone. "Yes, Mr. King," she said, "they're in the county jail tonight. It's very uncomfortable, but they're safe." The woman was from up North. She spoke rapidly, in a flat tone of voice, and sliced off the beginning and end of each word with precision.

"There's no bail set so far, Mr. King," she said, and stopped to listen. "No, we don't know when they'll go to court. Someone will call you when that happens. But most of them are going to refuse bail. We can't bail out your son if he doesn't want it, I mean, we won't..."

There was a long silence. The white woman tapped her pencil on the desk as she listened. Mr. King was talking so loudly that Tommy could hear his voice from the earpiece across the room. The white woman struggled to remain calm. "I understand that, sir. It's difficult for everyone..." The voice sounded from the earpiece again. "I have to hang up now Mr. King... Yes... Someone will stay in touch...It's (601) 634-5789...Goodnight, Mr. King."

She hung up the phone and sighed. Tommy coughed loudly and stepped into the room. The woman turned around. She was small and pale. Her hair was almost black and completely straight except where it was curled under at the ends around her neck.

"Oh, hello there," she said, "can I help you?"

"Maybe. I'm Tommy Jackson." Tommy leaned over a desk chair and extended his hand. "I'm looking for Phil O'Toole or Will Richards."

The woman stood and shook his hand. She was wearing a loose, light-blue, sleeveless shift. There was dark stubble under her arms. "I'm Sarah Golden. Will and Phil and the others are in a meeting upstairs. They should be finished soon. You're welcome to wait out there," she said, pointing to the living room. "If you'll excuse me, I've got lots of calls to make, and it's getting late back East."

"Yeah, I guess it is," Tommy said. He retreated to the living room and closed the office door behind him. There was a newspaper on the table by the couch, and Tommy sat down to read and wait. The paper was a week-old Sunday *New York Times* opened to an article about the departure of the second Freedom Ride. It said that there were 49 Riders. They were all Northerners, mostly from New York or Boston, and 33 of them were white. The whites were mostly preachers and professors, and some of the blacks were staff members for national civil rights groups. Tommy didn't recognize any of the names. Another group from New York was coming in a month.

Tommy looked restlessly through the remains of the paper. He tried to concentrate on a long article about Cuba, but he was nervous and distracted by the sound of Sarah Golden's voice through the door. He gave up on the paper, lit a cigarette, and went to look for an ashtray. He found one on the dining room table and sat in the dark, smoking and watching the stairs.

The scuffle of feet came from the ceiling, followed by the scraping sound of chairs pushed across the floor. There were voices, and a group of a half-dozen college-age kids, black and white, appeared on the stairs. Tommy put out his cigarette and scanned the group. There was the black girl who had been at the meeting at Brooks, but there was no Will or Phil.

As the group descended the stairs, Tommy recognized someone at the back and he called out, "Hey, Sheila." She cut around the people in front of her and hurried down. She and Tommy stood looking at each other. They hadn't met since the night at J.W.'s. Sheila's hair seemed longer and blonder now, and her skin was tanned. She was barefoot and wearing a white t-shirt and her green Brooks College P.E. shorts.

"So here you are," she said. "When did you get in?"

"Just a few minutes ago. I was visiting my family up in Calhoun..."

"I know, Will told me," she interrupted.

"Where is Will, anyhow?"

"He's still up with Phil going over some details," she answered. "You want some iced tea?"

Tommy followed her down a narrow hall to the kitchen and watched as she cracked ice from the trays and poured two tall glasses. As she moved around the kitchen, Tommy found himself observing the details of her body. He watched the rolling movement of her shoulders. He tracked the muscles and tendons that spread out from her neck to her collarbone. He followed the flow of bare arms and legs from her torso. He lingered for a long sweaty moment over the curve of her breasts beneath the t-shirt. Tommy was in a state of heat and confusion. Sheila handed him his glass of tea. He took the glass clumsily and stepped back to let her out of the kitchen. Sheila brushed against him as she passed. Tommy held his breath and followed her to the dining room.

Sheila sat at the table and Tommy took the chair next to her. They drank, and looked at each other again. Tommy wondered if he was breaking out or changing colors or showing some signs of his disturbance. He caught Sheila's eye for a moment, and she looked away. He couldn't decide if this thing he was feeling was something inside himself or between the two of them. People passed around them without taking any notice.

"So, you're going to stay for the summer?" Sheila said.

"That's the plan," Tommy said. "How's it shaping up around here?"

"Well, did you know the second group came in today..."

"Just what I heard on the radio," Tommy said.

"Well, the whole bunch are in the county farm now. No room in the city jail," Sheila continued.

"What happened to the first ones?" Tommy asked.

Sheila took a drink from her tea. "Last Thursday they went to court and got convicted," she said. "Judge gave them a year and they went to the county farm. Then, just this morning, they shipped them up to Parchman, to make room for the new ones. They'll be up there for a while, at least a month, until the appeals go through. They say it's really tough up there."

"Yeah, I bet," Tommy said. "What are y'all doing about it?"

"Keeping in touch with the people in jail best we can, and with their relatives," Sheila said. "Getting out news to the papers and the TV people, and the supporters up North. We're trying to build up the local support. There's church meetings every week now, and a picket line at the bus station every day. It's a ton of work just keeping that up, and answering the mail and the phone; it rings about every five minutes."

"Who's working here?" Tommy asked.

"Lots of folks now, but most of them came along with the second group, and they'll be gone in a week. They'll come and go like that all summer. Phil works here, but he still lives in his place at Tucumbee. Permanent, here at the house, it's just," she started counting the people out on the fingers of her left hand, "me and Rebecca Carter, that's the girl from

Tucumbee, and Sarah Golden..."

"I met her," Tommy said.

"She's from Cleveland, Ohio," Sheila continued, "and Charley McGill..."

"Met him, too."

"...and Will, and now you," she said, pointing the index finger of her right hand at Tommy.

There were loud footsteps on the stairs and Will Richards appeared, followed by Phil O'Toole. Will bounded into the dining room in long-legged steps and grabbed Tommy's hand. "Tom-Tom, I heard your voice from the stairs. We didn't expect you for another couple of days. Did you hear about the second group?"

"Yeah, but only after I'd already headed back," Tommy said. "Calhoun was a drag, so I split."

"Good thing," Phil O'Toole said. "We need every hand we can get around here. Let Will set you up in your room, and then come by the office and we'll talk about your assignment."

Will took him around and introduced him to Rebecca Carter and to several of the visitors. Tommy followed him upstairs with his suitcase in tow. He and Will would share a room. Each of them had a single mattress on the floor for a bed. The room was plenty big for the two of them and there were even two closets. But there was a visitor's sleeping bag on the floor that night, which made it crowded. Tommy put a sheet on his mattress and emptied his suitcase into the closet. He grabbed the application form for Phil O'Toole and took it down to the office.

Phil was in the office alone. He was at his desk writing on an oversized monthly wall calendar. When he noticed Tommy, he stood and gestured down toward the calendar. "Duty schedules for next week," he said, "Who's covering the phones, manning the picket line, all that. There's another one in the kitchen for house work. You guys work that out."

"I'll check it out," Tommy said. He held the form across the desk.

"Here, this is the paper you wanted me to do."

Phil looked it over. "Who's this next of kin in Wellsburg? I thought you were from Calhoun."

"Those are some old friends," Tommy said. "I don't want my family to know what I'm doing."

"I understand," Phil said. "But if something happens, something bad..."

"Brenda and Jack can deal with it," Tommy said.

"OK, we'll leave it at that." Phil initialed the document, opened his right desk drawer, and put it in a file folder. "I'll put you on the work schedules, starting with this one," he said. "Everybody has a job they are individually responsible for, then, on top of that, we take turns at all these other things. Then there are the meetings. There's a house meeting every Sunday night, that's what we just finished, and committee meetings all through the week. They are all on this calendar, and it's always up in the office; check it first thing in the morning for any changes."

Phil paused for a breath. "You understand all that?" Tommy nodded, and he continued. "OK. Now I've been thinking about your main job. It's very convenient that you have a car with Mississippi tags and a local driver's license. Your car is all legal, isn't it?" Phil asked.

"Yeah, everything's up to date," Tommy answered.

"You know your way around the area, too," Phil said, "And, let's face it, a white boy won't attract nearly as much police attention as a Negro on those streets. So I want you to be on call as a driver. This will mean picking people up at the airport or the train station or whatever, taking reporters around, running people to the courthouse, delivering press releases, picking things up at the printer, all kinds of gophering and fetching. Is that OK?" he asked.

"Sure," Tommy said. "I love to ride."

"Good. Now the main thing we expect is that you keep up a decent appearance and obey every traffic law ever written to the absolute letter. Also, just for safety, when you have Negro passengers, make sure they sit in the back seat, to avoid suspicion. Most of them will understand, most of them will do it themselves for the same reason. But if they don't, you'll have to explain, and you'll have to explain very nicely."

Tommy nodded gravely. Phil O'Toole waved at the door. "All right, be gone," he said, "I've just got to write you in here and I'm going home."

When Tommy emerged from the office, there was no one else around. The living room and dining room were dark but the front door was still open. He stepped out to the porch. Sheila was there sitting on the steps. Tommy sat beside her. They listened to the noises for a while, the frogs and crickets from the Freedom House trees, and the voices from the other houses on the block. An old car with a bad muffler roared by and they listened as it slowly faded into the night.

"What was it like back home?" Sheila said.

Tommy told her about his encounter with Barry Kimbrough at the roadhouse. "Then," Tommy said, "my own best friend told me there was going to be nothing but trouble coming from all this 'colored stuff.' After that I had to get away. So I decided to come back here and get to work."

"It must be hard for you to do this," Sheila said. "I can go back to California. Will has family up North. You don't have any protection like that."

"I feel like I don't have any choice," Tommy said.

Sheila put her arm around his shoulders. "Well, I'm glad you're here," she said. She leaned over and kissed him lightly on the cheek. When she didn't pull away, Tommy put his arm around her, turned his face to meet her and they kissed on the mouth with lips parted. Then Sheila did pull her head back, but they kept their arms around each other for a long moment. She squeezed and Tommy squeezed back. "Goodnight, Tommy," she said, and stood to go inside.

Tommy sat for a long time in stunned euphoria. He was only a few hours away from Calhoun, and already it seemed that light-years had passed and he had landed on another planet. Here, at last, in this world, things made sense.

When his euphoria began to subside, Tommy noticed that he was very tired. He went in to the kitchen to see if there was any beer in the refrigerator. There wasn't, so he went back to the porch and lit one last cigarette. He sat and smoked it all the way down and listened to the noises of the city night. There was a distant jumble of voices and radios and car engines, and every once in a while the louder voices of black people walking on the street beyond the Freedom House yard.

Tommy ground out the butt of his cigarette and went upstairs to his room. He carefully stepped around the sleeping body on the floor. It was hot upstairs in the closed-off bedroom and there was an electric fan blowing from the window. Tommy stripped to his underwear and laid on top of his bed sheet. He let the noise of the fan fill his head while he drifted off to sleep, wondering what incredible thing would happen next.

- Fifteen -

Tommy had never been to the Jackson airport, and that's where Phil O'Toole sent him at 8:00 a.m. on his first day as a driver. Two men from the National Lawyers Guild were coming from New York to defend the second group of Freedom Riders. Rather than admit his ignorance, Tommy got a map from a gas station and figured out a route.

He was only ten minutes late and the lawyers were easy to find outside the terminal. They were white men in black suits and shiny shoes. One of them was short, thin and pale, with black, slicked-down hair and thick glasses. The other was tall and broad-shouldered, with olive skin and enormous hands that waved in the air as he talked. The big one had glasses, too, propped on his forehead and almost buried in a wiry bush of brown and grey hair. Both were carrying leather briefcases.

Tommy pulled up beside them. "Y'all the Lawyers Guild guys?" he called through his open window. The two men looked around nervously. The short one made a hushing motion at his mouth.

"Yeah, but don't tell the world, kid," the tall one said. He had a gruff and speedy way of talking that Tommy had only heard in old gangster movies. The two men tossed their bags in the front, sat in the back, and continued their conversation.

"By the way, I'm Tommy Jackson," Tommy said over his shoulder. The lawyers stopped talking long enough to say, "Hi," but didn't introduce themselves. When they reached cruising speed on Highway 25, Tommy turned the radio on to the Jackson rhythm and blues station. He lit a cigarette and left his window down for the smoke.

"Could you turn that off, please?" the small lawyer said, "We're trying to talk about something important."

"While you're at it, could you roll up your window?" the tall one added, "The wind is terrible back here." His glasses had blown out of his hair and onto the shelf behind the back seat. "Don't you have air conditioning in this thing?" he muttered, as he groped for his spectacles.

"No, sir, I don't," Tommy answered, "But I'll keep things as quiet as I can." He turned off the radio, threw out his cigarette, and closed the window. Tommy delivered the two men to the NAACP office on the black side of downtown Jackson and drove back to Freedom House. There Phil O'Toole handed him a piece of paper that said, "Ralph Powell, Rm. 227."

"It's a *New York Times* reporter," he said, "Pick him up at the Sun 'n' Sand and take him to the Tucumbee College chapel. He's interviewing Josh. Here's five bucks for gas, and lunch, if he keeps you that long."

Ralph Powell was waiting in the hotel lobby with a notebook and a copy of The *New York Times* on his lap. He was a white man in his 40s, deeply tanned, balding, and dressed in a blue seersucker suit. Tommy introduced himself.

"My goodness, you're a Southerner," Powell said as he stood to shake hands. "I'm from Alabama, myself." They walked to the car and the reporter sat in the front. "I didn't expect to see one of us on this side of things."

"I didn't expect a New York reporter from Alabama, either," Tommy answered.

"Oh, they sent me North to college, and I never came back. I haven't actually lived in Alabama for 20 years."

They drove north on State Street past the back side of the Brooks College campus. "You a student there?" the reporter asked.

"No, sir," Tommy answered.

"How did you get involved in this stuff?"

"I don't know," Tommy said, "when they came down here it just seemed like the right thing to do." He saw that the reporter had his notebook open and his pen out. Tommy remembered his friend's warning about keeping his name out of the papers.

"Where you from?" the reporter asked.

"Oh, not far," Tommy said.

"Mississippi?"

"Not really."

The reporter closed his notebook and put the pen in his pocket. "You don't want to be written about, do you?"

"No, sir," Tommy said. "I don't want that."

"Might cause trouble at home?"

"That's right, sir."

They stopped at a red light and the reporter put his hand on Tommy's shoulder. "Last thing I'd want is to make trouble for you," he said, "Off the record, I want you to know that I'm damned proud of what you're doing."

"Thank you, sir," Tommy said.

"And knock off the 'sir' stuff." Tommy nodded. "And turn on the radio," Powell said, "I want to hear some hillbilly music."

Tommy tuned in the country station and they drove past the university hospital and the old residential areas, and on beyond the outskirts of town where State Street became Highway 51. After two turns off the highway, they reached Tucumbee. The chapel was at the center of the campus, with a cross on top. Tommy parked under a shade tree across the street.

"You coming in?" Powell asked.

"Naw, I think I'm supposed to wait," Tommy said. When the reporter was gone, Tommy switched the radio back to rhythm and blues and read the newspaper Powell had left behind. An hour passed and most of another. Tommy turned off the radio to save his battery. School was out at Tucumbee and the place was quiet. Lulled by the mid-day warmth and the singing of birds above him, Tommy fell asleep. When he woke he was hungry, but there was no place to spend the money Phil O'Toole had given him.

Ralph Powell emerged from the chapel with his suit jacket slung over his shoulder and walked quickly to the car. "Get me back as fast as you can," he said, "I've got one hell of a story to call in." Tommy drove away and forgot about eating.

"Have you met that Robinson fellow?" Powell asked when they reached Highway 51.

"Naw, I just heard him speak at a meeting once," Tommy said.

"He's really something," Powell said. "This country is going to hear from him." They drove through the outskirts of Jackson past garages and pool halls. "Was hearing Robinson what roped you into all this?"

"It didn't hurt," Tommy said. "But I couldn't begin to say what all roped me into this. Tell you what; I'll call you when I figure it out myself."

"You do that," Powell said. He spent the rest of the trip working on his notes until they pulled up at the Sun 'n' Sand. "Thanks for the ride," the reporter said. "Listen, I was serious about you calling me." He handed Tommy a business card. "Use that number anytime you want to talk. Call collect."

Powell rushed into the hotel, his jacket flapping behind him. Tommy pulled out of the circular driveway and into the Esso station across the street to fill up his car. While the attendant pumped the gas, Tommy looked at the business card in his hand. Big letters in the middle said "Ralph Powell, National Correspondent, The *New York Times*." There was a New York address and phone number across the bottom. Tommy stuck the card into his wallet when he paid for the gas.

Back at Freedom House, Tommy parked in the driveway and honked his horn at Will Richards, who was out back cutting tall weeds with a swing blade. "What did you do to deserve that job?" Tommy asked.

"This is what the house manager does," Will said. "Keep up the physical plant, lie to the landlord, plunge the toilet, cut the weeds, all that managerial stuff..."

"Guess I got lucky, sitting around in my car all day," Tommy said, "See you around, I got to check with my dispatcher."

Tommy walked in to the office. The place hummed like a big machine. Phil was typing rapidly at his corner desk. Charley McGill had his back to the room, writing out something by hand at a long folding table against one of the walls. Sarah Golden was at a desk in the middle of the room making phone calls. Tommy picked his way through the clutter and tapped Phil on the back. "Here's the change from the gas," he said, "What next?"

"Did you eat?"

"Naw, no chance," Tommy said.

"Well, go get something," Phil said, "then come back and help Charley. He's doing envelopes for a big mailing." He returned to his typing and Tommy headed toward the kitchen.

Sheila and Rebecca Carter were bent over the dining room table painting on poster boards.

"Hey, what's up?" Tommy said.

"Not much," Rebecca answered without stopping her work.

"Well, hey, yourself, Tommy Jackson," Sheila said as she turned to face him. "We're painting signs to use at the courthouse when the new group goes on trial. What you been doing?"

"Oh, riding around," Tommy said, "with people from New York mostly. Got to get some lunch now."

"Well, go ahead," Sheila said, "There's cheese and baloney in the refrigerator and tea made, too. I'll talk to you later."

"Yeah, later," Tommy answered. In the kitchen he made a sandwich and sat to eat in a position that allowed him to watch Sheila at her work.

Back in the office Tommy sat in a chair alongside Charley McGill. "Remember me?" he said. "I'm supposed to help you out again."

"Yeah, sure," Charley answered, pushing round glasses back up on his nose. "How's your handwriting?"

"Lousy," Tommy said.

"Then you do the stamps. Wet 'em on this." He shoved a sheet of stamps down the table and handed Tommy a bowl with a wet kitchen sponge in it. "Stick 'em on the envelopes and pile 'em up here. I'll write addresses."

Tommy pulled a stamp from the sheet, wet it, and placed it on an envelope. He tried to pull another and the entire sheet stuck to his damp hand. "What's this for?" Tommy asked, as he wrestled the stamps.

"Fundraising appeal," Charley said without looking up. "New York people gave us a list from some civil liberties committee."

"You been doing this all day?"

"Naw, I got in just before you," Charley said. "I've been putting up posters for the mass meeting Sunday. Hot as hell out there, ain't it."

"Yeah, but it's early yet," Tommy said, "another month it'll be hot as hell in here, even at night."

They worked away for a while. "Where you from, Charley?" Tommy asked.

"Maryland," he said, "Near Salisbury, on the Eastern Shore. Been at Morgan State near Baltimore."

"What year are you?" Tommy asked. The work was going better. His hands had learned the job and his mind was free.

"Just graduated. I was planning on going to law school this fall, even took the test for it. But then the sit-in movement started last year and I got involved in that." As he talked, Charley kept writing out New York City addresses.

"You were in the sit-ins?"

"Twice, up home."

"I didn't know they had Jim Crow up there."

"Not as much anymore around Baltimore," Charley said, "but the Eastern Shore is plantation country, not much different from Mississippi."

"Did you go to jail?" Tommy said.

"Just overnight both times."

"What was it like?"

"Sort of fun," Charley said. "We were all together, 10 of us in a little two-room jail. We sang and played cards and fooled around all night."

"Don't think it's like that down here," Tommy said.

"That's what I hear."

They worked quietly for a few minutes. "So what about law school?" Tommy asked.

"Oh, maybe some day, but not now. I've signed on with the movement full time."

"You're not just here for the summer?"

"Naw, I'm here for as long as it takes. I'm training to be field staff for the student committee," Charley said.

"A professional agitator, huh?"

"You bet."

They worked some more. "Where you from?" Charley finally asked.

"Calhoun, up in the Delta," Tommy said.

"Oooh! The hardcore country, up there," Charley said. "Josh told me about the Delta. Said it's worse than slavery days."

"You talk to Josh Robinson?"

"Yeah, he schools me. He recruited me to come down here in the first place. Thought I'd be working in the Delta with him, then all this happened."

All the envelopes were stamped and Tommy took a pen and began addressing. He printed out the words, one letter at a time, as carefully and clearly as he could.

"How did you get hooked up with this stuff?" Charley asked.

"I go to Stillwater, so when they started coming, here I was," Tommy said.

"Yeah, but why?" Charley said, "Not many local white folks on our side here, in case you didn't notice."

"I don't know," Tommy said, "The whole thing has never seemed right to me. You ever hear of Darrell Farmer?"

"Was that a lynching case?" Charley said.

"Yeah."

"I remember the name."

"Well, it happened in my hometown, when I was 15," Tommy said. "The guys that did it got away with it. They killed this kid, and the sheriff and everybody looked the other way. The Klan put out a threat on anybody who talked. It was awful, and scary." Tommy's voice broke; he paused for a moment. "I guess I've looked at everything different since then."

"People in town knew who did it?" Charley asked.

"Everybody knew," Tommy said.

"But there weren't any witnesses?"

"Nope, not any that saw who they were," Tommy said. He felt blood rising in his face. "They had masks on when they took the kid."

"Damn shame. They'll pay some day, man," Charley said.

"Yeah, some day," Tommy whispered. He squeezed his pen and stared at the wall in front of him. It suddenly felt very hot in the crowded office and it was hard for Tommy to breathe. He stared down at the address list before him. The words and numbers were all a blur, but Tommy put the pen to the paper and tried to write, just to keep from talking.

After a few minutes of silent work, Tommy changed the subject. "The other thing that got to me," he said, "was music. I'm a big rhythm and blues fan, and rock and roll when that came along. That made me think different about Negroes, too. Once I went to see Bo Diddley up in Memphis and they had a rope across the hall to separate white and colored. But when Bo had played two songs, that rope was gone, man."

"No kidding," Charley said.

"Really," Tommy said. "Cops came in and stopped the show. It was wild. I guess somewhere along the way I said to myself, if it comes to choosing sides, I'm on the side with Bo Diddley."

"That's cool," Charley said, "but you know it's not anything new. There's always been white hipsters hanging around black music. I used to see those beatniks at the clubs on 7th Street in D.C. My uncle's a musician, and he said they had 'em way back in the '30s, too, coming around looking for reefer and stuff. He said they slum around for a while, then they go back to Daddy's money. We're not going to get free by dancing or playing any guitar."

Tommy felt hot and flushed again. He turned to his work and tried to stay calm. "I know it's not enough," he said quietly, looking down at the pen in his hand, "but it means a lot to me. And my daddy doesn't have any money."

"I'm not putting you down, man," Charley said, "I'm just telling you what I've seen."

"OK," Tommy said. He tried hard to concentrate on names and addresses. There was no use in talking, he thought. Nothing he said seemed to say what he meant. He couldn't explain himself without telling everything. But if people at Freedom House knew everything, they would start talking about public statements and lawyers and testifying.

At supper time everybody stopped work and ate together around the big dining room table. The meal was macaroni and cheese, out of a very big box, and string beans, out of a very big can. The table was crowded with visitors, and the room was hot. But there was laughter and loud talk about the events of the day.

Charley McGill told of outrunning some cops down an alley while he was putting up posters. Sarah Golden told about the mother of one of the Freedom Riders who insisted that it was all a mistake. "Our Richard is in Fort Lauderdale with his friends," Sarah reported in a nasal imitation of the mother's voice, "He's never lied to us."

"Well, that's nothing," Tommy said. "I'm in summer school as far as anybody back home knows."

"Well, you'll learn a lot," Will said.

There were no meetings or work assignments for Monday night. After supper was cleaned up, the day was done. Tommy looked in the refrigerator again and saw nothing but food and milk and iced tea. He drove away in his car and returned with a six-pack of beer in a paper sack. He went upstairs to get his bedside radio and he set it up on the dining room table.

With the dining room lights turned out, Tommy sat facing a window, with his feet propped on the window sill and the radio playing behind his head. He pulled a beer from the sack beside him as the night noises from outside mingled with the music. He drank the first one quickly and started a second, putting the empty can on the floor beside him for an ashtray.

For the next half hour Tommy sat, drank, smoked and listened to the music. People came and went in the area outside the dining room and Tommy looked over his shoulder. "Want a beer?" he offered, but nobody took.

Time passed peacefully. Tommy was on his third beer and getting a buzz when the d.j. played a new Elvis Presley record, "Little Sister." Elvis was just out of the army that year. Tommy felt like he'd been released from something, too. He also thought this song was really great. It had a rattling, serpentine guitar riff all through it and heart-stopping pauses in the rhythm. The guitar played and Tommy turned up the volume. The drums crashed and he turned it up a little more. The guitar solo came in the middle and Tommy turned the radio up so loud that the speaker hissed. He turned and drummed on the dining room table. When the song ended, Tommy turned the volume down. He heard footsteps as he propped his feet back on the window. Will Richards tapped him on the shoulder from behind.

"Buddy, we've got complaints," he said, as he switched off the radio. "This isn't what people want to hear in the house. I don't mind, you understand. But some people are upset, and it's my job to talk to you."

Will picked an empty beer can off the floor. "Also, house rule is no alcohol except for special occasions. Lot of our church supporters wouldn't like it. They're already suspicious of us all living together. We can't let them think we're running a juke joint."

Tommy was shocked, and his thinking was slowed by the beers. He fumbled for words. "Well, I can keep it down," he said, "I could use an earphone..." As he spoke a shot of adrenaline cut through the alcohol fog. "But why should I? I thought this was Freedom House. How come you call it that if we ain't free?"

"Tommy, this isn't about your freedom," Will said, "it's about freedom for the Negroes. You've got the rest of your life to be free and the whole world to do it in. They don't and we have to sacrifice to give it to them."

"OK, OK," Tommy said. "The rules are the rules."

"No offense, then?" Will said, extending his right hand.

"No offense," Tommy answered. He unplugged the radio, put the empty cans in the trash, and stood, for a moment, alone in the dark dining room. He took a deep breath and stepped onto the front porch.

Sheila was sitting on the steps again, in her gym shorts and t-shirt. "Hi," she said.

"Hi, yourself." Tommy sat down heavily beside her.

"I heard all that," she said, "It's hard, isn't it?"

"He doesn't get it," Tommy said. "He acts like I've got it made, like I got nothing to worry about but Negroes. I've never been free, either. I feel like the whole rest of my life is going to be a war just to keep from going crazy, much less make a living and stuff."

"I understand, Tommy," Sheila said. "You need to express yourself. That's what that music is for you, self-expression. Like my painting. People never understand. Back home I could go into the city and meet other artists. There was one, a woman, who was my teacher. She understood and helped me and introduced me to people. She said that people like us have to make corners in the world where we can be ourselves. You're not crazy, Tommy. You're just misplaced."

Tommy choked on a sob. Sheila put an arm around him and he leaned his head on her shoulder for a long time. When Tommy felt better he straightened and stretched. "Why did you leave California?"

"Daddy thought my friends were beatnik drug addicts and my teacher was a lesbian," she said, "so he sent me back here. I had to come, or else run away, and I'm not ready for that yet. I need school to work on my painting."

"Was your daddy right, about your friends?"

"Oh, they were all beatniks, but I never saw any drugs. Myra, my teacher, I don't know, she might be a lesbian. She lives with another woman. But she never made a move at me."

"You have any of your paintings here?" Tommy asked.

"A couple of things in my room, one that I'm still working on."

"I'd like to see them."

"Rebecca and a visitor are asleep up there now. But I do want you to see them, soon," she said. They sat quietly looking into the night. Tommy took her hand and held it. After a while Sheila freed her hand and stood up. "It's getting pretty late."

Tommy stood, too. "Yeah, I guess so."

Sheila put a hand on his shoulder. "Tommy," she said, "You're a very special boy."

"You're pretty great, too," he said.

They stood looking at each other awkwardly. Tommy put his arms all the way around her and pulled her tight against him. She felt warm and firm. He rubbed his hands over the ridges of her back and the curve of her sides. They placed their heads face-to-face and mouth-to-mouth, and kissed, wide open and all the way in, tickling and tingling deep to the bones. His hands were in Sheila's hair. She scratched at his shoulders through his shirt and rubbed up and down against him as she rose and fell from her barefoot tiptoes. They could each feel the other's heartbeat pounding on the skin of the chest.

Sheila sank flat-footed and dropped her arms. "Oh, Lord," she sighed.

"Lord, Lord," Tommy said, and took her hands. "Thank you, Lord."

They laughed and looked in each other's eyes. They were on the verge of starting again when Sheila pulled back. "I'll see you tomorrow, Tommy Jackson," she said.

"And tomorrow night?"

"And tomorrow night."

Sheila walked up the dark stairs inside. Tommy collected his radio and went to his room.

The second group of Freedom Riders went on trial at the Hinds County Courthouse that Wednesday, and the Freedom House crowd organized a picket line to support them. Sheila and Rebecca's new signs were ready. They said things like "Free the Freedom Riders" and "Put Jim Crow on Trial." They also designed a leaflet to give to reporters and people on the street. Phil O'Toole wrote the words.

Will and Tommy gathered water coolers and blocks of ice. Tuesday night they all gathered in the kitchen and made peanut butter and jelly sandwiches. Wednesday morning Tommy was up at 6:30 to get the leaflets from the printer. At 7:30 Phil O'Toole arrived, driving the same navy blue Tucumbee College van that had been at the bus station. Some older black people, other Tucumbee faculty and staff, rode with him in the front seats.

In the back of the van were stacked the same picket signs they had carried at the bus station. They added the new ones to the pile, and some of the Freedom House people sat on the floor of the van. The rest piled into Tommy's car and followed the van downtown.

They arrived at the courthouse and newspaper people were waiting outside with cameras. Tommy parked his car and they unloaded the van. One by one people grabbed picket signs from the stack and took their places in an oval line on the sidewalk. Tommy took a sign and hung it around his neck by a string. Soon everyone was in place, and they started to walk around and around. Someone started singing, "Oh, Freedom," at a slow, rolling tempo. Tommy clapped in time and walked along. Sheila was in front of him and Charley was behind. Tommy was carrying the sign that said "None Are Free Until All Are Free."

It was a long, hot morning. Tommy mostly walked with his head down looking at the sidewalk because he didn't want his face to be in any of the pictures. But inside he was proud of himself and what he was doing and who he was with.

There was a line of police on the sidewalk to keep order, but white people still walked by and spat at the picketers or tossed garbage and lit cigarettes. They said nasty things about "niggers" and "communists." When this happened, Tommy didn't look down at the sidewalk. He looked up strong and straight into the faces of the angry white people.

One older man, about 60, picked Tommy out for special attention. He was a short man and he got right under Tommy's face and walked beside him. "You a niggerlover," the man said. "Nothing worse than a nigger except a niggerlover. Niggerlover, niggerlover," he repeated. Tommy ignored him. "Damn Yankee niggerlover," he said loudly.

Without breaking stride, Tommy looked directly down at the man. "Yes sir, that's what I am," he said, "except I ain't no Yankee." The man looked stunned at the sound of Tommy's voice. He froze in confusion for a second, then spit in Tommy's face and walked away.

Tommy wiped his face with his shirtsleeve and kept walking, a little taller and straighter than before. He joined in singing, "We are not afraid, we are not afraid..."

At 2:00 p.m. word came from inside the courthouse. The Freedom Riders were all guilty on every count. The sentence was a year in jail, same as the first group, and they were all going to Parchman.

A few minutes later a grey-painted school bus appeared from behind the courthouse. The Freedom Riders were packed into it and they waved to their supporters from behind the windows. The people in the picket line stopped and cheered. The bus stopped at a red light and the picketers ran to stand beside it. They held their signs above their heads so that the Freedom Riders could see them. The signs swayed in the hot wind as the people inside and outside the bus sang together, "We shall overcome, we shall overcome..."

The light changed and the bus was gone, weaving through the downtown traffic, headed for Highway 49, and the long haul up the Delta.

- Sixteen -

The Fourth of July came and went. Wave after wave of Freedom Riders came to Jackson. They were all arrested and shipped to Parchman. Summer was slipping away, the jails were full, and nothing had changed.

When the Freedom Ride prisoners left Jackson, nothing was heard from them. There were no letters, no phone calls and no visits. Up in the Delta the Freedom Riders were out of sight and out of mind. News coverage stopped, because there was no more news. Publicity began to die down, and so did the number of volunteers from up North. There was talk in the movement about doing something new and dramatic to break the stalemate.

That talk got louder when the first group of Riders left Parchman on a federal appeal bond. The 27 prisoners emerged looking like survivors of a long, brutal war. Their faces were lumpy and discolored. All of them had lost a lot of weight. Skin sagged on their limbs. Their clothes hung on them loosely. Some of the men's suit coats looked like over-sized bathrobes.

At a press conference in Jackson, a few of the released prisoners told what happened in their 40 days at Parchman. The whole time they were kept naked, sleeping on the cold, cement floors in cells on Death Row. They were given food that had been made inedible by gross amounts of hot pepper or other unknown additives. They reported that once Governor Ross Barnett himself visited their cellblock and approved their treatment.

The prison horror stories drew national attention back to Mississippi.

The stories also raised fears about the fate of all the other prisoners at Parchman, and questions about whether the movement should keep sending people up there.

Finally a meeting was called to hash out all these strategy questions. It was held at Freedom House on a Friday night at 7:00. All the full-time workers came, including some from Atlanta and Washington and New York. Leaders of all the black organizations in Jackson were there, and some of the preachers.

At Freedom House they moved the table out of the dining room and filled it with rows of folding chairs. More than 30 people were crammed into the stifling hot room that night. Electric fans blew at top speed from each corner of the room, but it was still hot. As the talk went on, body heat accumulated, and even the preachers took off their jackets and ties.

Josh Robinson chaired the meeting. He stated the problem at the start and called on people to talk as they raised their hands. People from up North were the first to speak. One of them was the short New York lawyer who'd been in Tommy's car. "This battle will be won in federal court," he said, "It's a perfect case. We'll win all the segregation issues, and we can bring civil suits against the state prison system and Ross Barnett himself. We can tie them up in court for years and cost them more than a million Freedom Riders ever would. I say suspend the Rides and let the law take over."

A white lady from Washington, D.C. stood, still wearing her hat and gloves and fanning herself with a copy of Time magazine. "Some of our friends in Congress would like to hold hearings on this whole issue, and that would put us back in the news," she said. "But they're also afraid of Senator Eastland."

She was drowned out by laughter. "Forget that old toad," someone yelled.

"I'm not saying it's right," the Washington lady responded. "But he's a real power up there. They have to work with him, and it would help if things cooled down for a while."

A local preacher got up, a short, stocky bald-headed black man with the voice of a Shakespearean actor. "My good people," he said, "it is not yet the fullness of time. No tree bears fruit before due season. These Freedom Riders came from the outside. They meant well, but they never understood the situation down here. What they're doing with Ross Barnett is waving the red flag at a mad bull. He's just going to get madder, and more stubborn, and dangerous. And we have to live with that old bull when our outside friends are gone."

Other preachers said, "Amen." At least a dozen hands shot into the air, and a dozen voices began to speak at once. Josh Robinson stood and stomped his foot loudly on the wooden floor. "The chair recognizes Charles McGill," he shouted above the uproar.

Charley was sitting at the back of the room with the other Freedom House residents, almost out of Josh's sight. His hand was up to speak, but he was sitting quietly when called upon, while others at the front of the room were standing and shouting to be heard.

Charley stood and waited for the room to get quiet. With everyone turned to watch him, he cleared his throat. "With all due respect to the Reverend," he nodded deferentially toward the bald-headed preacher, "I rise to say that the fullness of time is at hand. I admit that I am from outside. My home is in Maryland. But segregation and discrimination are not just problems for Mississippi. They are problems for my state, for all the Southern states, and for all America.

"Like many of you," he continued, "I am a country boy. I grew up hunting and fishing on the Eastern Shore, and my daddy taught me if you want to kill a deer, you shoot at the heart. The heart of Jim Crow is in Mississippi, and if we are going to kill the beast, that must be our target."

There was applause, and Charley waited for it to end. "Today, for the first time in almost a hundred years, the whole country is watching Mississippi and asking whether racial discrimination is compatible with American democracy. For the first time since the Union troops went home, it's possible that the weight of the federal government could come down on the side of Negro rights. This isn't time to retreat, it's time to push harder."

There was more applause, but Charley was impatient with it and raised his voice to be heard. "The clock is running down, people." The applause stopped. "I played a little basketball in school," he paused for a scattering of laughter. "When the clock was running down and we were behind, we didn't talk about holding hearings or suing the referee. We went to the full court press. We put on the pressure from baseline to baseline. Every time the opposition drew a breath, one of us would be up in their face. That's the situation we have in Mississippi. The clock is running down. Old Ross Barnett has us by two or three points. But we're stronger than he is. We're hungrier than he is."

The applause rose, and with it scattered cries of "Amen!" and "Tell it!" Charley raised his voice to a crescendo. "It's time to put Jackson, Mississippi under the full-court press. Take the battle out of the bus station. Take it to the cafes and stores and movie houses, and even to the white Jim Crow churches. Everywhere that white Mississippi tries to draw a white-only breath, they ought to see a bunch of us, right up in their face." The applause and cries of support started again.

"We can do it people," Charley continued. "For the next six weeks-- till the schools start-- we've got a ready supply of volunteers. We've got the organization in place. There will never be a better time. I say we call a campaign of daily sit-ins at all segregated places of business in downtown Jackson until Jim Crow is abolished, at the bus station, and everywhere else."

Charley sat down. At least half of the people in the crowded room stood to cheer. Charley looked to Josh Robinson at the front of the room. Josh nodded back and looked to another young black man, a fellow in a white shirt and blue necktie who had not been seen in Jackson before. When the cheering dissipated, the young man in the necktie stood on his chair and raised his hand.

Josh called for order. "The chair recognizes Lewis Johnston," he said, "an officer of the student freedom movement visiting us from Nashville."

Johnston stepped down from his chair and spoke in favor of Charley's proposal. He turned to the bald reverend. "Brother, it is true that no tree bears fruit out of season. But didn't Lord Jesus also say that some demons can only be driven out with prayer and fasting, and even the shedding of blood?"

There was a sprinkling of applause, and many amens. "That's the kind of demon we're up against. I'm with the young brother. Full Court Press! Full Court Press!" Lewis Johnston climbed back onto his chair, waved both fists in the air and chanted, "Full Court Press!" Charley joined him, then Rebecca and Phil and some other people from out of town. The local NAACP president joined the chant.

All the Freedom House people stood and chanted, Tommy included. Tommy was dazed; he couldn't keep up with the words that flew around the room, or what their consequences might be. He was moved by Charley's speech, but Lewis Johnston's brief words spoke to him even more. They rang deep in his heart, down where his Baptist church upbringing was stored.

The strategy meeting had turned into a revival service. Tommy felt pushed along by the tide of feelings in the room, just as he'd felt some invisible thing push him down the aisle of the First Baptist Church on a summer night ten years before. Back then he didn't know where he was going, or why; he just put one foot in front of the other until he was face to face with the revival preacher. Now he heard his voice joined with the crowd chanting "Full Court Press!" and singing "We Shall Overcome," and again he surrendered to the current.

When the chanting and singing died down, Josh called for a standing vote on the sit-in proposal. The motion carried with only the preacher, the lawyer and the Washington lady opposing. A committee was named to make a detailed action plan. Charley McGill was on it, along with Phil O'Toole, Lewis Johnston and a couple of the local preachers.

After the meeting people milled around and talked excitedly for a while. When the last of the guests were gone, Phil called the Freedom House residents together. "No work tomorrow," he said. "Everything's off until we have a new plan. I'll see you in church Sunday night at the mass meeting."

Phil went home and the group went to work putting away folding chairs, rearranging furniture, sweeping the floor and emptying ashtrays. When the work was done, all six of the young people plopped down in the living room. It was the first time they had been at rest together in weeks, and after the excitement of the meeting there was adrenaline to work off.

After several minutes of congratulating Charley on his triumph, the talk among them petered out into awkward silence. The atmosphere was cloudy, as if the reality of what this new campaign might mean had suddenly sunk in upon them.

Tommy stood from a faded gold easy chair and broke the silence. "People," he announced dramatically, "what we need is a party. We've got something to celebrate, one of our own here has become a genuine movement star. And besides, let's face it, if things go the way it seems, there ain't going to be another chance this summer."

"I think my man's onto something," Charley said, "It's only nine o'clock, let's do it."

"I vote yes," Sheila said.

"What do you say, Will?" Tommy asked, "Is this a special occasion?"

Will looked around for objections and saw none. "Yeah, let's do it," he said.

Tommy collected for the beer fund, Will chipped in a few bucks from the house cashbox, and Tommy returned from the store with two cases. He brought the radio down from his room, placed it on the living room mantle, and carefully tuned it to WDIA. He held up a foaming can of Falstaff and addressed the room. “Friends, Romans, et cetera, let the good times roll.”

They sat around the room drinking and talking. They talked about personal things, families, studies, friends, things that got lost in days of hectic activity and big ideas. The beer took hold, and when James Brown came on singing “Think,” all barriers among them fell. They pushed aside the chairs and danced, not in couples, but all together, in a circle. They sang with the chorus, “Freedom, freedom, freedom...” and screamed with every James Brown scream.

The radio played “The Stroll,” and Rebecca tried to teach them the line dance that went with the song. They fumbled and stomped their way through it and laughed at their mistakes. When the disc jockey played “In the Still of the Night,” people moved toward their seats. Tommy and Sheila looked at each other and gave in to the moment’s heat and glory. They pressed their bodies together for a slow dance that announced their feelings to the world. As they swayed together Tommy felt the eyes of his housemates upon them, but he was more proud than embarrassed.

The dancing ended when a string of commercials came on. It was almost midnight and everyone was at least a little drunk. Voices were raised above the radio. The room was littered with empty cans, many of which smoldered with discarded cigarette butts. A lull came in the laughter and talk and Sarah Golden yawned loudly. “My head hurts,” she said, “I’m going to bed.”

She climbed the stairs. “Maybe we better hold it down and let her sleep,” Will said.

“Screw that,” Tommy replied, joyously drunk. He felt touched by magic.

He had a place, a partner and a mission, and he felt a deep contentment. He was oblivious to anything except keeping that feeling alive. "Let's get out of here instead," Tommy said, "Let's go to Vicksburg."

"What's at Vicksburg?" Charley asked.

"Nothing, at this hour," Will said. "It's just an old river town, with some historic stuff."

"That historic stuff is a national park," Tommy said, "There was a big Civil War battle there and now there's a park with a lot of monuments and a huge graveyard. They never lock it. Me and my friends at Stillwater go over there late sometimes and drink on these high bluffs over the Mississippi River. It's cool, especially when there's stars and stuff."

"Sounds good to me," Sheila said.

"I don't know, man," Charley said, "maybe a Civil War monument isn't the best place for us to be hanging out together, you know?"

"It's OK," Tommy said. "I've never seen anybody else up there this late. It'll be great. There's nobody there but ghosts. You stand on those bluffs and feel the wind, and I swear you can hear those ghosts fighting and crying."

"Who won the Battle of Vicksburg?" Charley asked.

"The Union," said Tommy.

"OK, I'll go," Charley said, "as long as the Northern ghosts are in charge."

"Oh, what the hell," Will said. "I've never been over there. Let's do it."

They gathered a grocery sack full of beers from the refrigerator and piled into Tommy's car. Charley and Rebecca sat in the back, for safety's sake. Sheila took the middle spot up front. Tommy headed for the driver's side. Will laid a hand on his shoulder. "Maybe I ought to drive?" he said.

"Shit," Tommy said, "I drive better drunk, makes me pay attention. Quit being a worry wart."

"OK, if you're sure it's safe," Will said.

"Yeah," Tommy said as he slid behind the wheel, "I'll drive like your granny." Tommy crawled through the city streets to Highway 80, where he kept the speed at a steady 45. He passed the sign marking the turnoff for Stillwater College. "My alma mater," he said, "I think I need a drink." He reached his right hand over the back of the seat and Charley put a cold, open can in it. Tommy took a long drink, put the can between his legs and reached his arm around Sheila. She leaned against him.

"We OK, baby?" Tommy whispered into her ear.

"A-OK," Sheila answered.

With no traffic on the road, they coasted to Vicksburg in half an hour and pulled into the battlefield park. Tommy inched through the looping road, past the shadowy monuments and statuary. He finished his beer and reached back for another. "This is where it happened," he said. "This is where they fought like wild animals to see which vision of the New World would rule the big river."

"And the best men won?" Sheila asked.

"The best vision, anyhow," Tommy said. "Or the least bad one."

"Tommy, were your ancestors in the war?" Rebecca asked.

"We don't really have ancestors in my family," he laughed, "Daddy's people came down from the hills somewhere. So who knows? The Southern hill people didn't have slaves, and some of them were for the Union. Some didn't fight, some did, some got drafted."

Tommy stopped the car at the edge of the military cemetery. The cemetery gate was locked, but the moon was bright and it shone on the endless expanse of headstones. Tommy drove on to an empty parking lot off the road. They all got out and walked to the edge of the bluffs. They sat in silence for a long time, listening to the wind and the frogs and looking out at the great meandering river.

Tommy began to quietly hum a tune. It was "Stay" by Maurice Williams and The Zodiacs. As he hummed the words came into his mouth "...just a little bit longer... please, please tell me that you're going to..." Charley McGill joined in with a high tenor, "... `cause your mama won't mind..." Tommy dropped down to the bass part. Soon all five of them were singing a ragged harmony to the river and the moon. At the end of the song they put their arms around each other and giggled.

"Amen!" Charley pronounced. It was almost 2:00 a.m. They stood up slowly and trudged toward Tommy's car, still giggling and humming the song. The parking lot came into view and the singing stopped. A pick-up truck was parked next to Tommy's old Chevy and three young white men sat on the tailgate drinking beer. In the rear window of the truck was the outline of a rifle in a gun rack.

Tommy, Sheila, Will, Charley and Rebecca all stopped dead still for a long moment. Tommy resumed walking briskly toward the car and the others fell in line behind him, with Charley and Rebecca at the rear. The truck was parked along the driver's side of the car. Tommy led his friends to the passenger side of the car. Will got in the back seat first, and Charley and Rebecca rushed in behind him. Sheila got in the shotgun seat. Tommy walked around the front of the car to his door, hoping that Charley and Rebecca had escaped the three men's notice.

"Good evening," the biggest of the three men said, nodding to Tommy. He was a heavy-set fellow, about Tommy's age and about 6'2" tall. He had long hair greased back in a ducktail and he wore a white t-shirt and blue jeans. His two friends were about the same age and also wore t-shirts and jeans, but had flat-top haircuts.

"Yeah, it's a good one, ain't it?" Tommy replied, looking up at the stars.

"What y'all up to?" the big man asked. He stood from the tailgate and stepped around the truck to face Tommy.

"Not much," Tommy answered, "just riding and drinking beer, and sitting out under the moon."

"Heard y'all singing," the big man said.

"Pretty bad, huh?" Tommy said.

"Oh, I don't know. At least one of you sang pretty good," the big man answered.

"Well, thanks," Tommy said. He paused for a moment. "Guess we'll be moving on, nice talking to you guys."

"See you around," the big man said, studying Tommy and his car intently.

Tommy opened the door and jumped inside. When he did, the interior light came on and the big man saw Charley and Rebecca. He stuck a work-booted foot into Tommy's door before he could shut it.

"Look here!" the big man called to his friends. "Y'all see what I see?"

"Sure do," said the smaller of the two, "and here of all places."

Tommy started the engine and turned on his headlights.

"Y'all get out," the big man ordered. His other friend pulled a sledge hammer from the bed of the truck and walked toward the car.

Tommy threw the car into first gear, stomped on the accelerator and surged forward a few feet. The big man fell to the pavement on his rear end and Tommy slammed the door and threw the car into reverse. The man with the sledgehammer kept coming and swung at the windshield, but the blow fell short and only left a crumpled dent in the hood.

Tommy threw the car into first again and tires squealed as they roared down the narrow road. The truck headlights appeared in the rear view mirror. The car tires screamed around the curves. They ran off onto the grassy shoulder of the road, but Tommy steered back onto the pavement without slowing down. The rear end of the car scraped loudly at the bottom of a hill. In the mirror Tommy saw sparks fly from the back, but he kept driving in a panic. He tried to think of a way to elude the truck, but his mind was still clouded with beer.

"Oh, Lord, we're going to die," Will cried in the back seat, "Jackson, you've really fucked us up."

"It's not his fault," Sheila said, "You came of your own free will, we all did."

"Both of you shut up," Charley said. "We'll have that talk later." He leaned over the front seat. "Jackson, turn off your lights," he said. Tommy obeyed. "Can you drive this thing?" Charley asked, "or should we lose them long enough to make a switch?"

"It's OK. I'm stone cold sober now," Tommy answered.

"About time," Charley said. "Keep the lights off and drive as fast as you can. Screw the speed limits and the police. We might be better off if we get pulled over."

They reached Highway 80 well ahead of the pick-up truck and turned east toward Jackson. Five minutes passed and the rear view mirror was empty. Tommy let out a little of his breath and noticed that the car radio was on. It had come on automatically when he started the engine and was playing a series of commercials for skin creams and hair gels.

"Think I can turn the lights back on?" Tommy asked.

"Not yet," Charley said, looking at the road behind them, "Somebody's back there."

Tommy saw the lights, too. He was driving 85 but he pushed the accelerator harder and got the Chevy up above 90. The lights in the mirror were still gaining on them. Tommy pressed his right foot hard into the floorboard and kept it there. The muscles in his leg trembled as he held the pedal all the way down, even around the curves. The car fish-tailed wildly and threw the passengers across the seats.

"You're going to kill us before the rednecks get a chance," Will said.

"Shut up, Will," Charley replied.

Tommy kept driving without lights. He held on to the darkened road by hugging the yellow line that reflected the moonlight. The car topped out at 95 and would go no faster except on a downhill stretch. The lights in the mirror were a little closer every time Tommy looked.

They sped past the little town of Edwards. They were more than halfway home, but the lights were still there in the mirror. The radio played "Mother-in Law" by Ernie K. Doe. Bass and falsetto voices sang the silly call-and-response refrain. Tommy's hands were glued to the wheel. He couldn't pause to turn off the radio. He tried to will the song away, to clear his mind, to concentrate on the moment. But the song wouldn't leave, it kept grating on his brain.

"Mother-in-law, mother-in-law. Mother-in-law, mother-in-law..." Over and over it played. The truck headlights filled up the rear view mirror, then they filled the rear window of the car, silhouetting the heads of Tommy's three friends.

"Everybody down," Charley said. "Remember they have a gun."

Sheila was already crouched on the floor in front. The others put their heads below the seat. Tommy kept driving. The truck was about 20 feet behind them. The radio kept singing, "Mother-in-law, mother-in-law..." There was a clank against the trunk of the car and the sound of breaking glass. One of the men in the truck had thrown a beer bottle at them. Another clank sounded from the roof. A brown bottle rolled down the windshield and smashed on the pavement as they drove over it.

Another bottle hit the back of the car, and a crack formed across the rear window. Another struck the same spot and the glass shattered. A bottle whizzed through the jagged glass and Rebecca started to cry. "Oh Lord," she said, "I'm bleeding."

"Let me see," Charley stretched across the backseat to examine her. "There's some pieces of glass in her face," he said. "Those bastards are serious, man. Are there any back roads you could take?"

"Not that I know, but I could try one," Tommy said. He stared at the dark road ahead of him and tried to concentrate on his driving. He tried to ignore the crying from the back seat, the silly music on the radio, and the roar of the truck engine that came through the hole where the rear window used to be.

"No good," Charley said, "You get on a strange road it could be a dead end."

"Literally," Will said.

The pick-up truck was close enough for Tommy to see the men's faces in his rear view mirror. They blew their horn. The truck bumped its front end lightly against Tommy's rear bumper. Another bottle hit the roof of the car. Then another sailed through the rear window and hit Tommy on the back of his neck.

The bottle bounced off without hurting Tommy, but it caused him to swerve momentarily, and the pick-up truck bumped him from the rear again. This time they hit harder. The rear bumper crumpled and the impact sent the car careening into the west-bound lane. The truck kept coming. It pulled even with Tommy's car, then pulled a little further to the left and sideswiped them.

Metal crunched and the car shuddered but Tommy managed to keep it on the road. As they drove a grinding noise came from the direction of the right rear wheel. The truck veered left again and struck harder. The front passenger side door crumpled inward and the glass inside it popped. The car was shaking badly and weaving in and out of the lane. Tommy tried to slow down so the truck would pass, but the truck slowed down with him.

In the distance west-bound headlights were coming at Tommy's car. The truck bumped them in the side again. Tommy was going 75 when he finally lost control. The car went onto the gravel shoulder and Tommy stomped the brakes. The rear end swung around and they spun down the grassy embankment into the ditch at the side of the road. When they came to rest, the nose of the car was buried in mud at the bottom of the ditch, and the rear end was stuck in the air.

Tommy took a breath. The car was silent. The engine and the radio were dead. "Is everybody still here?" he asked.

"We're all here," Charley said.

"Sheila?"

"I'm OK," she answered from the floor.

Another beer bottle hit the rear end of the car. Tommy ducked below the seat, waiting for the next assault, but there was only silence. Tommy peeked out his window and saw that the three men were on the roadside above them, standing beside their truck, waiting for the oncoming car to pass. The car slowed down, but didn't stop.

When the engine noise of the passing car faded, another rain of beer bottles fell on Tommy's car. "So long niggers, and niggerlovers," the big man shouted, "have a nice walk!" The truck engine roared and the roadside gravel crunched. A few seconds later Tommy peeked again and saw the truck's tail lights receding to the west.

"They're gone," he said.

"Thank God," Will said. "We're going to live. I can't believe we're going to live."

"We're not home yet," Charley said. "We've got to get away from this mess before a cop comes by. And we have to call O'Toole to come get us." He paused and thought for a moment. "We'll split up," he said, "me and Rebecca will walk toward Jackson, the rest of you go back to that little crossroads. When either of us reaches a phone, we'll call Phil for help. If you don't get an answer that'll mean he's already on the way, so wait on the roadside where he can see you."

None of the car doors would open. They climbed out through the windows and started walking. Charley's plan worked. Twenty minutes later Phil O'Toole arrived, driving his great, red Oldsmobile which still had its Illinois tags. He was dressed in a bathrobe and slippers, his face was bristly with beard and his red hair looked like a rag mop. He collected the five of them from along Highway 80 and they abandoned Tommy's car for the time being.

The crew came through the ordeal intact. Rebecca had picked the small pieces of glass out of her face and washed away the blood at the water spigot of a closed gas station. The others were unhurt. Tommy feared O'Toole's reaction, and it wasn't long coming. "OK, Jackson, what happened here?" he grumbled on the way back. "You were driving, right?"

"Right."

"What were you guys doing out at this hour?" O'Toole asked, "and smelling like a brewery, to boot?"

Tommy told about the party, and his idea to end the night at Vicksburg.

"Why Vicksburg?" O'Toole asked.

"There's this really cool national park there," Tommy said, "right up over the river. It's a Civil War memorial..."

"Holy shit!" O'Toole said, "A Civil War memorial! Jackson, you're not just drunk, you're crazy. You can't fuck around with that stuff. You're on the other side now, the side that won the damn war, and your people are never going to forget it."

- Seventeen -

"You're on the other side now." Tommy woke Saturday morning with those words sounding in his head. His eyes opened and he lay on his mattress looking up at the cracks and holes in the plaster ceiling. He stayed there, half-asleep, playing the words over in his head and wondering what they meant. He knew that O'Toole was right. He was on the other side, and nothing could ever be like it was.

He had thought this was what he wanted. He knew what the old ways did to Darrell Farmer and to Wade Suggs and to Dicky White. He knew what it did to him to be a false witness, to know the truth and be afraid to say it. He hadn't wanted to live like that and now he wasn't. He was on the right side now, but it didn't feel right. Tommy had thought that it would at least feel good to be right. But it didn't.

The sun was shining through the bedroom window, bright and hot. As Tommy woke his head began to hurt and he had to pee. He pulled himself to his feet and tried to walk. His back was stiff from the impact of the car wreck, and his neck hurt where the beer bottle hit him. His head throbbed and his stomach was queasy. His mouth was dry and foul-tasting.

He inched his way to the bathroom in the hall, drank two glasses of water and took three aspirin. He splashed his face with cold water, and as he did, details from the night before drifted up in his mind. Tommy saw the picture of his car dented and battered, with windows smashed and its nose in a muddy ditch. He groaned out loud.

Tommy dressed and made his way down the stairs, where the house was filled with the usual bustle. Rebecca and Will were eating breakfast at the dining room table. Rebecca had two band-aids on her face.

"How you doing?" Tommy asked.

"Oh, it's OK," she said. "They're just little cuts; they didn't bleed much. It was just scary at the time."

"Yeah, I know," Tommy said.

"So how'd the old Confederate pull through?" Will asked.

"OK, I guess," Tommy answered. "Listen, any chance you could help me with my car today?"

"What you got in mind?" Will asked.

"I want to see if we can get it out and running. I figure O'Toole's car could pull it," Tommy said, "if we got some chain or rope or something."

"What you want me to do?" Will said.

"Call O'Toole for me. I don't think he'd talk to me right now."

"Yeah, I guess," Will said. "We can't just leave it there like it is. The cops might trace it from the tags or something."

"Thanks, buddy," Tommy said. He turned toward the kitchen but heard footsteps on the stairs. He stopped and saw Sheila headed for the door with an overnight bag.

"What's up?" Tommy said to her back.

"Oh, Tommy," she said. "I was just in your room looking for you. I'm going to visit my grandmother in Brandon today. She's picking me up at the Brooks campus in half an hour. I gave her the summer school story."

"Guess that makes us classmates," Tommy said. He followed Sheila onto the front porch. "Are you OK?" he asked.

"Yeah, I'm fine. How about you?"

"A little stiff and sore, but alright. Will's going to help me get the car out of the ditch," he said. "When will you be back?"

"Tomorrow afternoon," Sheila answered, "I'll have to go to church with Granny before I can get away. We'll talk about everything then, OK?"

"OK," Tommy said. He laid a hand on her shoulder. She touched his face, kissed him lightly on the mouth and took off across the yard and up the street. The top of her disappeared behind the tree branches. Tommy stood on the porch and studied the movement of her legs walking away. They were long and tanned, and the sunlight caught the ripple of her calves.

In the light of day Tommy's car looked pitiful. Overnight it had sunk deeper into the mud, and the front tires were buried. The rear bumper was mangled and the top of the trunk was bent. The doors and fenders on the passenger side were dented and torn. Much of the paint was scraped off and that whole side of the car bent inward at the frame. The roof was dented from the beer bottles, and the front windshield had a long crack down the middle. The inside of the car was strewn with their empty beer cans, the bottles that were thrown, and shards of glass from the broken rear window.

Will and Tommy had a heavy rope they'd found in the attic at Freedom House. With that and Phil O'Toole's V-8 engine, they pulled the car free of the mud and got it onto level ground below the highway. The doors still wouldn't open, so Tommy climbed in through the window and tried the engine. It wouldn't crank.

He lay his head on the steering wheel. "They killed it," he muttered. "Sons of bitches killed my car."

Tommy climbed out. "What do you think?" he said to Will.

"For one thing, the frame is bent and that can't be fixed," Will said. "We can't even tow it. The wheels on the bent-up side won't turn with that metal pushed down on them. I'd say this car is totalled."

"Yeah, you're right," Tommy said. "But I hate to leave it like this. I've driven it ever since I got my license. It's part of me."

"It's part of your past now," Will said as he walked up the embankment toward O'Toole's car. Tommy followed him and took a screw driver from the tool box in the trunk. He used it to scrape the inspection sticker off his windshield and remove a crumpled 1961 Mississippi license plate from the rear bumper.

Tommy climbed back into the car, took the registration papers from the glove compartment and searched the interior for anything suspicious. There were some "Free the Freedom Riders" leaflets under the seat and an old copy of The *New York Times*. He grabbed it all up and crawled out the window.

He stood beside his car and banged the hood with his fist. "Bye, old buddy. Rest in peace," he said, and returned to O'Toole's car. As Will drove away, Tommy looked back at the wreck by the roadside. He strained his eyes and kept looking even when the old car was just a distant speck. When he wasn't sure which speck it was anymore, Tommy let the car recede into the invisible past, and he turned to face forward.

Back at Freedom House it was only three in the afternoon. Tommy was left alone for the rest of the day. He wanted to get away from the house. Any other time he'd have gone for a long solitary drive in his car. Tommy felt trapped. He turned on the radio and paced his bedroom, but that didn't help. He sat on the porch and smoked, but his legs crawled inside their skin. Finally he surrendered to the urge for motion and set out walking up the hill toward Brooks College.

Tommy didn't stop at the Brooks campus. He kept walking all the way to State Street, turned right and continued up the commercial strip for several blocks to the Old Capitol. The Old Capitol was a small, white-domed, brick building that housed the state government before, during and immediately after the Civil War. It was built by slaves and later became a museum for memories of the old days and the old ways. It was a hot day, well into the 90s, and Tommy was thirsty and soaked with sweat from his long walk. He went inside the Old Capitol for the first time in years.

Tommy walked through the building without looking at the exhibits. He drank deeply at the "white" water fountain and rested in one of the cushioned seats of the quiet, carpeted old House of Representatives chamber. The Old Capitol was deserted except for a black man who swept the hall outside the House chamber. As he worked, he sang "Rock of ages, cleft for me..." Tommy listened and closed his eyes. The room was cool and dimly lit.

When he felt refreshed, Tommy re-entered the sunshine and walked up Capitol Street, past the Lamar Life Insurance Building and St. Andrew's Episcopal Cathedral. He crossed the street and stood in front of the Governor's Mansion. For a long time he watched the windows and doors for some sign of Ross Barnett. But he only saw one of the black prisoners sent from Parchman to work at the mansion. The man wore blue denim prison clothes, with a number printed on the shirt, as he mowed the governor's lawn.

After several minutes out in the sun, Tommy was thirsty again. He walked into O'Shea's department store. The place was crowded with Saturday shoppers, black and white. Tommy passed among them and continued on to the "whites-only" lunch counter at the rear of the store. He ordered a Coke and sat at the counter long enough to drink it.

Tommy left the store through a rear exit that opened onto a side street. He walked a meandering path past the bus station and around the corner to the spot where he had stood watching the demonstrators on that morning in May. This was still the "colored" entrance to the bus station. Tommy stood for a moment and watched the black people go in and out.

He walked back to Capitol Street. He was hungry and he went into the white, metal box of a building that was called "The Krystal." He sat on a stool at the counter, directly under the cold blast of an air-conditioner vent. He felt sweat evaporate from his skin as he ordered three of the tiny square Krystal-burgers, and another big Coke, to go. While waiting for his food,

Tommy spun halfway around on the stool. He watched the black people lined up for hamburgers at the carry-out window in the rear of the diner.

His order arrived and Tommy carried the greasy paper sack and the sweating, waxed-cardboard cup into the street. From a corner box he bought a *Jackson Daily News*, stuck it under his arm, and walked to the park outside the new, golden-domed state capitol. He sat on a bench and ate his burgers and read the newspaper. First he read the comics, then, his fingers stained with grease and ink, he turned back to the front page and read the latest editorial about the freedom movement. The editor said it was a movement of dupes, manipulated by cold-blooded subversives and homosexuals. Tommy folded the paper and put it into the grease-soaked bag with the other garbage.

Across the street the bells of the First Baptist Church rang five o'clock. Tommy sat and rested and studied the reflections of the late afternoon sun on the Capitol dome. When the bells rang 5:30 he stood up, dumped his trash, and began the long walk back to Freedom House.

The house was quiet and shady and cool. Tommy went to the kitchen and poured a large glass of iced tea to take upstairs. He went to his room, undressed, and turned on the radio. It was tuned to the Jackson rhythm and blues station, which went off the air every day at sunset. He rummaged through the books in his closet, pulled out a paperback copy of *1984*, and lay down to re-read the story of Winston Smith and Big Brother.

The radio played two Bo Diddley songs in a row. Tommy lay the book across his chest and listened. He closed his eyes and pictured Bo Diddley in Memphis, standing like a great black mountain with the ocean of young people coming together before him.

The music changed to something new by The Ronettes, and Tommy picked up the book again. He read the part where Winston Smith hid from the telescreen and wrote over and over in his journal, "I hate Big Brother." Tommy went to his closet and found an ink pen. The radio was playing

"The Star Spangled Banner" to end the broadcast day. Tommy turned to the blank page at the back of the book and wrote, all at once, in a rush:

"I hate Ross Barnett. I hate Ross Barnett. I hate Ross Barnett.

"I hate Jim Crow. I hate Jim Crow. I hate Jim Crow.

"I hereby declare that I, Thomas Jefferson Jackson, will be arrested in the sit-ins. I will go to jail. I will become a Thought Criminal.

"God Bless Elvis. God Bless Bo Diddley. God Bless Little Richard.

"Go Mississippi!

"Signed: Thomas Jefferson Jackson,

"July 19, 1961 A.D."

Tommy closed the book and put it under his pillow. He turned off the light and the radio and went to sleep.

Sunday morning Freedom House was still quiet. Will was out early, visiting college friends on the east side of town. Rebecca was at church for most of the day. Charley was in a meeting out at Tucumbee to hatch the sit-in plan. By late morning, Tommy was alone. He took his radio downstairs and listened to gospel music while he ate baloney sandwiches and read the Sunday funnies.

When the paper was used up, and the music was replaced by a preacher, Tommy turned the radio off. He sat on the porch and smoked cigarettes and waited. At about 1:30 he saw Sheila's legs through the trees again, walking toward him. She was still dressed for her grandmother's church, in a short-sleeved blue dress that covered her knees.

Tommy stood in the yard under the trees to wait for her. When she arrived he wrapped her in his arms and held on tight for a long time. "I'm so glad you're back," he said. He kissed her hard on the mouth, then on each cheek and on her nose and chin. "I missed you so much. I need to talk to you."

"I was only gone for 28 hours," she said.

"Yeah," Tommy said, "but the whole time I've been thinking and thinking, till I thought I'd go crazy. I've got so much in my head."

"Well, let's go inside and sit down," she said, "I'm tired and thirsty."

"OK. Rebecca's gone you know," Tommy said. "Everybody's gone. We can go up to your room if you want to. Maybe you can show me your paintings later on."

"That would be good."

They walked into the kitchen and Sheila got some cold water. "I want to go upstairs and change clothes," she said, taking the glass with her. "I'll call for you when I'm ready."

Tommy sat by the stairs. A few minutes later Sheila called "OK," and he ran up to her room. She was dressed in her gym shorts and t-shirt again and sitting on the edge of her bed. Tommy stopped and looked at her for a long time. With everything else that was on his mind, he found himself studying her tanned legs.

"Well, what's on your mind, big boy?"

Tommy looked up. "I've decided to be arrested in the sit-ins."

"Hold on, what got you started on that?"

"It was what Phil said about being on the other side. I got to thinking yesterday, when I was by myself," Tommy said. "He was right. This is war now, it has to be, and this is the side I'm on."

"Yeah, but there are a lot of things you can do besides go to Parchman. Won't that make it hard for you with your family?"

Tommy told her about reading *1984*. He tried to tell her again about Darrell Farmer and Bo Diddley.

"That's old stuff," Sheila said. "You told me all that the first time I met you, at J.W.'s. Something else is going on with you. What's got you all worked up to be a martyr?"

Tommy looked down and gritted his teeth. He clenched his eyes shut and tried to swallow the thing that was rising from his chest to his throat.

He couldn't hold it in anymore. All at once, everything came out. Tommy sat on Sheila's bed and cried uncontrollably for several minutes. She held his head against her chest and stroked his hair and rubbed his back.

"It's all right, baby," she said, "cry it all out and then tell me."

Finally Tommy got control of himself. He sat up straight, held Sheila's hand, and looked at the floor as he began to talk. A few times he sobbed and started to cry again, but he stopped and took a drink of water and kept talking until he had told it all, beginning with the night he saw Elvis, and the night after. He told everything, down to the moment when Wade Suggs lay curled up in the dirt on Dicky White's grave.

When it was all told, Tommy threw himself down face-first on the bed and cried again. "I'm an awful person," he said into the covers. "I've never been strong enough to do what's right. But now I'm going to do what's right if it kills me."

Sheila lay down across his back. "Tommy," she said, "you're the best person I've ever met. If you'd told those things before, you might be dead already, and I wouldn't have liked that. I'm proud of you, Tommy. I'll stand up for you. But I'm not going to let you get killed. That would mess up too many of my little plans."

Tommy pulled his face from the bedspread and rolled over to face Sheila. They lay side by side, touching chests, bellies and legs. He wasn't crying anymore, but his face was still wet. The tears rubbed off on Sheila as they kissed long and strong, until they seemed to melt together in the heat.

Tommy broke off the kiss for air and laughed. "Tell me about those plans," he said.

"Uh, uh, none of your business." Sheila wrapped her legs around Tommy and they kissed again. They writhed together on the bed, side by side. Hands went everywhere. Clothes slid off. Sheila raised up on her elbow and looked deep into Tommy's eyes. "I love you, Tommy Jackson," she said.

"I love you, Sheila Bissell," he answered. She rolled onto her back, and Tommy positioned himself above her.

When it was all over, they lay naked together for a long time, tangled around each other on the narrow single bed. Their sweat ran together in the afternoon heat. A fly buzzed somewhere in the room. There was a distant rattle of dishes from the kitchen below.

"That was beautiful," Sheila said.

"Yeah, I'd say so," Tommy answered. "Did you ever do it before?"

Sheila took a deep breath. "Once," she said, "but it wasn't like this. It was back in California, with an older guy from USC. It was a party, we were both drunk, and he was obnoxious. I guess I ended up letting him do it so I could get rid of him. The next morning I could hardly believe it had happened. It didn't seem real. I never saw the guy again."

They were both silent for a minute or so. "So this is the first real time," Sheila said. She rolled over and looked up at the ceiling, with her head on Tommy's chest. He ran his fingers through her hair. "What about you?" she asked.

"Huh?"

"You ever do this?"

"Uh, no, not all the way, anyhow," Tommy answered.

"So, what do you think?"

"I think it's great."

"I mean, what does it mean?" Sheila said, "What do you think is going to happen?"

"Well," Tommy said, "We know one of the things that could happen."

"No, that's not likely this time of month," Sheila said. "But what if it did?"

"I could handle that, I think," Tommy said, "but I'd rather be more careful..." Tommy stopped mid-thought and caught himself, "...if there's a next time."

Sheila laughed. She rolled onto her stomach and planted her chin on Tommy's chest. "There will be a next time. And there won't be any shotgun weddings. But besides that, what does it mean?"

Tommy paused and tried to think of words that went with these feelings. "I guess it means that we love each other. That we're all wrapped up in each other, all the time."

"Yeah, that's it," she said, putting her arms and legs around Tommy. "All wrapped up, all the time."

They lay that way for a while longer. The fly was still buzzing. They heard it bumping the window screen, trying to escape. The noises in the kitchen were louder. There were voices now. Sheila sat up on the bed. "I hear Rebecca down there," she said, "we better get up."

They stood, back to back and put on their clothes. Tommy sat on the bed tying his shoes. "How about those paintings?"

"Oh," she laughed, "wasn't that just an excuse to get into my room?"

"No, it wasn't," he said.

"Well, that's one right there," she said, pointing to an impressionist magnolia tree that hung over her bed. "From my first year at Brooks. It's very peaceful, that's why I keep it there. She pulled some frames from the top of her closet. "Here are some more."

She laid five paintings across the bed. "This is in the order that I painted them." She waved her hand from left to right. The first one was a realistic ocean scene.

"From California?"

"Yeah, Venice Beach," she said.

The next two were fuzzier, like the magnolia, and seemed to be tall trees and rock formations. "Those are from Yosemite," she said. The last two were jagged slashes of black and red, with splotches of white buried in the background.

"Those are 'Night Riders, I and II.' I did them this year, after I got into the movement and read about the history down here."

Tommy wasn't sure what he was looking at. He could tell that the realistic ones were good, so he figured the ones he didn't understand were, too.

"You're really an artist," he said, "You're not just messing around with this."

"Of course I'm not," she said. "What did you think?"

That night Tommy and Sheila went to church. It was the mass meeting to announce the sit-in campaign, but the meeting was held at the Zion African Methodist Episcopal Church and it had all the hymns, prayers and preaching that came with church. Tommy and Sheila arrived in the Tucumbee College van with the rest of the Freedom House people. Inside the church was already very full. A quartet was onstage singing "Do Lord (Oh Do Remember Me)." Tommy remembered the song from Vacation Bible School, though they had changed a few of the words.

Tommy and Sheila walked, hand in hand, down the side aisle of the church, looking for two seats together. There were not more than a dozen white people in the church, not counting the reporters in the balcony. But people welcomed them as they passed, and up near the front some older ladies moved closer together to make space for Tommy and Sheila on their pew.

The Zion A.M.E. Church was one of the oldest buildings in Jackson. It was brick on the outside, with stained-glass windows, but the inside of the church was made from rich, caramel-colored wood. The high arched ceiling was built from four-inch boards. The wood pillars and exposed beams were single pieces carved from tree trunks sometime in the last century. The wood gleamed with decades of polish. It gave the church a magical glow and the music a special resonance.

Tommy was inspecting the boards of the ceiling and studying a stained-glass window of Jesus at Gethsemane when he was startled by a bony elbow in his ribs. It was the old lady next to him on the pew, swinging her arms and clapping time to "This Little Light of Mine." Tommy edged away from her, took Sheila's hand and joined the singing. The church grew hot as the congregation, crowded armpit to elbow, got worked up with the music.

After half-an-hour of singing, a preacher from somewhere in Tennessee was introduced. The preacher was tall and thin and grey-haired, with a white mustache, and he wore a blue pin-striped suit. He asked everyone to bow their heads, and he prayed over them for a long time, telling God about all the troubles black folk had in Mississippi, one by one.

After a big "Amen," the preacher stepped back and spoke about standing brave in the Spirit. Waving a Bible in his right hand, he talked about Daniel in the Lion's Den, and Shadrach, Meshach and Abednego in the fiery furnace, and Peter standing up preaching in the Temple. He talked about Paul and Silas freed from the Philippi jail, and led them into the song "Keep your eyes on the prize, hold on..."

Tommy was stirred by the man's preaching. Still during the singing, he whispered into Sheila's ear, "Wonder why there haven't been any earthquakes up at Parchman?"

"Hush up, those ladies can hear you," she whispered back.

After the song Josh Robinson stood to outline the new plan of action. He said the sit-ins would begin in a week and the Woolworth's lunch counter would be the first target. They picked Woolworth's because it had been desegregated in some Southern cities, and, as a national chain, it would be vulnerable to national pressure. They would move on to target other businesses, large and small, at least one per week, until every door in downtown Jackson was open to Negroes and whites on the same basis. The Freedom Rides into the bus station would continue, too.

Josh sat down, and everyone applauded. Then the crowd broke into

"Ain't Going to Let Nobody Turn Me Around." Verses were sung about segregation, Ross Barnett, the police, and Parchman farm, then the Tennessee preacher took the podium again.

"It's altar call, church!" he proclaimed. "You've heard the prayer and the preaching and the plan, now it's time to put it all on the line. Please join me in 'Amazing Grace.'" They sang, and during the second verse of the song, the preacher began to talk over the music.

"This great undertaking is going to need witnesses," he said, "We need prophets, messengers of freedom, who will go into the fiery furnace and shake the walls of the prisons with song. If you're ready to be a witness, I want you to stand up right now."

Tommy was sitting and humming the familiar tune with his head bowed down. He looked up at the sound of the call. Josh Robinson stood from his chair on the stage. Lewis Johnston was there standing in the front row. Tommy looked back across the rows of pews. Charley McGill was standing. Dozens of local high-school-aged black kids stood, and a few of their elders after them. Sarah Golden stood, and Phil O'Toole.

The congregation was singing the verse about "ten thousand years." Tommy took Sheila's hand again and looked in her eyes. She squeezed his hand and nodded, and he stood, too.

When they had been twice through all the verses of "Amazing Grace," the preacher stopped the singing and the organ continued to play. "All who are standing," he said, "if you are ready to make a commitment tonight, please come forward."

Tommy answered the call. "Here we go again," he said to himself as he walked down the aisle of the church.

- Eighteen -

Monday night Phil O'Toole met with the Freedom House residents over a spaghetti supper. They sat and talked until the tomato sauce and leftover noodles made a hard crust on their plates. At the start of the evening, O'Toole went through details of the sit-in plan, including the schedule of targets. Later they turned to the big questions: Who from Freedom House would be arrested? And when?

The summer commitment they had all made ended August 15, and a lot of schools started the week before Labor Day. People had plans to visit family. Sheila had a pre-paid plane ticket to California for August 10. But Tommy, Sarah and Charley were firm in their commitment to the sit-ins. Phil questioned them each in turn. "Don't do this," he said, "unless you really have to, unless that voice inside won't let you sleep."

At the end of the night nothing had changed, and it was agreed that those three would be arrested, and they would go together, on August 9. The target for that day was the coffee shop at O'Shea's department store.

As the time for the O'Shea's action drew near, tensions in the movement, and in the city of Jackson, were high. The first three sit-ins met violent reactions from local whites. At the Krystal hamburger place on Capitol Street, all the windows were broken by white men who tried to attack the demonstrators after police had locked the doors.

As a result of the violence, the movement was back in the news. The number of volunteers coming to Jackson was growing again. The strategy seemed to be working. As it became clear that the sit-ins would continue, the police stopped holding demonstrators in Jackson for trial. Instead they were arrested and sent directly to Parchman.

Training for the O'Shea's sit-in began August 6, in the basement of the Zion A.M.E. Church. Tommy, Charley and Sarah arrived a few minutes before the 8:30 a.m. starting time. There was no air-conditioning, but the basement was dark and cool, like a cave. There was a cold, cement floor and cheap cardboard tile on a low ceiling. The main room was about 20 feet square and lit by a single fluorescent fixture. There were two narrow windows high in the back wall of the room, but they offered no light and were closed against the August heat.

Thirty-two wooden folding chairs were arranged in an oval at the center of the room, and by 8:30 there was a body in each chair, 25 black and seven white. The session was convened by Lewis Johnston, who wore a short-sleeved white shirt and a red necktie that he never loosened. He would lead the training, and participate in the action.

The first thing Johnston did was ask for introductions. He said his own name to start and continued. "I'm a native of Nashville, Tennessee and I've worked full-time in the movement for the last year. Before that I was in seminary; I'm an ordained Baptist minister." In turn around the circle the rest said who they were and where they were from. There were 23 men and nine women. Sarah Golden and a history professor from up at Vanderbilt were the only white women. Besides Tommy, the other white men were two Quakers from Philadelphia and two guys from New York.

One of the Quakers was an older fellow who was at least 6'3", chubby and pink-skinned, with thick white hair. His name was George Miller. "He looks just like the guy on the oatmeal box," Tommy whispered to Charley.

"He's a legend in the movement," Charley answered. "He's spent more time in jail than you have in school, starting in World War II."

The black members of the group were all young. There were students from Tucumbee, Jackson State and the other black colleges in the state. There was a young woman from Atlanta who went to Spellman, and several teenagers from Jackson high schools.

That first morning Johnston gave a lesson on the ideas behind nonviolent resistance. "The tactics come from Gandhi's struggle with the British," he said, "We put our bodies in the way of injustice and refuse to cooperate with it. Freedom begins when the oppressed refuse to participate in their oppression.

"This is an infusion of the spiritual into the political," Johnston continued. "It is a religious act. It doesn't require a particular doctrine, but it does require an absolute commitment to Love and Truth. Whatever you personally believe or don't believe, in this action our God is Love and Truth. We stand for the Truth, without compromise, but we do it in Love, with our hearts open to the oppressor."

Later the group ate box lunches in silence, while Johnston read from the Bible and Gandhi and Thoreau. In these quiet times, and in his prayers offered before each session, Johnston hammered at the idea that even the cops and rednecks were children of God.

"The point," he said at the end of the reading, "is to reach that which is of God within our most violent opponent. Redemption is always possible. A change of heart may not come this week or this year, but grace is a surprising thing."

Tommy sat with the others in the hard wooden chairs and listened to the familiar talk of grace and redemption. The words fell over him like a cool breeze. They made him feel at home in this strange place. They made him feel that there was some common ground between where he had come from, and wherever he was going.

The next day they started the role-playing. This involved acting out the different scenarios they might face during the demonstration, from the time they entered the store, to the time they were in jail. It was a nightmare. The trainees simulated being beaten, cursed and insulted in every way imaginable. They took turns being the tormented and the tormentors.

In loud, rude, obscene voices, people talked about each other's sexual habits, religion, ethnic origin and female parentage. All the while Johnston pressed them to be tougher. "Believe it or not," he said, "the rednecks will give you worse than this. You've got to be ready to take it all, and heap coals of kindness on their heads. That's our power."

Through the days of training, Tommy stayed close to Charley McGill. Since his performance on the road back from Vicksburg, Tommy had begun to count on Charley's sense of what had to be done. During a break in the training, they ended up together, seated on the cold floor drinking Cokes. "Is this what your sit-ins were like?" Tommy asked.

"Almost," Charley said. "But Johnston's right about this nonviolent power. You can see it. Comes a time when they realize that you really won't move no matter what, and the power changes hands. They might start acting crazy, but it's because they're out of control."

"McGill," Tommy said. "I'm standing behind you when they say 'charge.'"

"Nowhere to hide in this army," he said. "But you'll do alright."

In the final stage of the training, they practiced going limp, being carried by the police and dropped. "Going limp," Johnston said, "is optional. Many feel very strongly that we should refuse any form of cooperation. We've all got to search our conscience and draw our lines."

At the end of the last day, Johnston had them stand in a circle, holding hands. "You're nonviolent soldiers now, people. You have nothing to fear," he said. Then he prayed, "Lord bring the power down on these children, like you did on Moses and Elijah and Peter. Make them brave and strong. Fill them with love and truth. Amen."

They remained in the circle, put their arms across each other's shoulders, and sang. "We shall overcome... black and white together... we are not afraid."

On the night before the sit-in, Rebecca slept on the floor in Sarah's room so Sheila and Tommy could stay together. It was a hot August night, and Sheila's room above the kitchen was stifling. Two electric fans worked to keep a breeze going, a box fan in the window and a small rotating one on Sheila's desk.

They sat side by side on the edge of the bed. A bedside lamp cast shadows on the wall behind them. "I'm sorry I'm not going with you," Sheila said. "You understand, don't you?"

"I understand," Tommy said. "We wouldn't go through it together, anyhow. We'd be separated from the arrest on."

"But I hate leaving here with you in jail," she said. "I'll be so worried."

"You wouldn't know any more if you were here, and couldn't do anything either way," he said.

They sat for a long minute in silence, listening to the hum of the fans. "Tommy," Sheila said, "something important is happening between us. I know it is. But there's so much happening all around us, it's hard to sort it out."

Tommy put his arm around her. "It's OK, I know what you mean. We'll figure it out when the dust settles."

Tommy woke still groggy at the first light of day. When they had finished making love, Sheila and he had slept naked and face to face, pressed together in the single bed. Tommy's arms were around Sheila's body and her head rested in the hollow of his shoulder. His left arm was beneath her, dead asleep.

He extracted himself from the bed and stood, still naked, shaking his numbed arm. Sheila half-woke, and mumbled something. The meeting at the church that morning was only for those who were sitting-in. Sheila yawned and stretched to fill the rest of the bed. Tommy knelt beside the bed, pulled the sheet over the length of Sheila's body, and smoothed it with his palms. "It's OK, baby, go ahead and sleep. It's time for me to go."

She put her hand on top of his head. "Take care of yourself." She leaned over the edge of the bed and kissed him.

Tommy dressed and slipped off to his room. He quickly brushed his teeth, changed shirts and joined Sarah and Charley downstairs for breakfast.

The meeting that morning was in the church sanctuary. The demonstrators were to gather at 7:45. They would arrive at O'Shea's just after it opened at 9:00. Phil O'Toole dropped them in front of the church at 7:40.

When they entered, most of the group was already clustered in three front and center pews. The sun was already hot outside, but the church still held the early morning coolness. Whispered conversations from the front pews made a distant and muffled sound in the expanses of wood and space.

Tommy sat in the third pew, next to Charley McGill. One of the New York guys was on Tommy's other side, and Sarah was on the other side of Charley. At 7:45 Lewis Johnston stood in front of the altar rail to address them. He was wearing a dark blue suit with his usual white shirt and red tie. He called on George Miller to lead an opening prayer.

Miller stood from his place in the front pew. "Close your eyes, please," he said. There was a long, long silence. After what seemed like five minutes of waiting, Tommy opened his eyes for a peek. Half the people in the room were doing the same thing. George Miller towered above them, his face turned to the lofty ceiling. His eyes were closed, his lips were smiling and in the quiet of the church his deep, rhythmic breathing could be heard. Tommy re-shut his eyes. He noticed his toe tapping and tried to concentrate on that to fill the silence.

"We turn to the ground of our being," Miller suddenly said, "and the source of our light. We seek the power of love and the strength to abide in love. We seek the power of truth for the truth will set men free. We seek freedom for the Negro people of Mississippi that they may walk in the light. We seek freedom from self and self-seeking. Join us in one beloved community. Amen."

Lewis Johnston started singing "We Shall Not Be Moved" and they all joined him. After three verses Johnston stood before the altar rail again and stopped the singing. "It's time for action," he said. "Remember that when we leave, you should walk in twos or threes at the most. Don't look conspicuous. Stay with people of your own race until you are inside the store; then look to me for the signal. I'll be at the tie rack in men's wear."

"You need a new one," someone said, and Johnston laughed.

"From there on we follow the plan," he continued. "If something comes up, look to me. If I'm not around, look to George Miller. Any questions?"

There was silence. "OK, then, move out," Johnston said, "I'll see you on the other side."

Sarah Golden was the only white person Tommy knew in the group, so he fell in beside her for the walk. She was talking to the New York guy who'd been beside Tommy in church. "OK if I walk with y'all?" Tommy asked.

"I guess so," Sarah said. They left the church and turned right, along with the 29 others. They held back and walked slowly to create some distance between themselves and the others. Tommy was nervous and exhilarated and could not hold himself back for long. He bolted into the street. "Come on, we can go this way," he said.

They crossed the street and Tommy led them on a zig-zag route toward O'Shea's. They walked on empty sidewalks along a side street of warehouses and loading docks. Sarah and the New Yorker were talking, and Tommy was walking faster. He got a half-block ahead, stopped, and waited for them to catch up.

"Y'all afraid to get there?" Tommy called back as he waited.

"No," Sarah said, "but it doesn't seem very inconspicuous to go darting down the street like wild people. Why are you in such a hurry?" She and the New Yorker kept walking.

"I'm fired up," Tommy said, "I can't wait to get on with the show."

"It's not going to be a show," Sarah said. "We're going to end up in jail. You won't be able to play that horrible music of yours in jail." They were together again on the sidewalk.

"Oh, haven't you heard?" Tommy said. He leapt several feet in front of Sarah and the New Yorker and turned to face them. In the middle of the sidewalk he assumed a half-crouched, hip-swiveling stance, slammed a chord on an imaginary guitar and sang, "Warden threw a party at the county jail. Prison band was there, they began to wail..."

Tommy continued backward, ahead of Sarah and the New Yorker, gyrating his hips clumsily as he walked. Sarah stopped to distance herself from him, and Tommy danced toward her, still singing, "... Let's rock. Everybody, let's rock. Everybody in the whole cell block was dancing to the Jailhouse Rock."

"Tommy, cut it out," she said. "This is not a party, and it's not a game." The New Yorker looked baffled and very nervous.

"It's not a funeral, either," Tommy said.

"No, but it could be," she said, "if you start acting like that at the wrong time."

"Yeah, yeah, yeah," he muttered. They continued their walk, with Tommy shuffling along just ahead of the other two. He sang, softly, to himself, "...don't be no square. If you can't find a partner, use a wooden chair. Let's rock..."

They reached the Capitol Street entrance to O'Shea's department store and Tommy stopped singing. The sign in the door said "OPEN" and they went inside. A few shoppers were scattered over the first floor of the store, but most of the faces were familiar. The clock high on the back wall above the coffee shop said ten after nine.

Tommy was the only one of the three who had ever been in the store. He led them through ladies' underwear and past children's clothing. Charley was there, looking through a rack of baby-sized overalls, and nodded as they passed.

Tommy kept walking to the edge of the men's wear section. Sarah and the New Yorker and he spread out and began investigating a row of summer suits. They came in tan, blue and white, with various shades of seersucker stripes. The tie rack was less than ten feet away, and Lewis Johnston was in place.

Men's wear was next to the coffee shop entrance. The coffee shop was separated from the rest of the store by a half-wall of fake brick with plastic plants along the top. The entrance was a break in the half-wall just wide enough for two people. In a few minutes a young black woman appeared and whispered in Johnston's ear. She left, and he turned away from the neckties and walked those last few yards. Johnston stood at the edge of the entrance and quickly, almost silently, 31 people formed a column behind him.

He led them across the threshold and up to a long counter with stools that stretched the length of the back wall. Two black women worked at the stoves in the open area behind the counter, along with two white waitresses. They all wore white uniforms and aprons.

Along the half-wall was a row of vinyl booths. Between the counter and the booths was a row of four tables, with four chairs at each one. Two white men in work clothes were drinking coffee at the counter. Two grey-haired white women were eating breakfast in one of the booths.

In a rush, the crowd of 25 blacks and seven whites fanned out and occupied every vacant seat. As the tide of black faces surrounded them, the regular customers put money beside their plates and escaped. Tommy ran to grab a stool at the far left end of the counter, next to Charley. Sarah Golden and the New York guy joined a young black man in one of the booths.

The two cooks disappeared through a door behind the counter marked "Employees Only." The waitresses were terrified. One of them, a heavy woman with curly black hair, grabbed the telephone from the back wall. The other one, a skinny red-headed woman, paced back and forth behind the counter, puffing furiously at a cigarette. A nameplate on her white uniform said "Earlene."

Earlene stopped pacing. "Can't you people read?" she said in a loud, high-pitched voice. With the hand that held her cigarette, she pointed to a sign above the counter, next to the luncheon specials of the day. It said "We Reserve the Right to Refuse Service To Anyone."

Lewis Johnston stood at the counter, by the stool closest to the cash register. "Ma'am, I can read very well," he said in a booming voice that carried to the rest of the store. "But I don't believe everything I read, do you?" The crowd of sit-inners laughed.

"Don't get smart, nigger," Earlene said, and her voice trembled. She pointed to her co-worker. "We're calling the police right now, so don't y'all try anything."

"Ma'am," Johnston said, "We won't try anything except your food and drink."

"You're not funny, boy," Earlene said. "We don't serve coloreds here."

"That's OK," Johnston said, "I don't eat them." His followers groaned. "I want the Hungry Man Special, with grits instead of hash browns."

Others along the counter shouted orders at Earlene. She raised her hands. "Shut up!" she yelled. "Nobody's getting nothing. Y'all can talk to the manager."

Earlene walked away from the counter. Her co-worker was finished at the phone, and they conferred in whispers. The bigger, dark-haired woman's name plate said "Iris." Earlene and Iris pulled chairs behind one of the stoves and sat, with their faces to the wall. Someone at the counter began a song. "Give us eggs and coffee, we shall not be moved. Give us eggs and coffee, we shall not be moved..." Then "fighting for our breakfast, we shall not be moved..."

The singing filled the store. Curious shoppers and white employees from other departments were gathering at the half-wall. From the counter Tommy could hear some of the on-lookers say, "Look at the niggers. Niggers everywhere. It's those damn sit-ins."

"Somebody get the cops," a voice in the crowd yelled. Several people dashed from the store to spread the word. While the sit-inners were still on their first song, angry white people began to come in from the street. They lined up at the half-wall to watch the action.

The store manager arrived. He was a tall man, over six feet, and somewhere near 40 years old. He was skinny, dressed in a grey suit, and had slicked-back blond hair. He shoved through the crowd around the coffee shop and walked in, waving his long arms. "What on earth is going on here?" he yelled.

At the sound of his voice, Earlene ran from behind the counter. "Mr. Culpepper, I'm so sorry. They got in so fast..."

"It's OK, Earlene," the manager said. "You and Iris go take a break while we clear up this mess." Culpepper wheeled around and examined the sit-in crowd. "Who's in charge here?" he called.

Lewis Johnston stepped forward. He looked across the row of faces at the half-wall and took a long pause. "I'm the spokesman, sir," he answered.

"OK, young fellow," Culpepper said, looking down at Johnston, "you're from out of town, aren't you?"

"Yes, sir, I'm from Nashville."

"Well, I'm assuming you don't know any better. If you're all gone from my store in five minutes, nothing'll happen to you," Culpepper said.

"I want some breakfast, sir. I'll be on my way when I've eaten," Johnston replied. He looked over Culpepper's shoulder at the spectators again.

"Don't be clever," Culpepper said. "Colored people don't eat here. That's our policy, and in Jackson that's the law."

"I know it's the law," Johnston said, still looking distractedly toward the wall. A group of white people came on the scene with notebooks and cameras, and his face relaxed. Johnston turned to address the reporters and Culpepper together. He raised his voice. "It was the law in Nashville until recently, but the law changed because good people took action. You're a Christian man, aren't you, Mr. Culpepper?"

"I'm a deacon in Calvary Baptist Church," Culpepper answered.

"That's good," Johnston said. "I'm ordained National Baptist myself. I'm sure you remember that when Christ appeared to the Apostle Paul, it was against the law for Jews and Gentiles to eat together." Johnston's preaching voice was at full throttle, reaching every corner of the store.

"Yes, it was," Culpepper answered.

"But the Lord Jesus Christ chose Paul, a Jew among Jews, to be the apostle who broke down those walls. He built a new community where there was no slave or free, male or female, Jew or Greek, but only free and equal brothers and sisters in Christ." Johnston paused to acknowledge the cheers and amens of the demonstrators.

"Mr. Culpepper," he continued, "today the Lord is calling you to be like Paul. You could be the Jew among Jews, the white man among white men, who turns to his people and says, 'Friends, it's just not right. Jesus died for these colored folks, too, and they deserve a place at the table.'"

The sit-in turned into a revival meeting as cries of "amen" and "tell it, brother" sounded in the coffee shop. Tommy caught himself saying, "Amen." Someone started singing an old spiritual, "We're going to meet at the welcome table, one of these days..."

Johnston raised his hands for silence. "Please, let the brother respond," he said.

"That's a fine sermon, boy," Culpepper answered, "but you'll have to give it to the judge. I'm calling the police." He waved his long, scarecrow arms for a path to be cleared, and stalked out of the coffee shop. Cameras flashed as he pulled and latched a chain across the threshold. A sign hanging from the chain declared the place "CLOSED."

Lewis Johnston took his place at the center stool and began singing again, "We Shall Not Be Moved." This time the song was not a joke. They sang "Fighting for our freedom, we shall not be moved," and they sang it like a vow.

When Culpepper was gone, the white spectators began taunting the sit-inners. There were at least 50 of them outside the coffee shop now, mostly men, spread along the barrier wall and the chain. There were still no police. The white men yelled to be heard over the singing. "Niggers go home!" they yelled over and over.

Tommy sat on the stool with his face to the counter. To his right Charley was pounding his fist in time with the song. Tommy tried to sing but he was too distracted by the voices of the white men behind him. He gripped the counter with both hands and stared at the stove behind it. He focused on an uncooked strip of bacon lying abandoned on the grill.

The voices from behind the wall grew louder and more insistent. They burned Tommy's ears.

"Go back to Africa, nigger!"

"Go back to New York, nigger-lovers!"

With his hands still gripping the counter, Tommy carefully turned to peek at the angry men. They were ordinary men; some big and some small, some Tommy's age and some older than his father. They wore short-sleeved shirts and slacks. A few wore ties, but most didn't. They had flat-tops and ducktails and bald heads. None of them wore hats. They were the salt of central Mississippi's red earth, but something had happened to them. Their faces were distorted with a rage that looked like pain. Their lips snarled and their throats strained and they made sounds like the barking and howling of midnight dogs. Tommy tried to turn away from those faces, but they filled him with pity and fear and he couldn't stop looking at them.

The spell was broken when the song changed to "This Little Light of Mine." Tommy turned his face back to the stove and began to sing, "let it shine, let it shine, let it shine." But the cheery song just made the voices angrier.

There was a clatter by the wall. One of the young white men had climbed on top and was sitting, among the artificial plants, with his feet dangling into the booth where Sarah Golden sat. He had kicked the glasses and silverware off the table.

The white man kicked at the head of the young black man in the booth. The black man dodged the kick. "Nigger, you're going to hang by your dick for this shit!" the white man yelled. He walked across the table and jumped to the floor inside the coffee shop. Sarah, the black man and the New Yorker ignored him and kept singing. He bent down to stare at them, and screamed into their faces, one by one. "Nigger dick! Nigger-fucking bitch! Jew bastard! You're all going to die." No one in the booth said a word or moved a muscle.

The man walked up and down the wall knocking water glasses and silver into people's laps and spewing curses. Others joined him, vaulting over the wall or crawling under the chain. They cleared all the tables and began to empty bottles of ketchup and jars of sugar onto the demonstrators. The singing continued, "let it shine, let it shine, let it shine."

One of the white men was working his way up the counter, and came to Charley's stool. He removed Charley's glasses. "You don't need these, you skinny baboon," he said. He took the tops off the salt and pepper shakers and emptied them into Charley's face. Charley groaned and covered his eyes. The man poured ketchup on his head and dumped the contents of the sugar jar onto the ketchup. Charley sat frozen, with his hands over his eyes, absolutely still.

The man moved on to Tommy's place at the counter. He threw water in Tommy's face. The water was cool and strangely refreshing. Tommy felt it trickle down his chest as the white man looked into his face and said, "Where you from, white boy?" Tommy said nothing. "I said, where you from, white boy? You're a nigger-loving Yankee, ain't you?"

Tommy remained silent. The man grabbed his shoulders and shook him hard, yelling, "Where you from?" The man shook so hard that he knocked Tommy off the stool. He landed with his rear end on the cold, tile floor. The man kicked him in the butt and looked down and spat as he walked away.

Tommy got back on his stool. He leaned toward Charley. "Have we got the power yet?" he whispered.

Charley was wiping his face and hair with paper napkins. "It was never like this in Maryland," he hissed through his teeth. "Where are the fucking cops?"

A booming male voice came over the store public address system, "Attention, attention, please," the voice said. The singing stopped. The spectators grew silent. The white men stood still in the middle of their violence.

"In the interest of public safety, O'Shea's Department Store is closed," the voice said. "All shoppers and members of the public, please leave the store. You have five minutes. At the end of that time police will clear the store."

Tommy looked over his shoulder. A ring of blue uniforms was moving through the store toward the coffee shop. "Here comes the cavalry," he said.

Charley took a peek. "That's nice," he said, "except we're still the Indians."

The white citizens fled the building and the police moved in. A dozen or so stood watch outside the half-wall. At least twenty more gathered inside. One of them had a bullhorn and a stop watch. The demonstrators sang, "We Are Climbing Jacob's Ladder," except they said "freedom" instead of "Jacob." The cop interjected his bullhorn squawk at 30 second intervals, counting off the five minute warning. "Two and half minutes... two minutes..."

The singing continued, low and sweet, "...sister do you want your freedom..."

"One and a half minutes..." the bullhorn voice said.

"...every rung goes higher, higher..."

"One minute!"

"...every rung goes higher, higher..."

"Thirty seconds!"

"...brothers, sisters, all."

"You are all under arrest," said the bullhorn. "Lie down on the floor with your hands in plain sight."

The row of cops along the half-wall drew their guns and held them at shoulder level, pointed at the ceiling. The cops in the coffee shop took out their handcuffs. The singing stopped and the only sound was the jingle of the hard metal cuffs.

Tommy looked around. No one was obeying the order to lie down. He remained on his stool. He glanced across the wall at the guns. Tommy was still wet from the glass of water thrown at him, but it was suddenly very hot in the air-conditioned store. His mouth was dry, his face burned and he began to sweat. Sweat mixed with the water and dripped from his nose.

The cop with the bullhorn whispered something to one of the others. The second cop pulled out his billy club and walked over to Lewis Johnston.

"Face down on the floor, nigger," the cop said, "with your hands in sight." Johnston said nothing and sat perfectly still. The cop raised his club high and brought it down on the back of Johnston's neck with a thump. Johnston crumpled and the cop pushed him off his stool. He fell to the floor and curled up in a fetal position.

"Lay flat out on your belly, nigger," the cop said, as he kicked Johnston in the rear end. Johnston didn't move. The cop kicked him in his belly. At the same time two other cops picked out victims at the counter. Thumps and groans were heard.

"Everyone lay face down on the floor with your hands in plain sight," the bullhorn repeated.

This time a couple of people obeyed, then a couple more. When Tommy saw this he stepped down from his stool. His legs trembled and almost gave way under him. He held the stool for support, lowered himself to a kneeling position and spread himself across the floor. The tiles were cold and made the sweat on his body go clammy. He trembled with the chill.

After lying in place for a few seconds Tommy reared his head for a look. The cops were dragging Lewis Johnston out of the coffee shop by his feet. His head dragged and bumped along the floor. Tommy looked directly above him. Charley was still fixed to his stool. A cop stepped toward him with his stick raised high. Tommy tried to bury his face in the cold, hard floor. There was a thump and a groan, and Charley was gasping for breath on the floor beside him.

While one group of cops got people onto the floor others made the rounds putting on handcuffs. One of them came to Tommy. He put the cuffs on tight, checked them, and tightened them again, hard, so that the metal seemed to cut into the bone.

Other cops took the handcuffed people out of the store one by one. A few of the demonstrators walked away. The cops led them by the collar. Most were going limp and pairs of cops carried them out, bumping them into the tables and sometimes dropping them.

They came for Charley. "Up and at 'em," one cop ordered. Charley didn't move. Two cops grabbed him under the armpits and pulled him upright. When they let go, Charley went limp and collapsed onto the floor. One cop grabbed his arms and the other held his ankles. They squatted and heaved, and Charley was on his way. His long body hung low between the two cops, just above the floor.

Across the room two cops lifted Sarah Golden from the floor. One held her under the arms and the other by the knees, with her legs together. They held her high, above the tables.

They came for Tommy. "On your feet, white boy," the cop said gruffly. Tommy refused. The cops pulled him upright, and he stood. One of the cops grabbed the collar of his shirt and tugged hard. The cop was short and had to reach up awkwardly to hold onto the collar. Tommy followed him.

The seven or eight demonstrators remaining on the floor were singing, "Ain't going to let nobody turn me around... keep on walking, keep on talking... marching to freedom land." The song followed Tommy across the empty department store. As he walked more voices dropped out and the song grew fainter. When he reached the doorway he could not hear the singing at all.

The cops opened the door and the hot August sun flooded down. They were on the Capitol Street sidewalk and it was almost noon. Somewhere dozens of voices were singing "We Shall Overcome." Tommy's eyes adjusted to the light and he saw that the singing was coming from two vehicles parked in front of the store. One was a grey school bus with bars on the windows, for the male prisoners, the other was a white paddy wagon with the city of Jackson insignia on the side, for the women. They all sang like school children loaded up for a field trip. "We shall overcome..."

- Nineteen -

The cop led Tommy onto the bus and up the aisle past the other demonstrators. The walk up the aisle felt like a victory march, as if all the people were singing especially for him. When they reached an empty row of seats on the left, the cop removed Tommy's handcuffs and shoved him into the window seat. His wrists were red and his hands were numb.

Another cop stood in the aisle with a clipboard and a pen. "Name, date, place of birth," he said, without looking up from his paper.

"Thomas Jefferson Jackson. January 12, 1940. Calhoun, Mississippi," Tommy answered in a loud, clear voice.

The cop lowered his clipboard. "My God in heaven, ain't that some shit. There was a white boy from Alabama in this mess the other day, but never one of our own." The cop looked at Tommy with disbelief. "You really grew up here?" he asked.

"Yes, sir. In Calhoun," Tommy said, "all my life."

The cop raised his clipboard and finished writing down the information. "Goddamn shame," he said.

Tommy was seated one row behind Charley McGill. From the back he could see the ketchup and sugar in Charley's hair. "How you feeling?" Tommy asked over the loud singing.

"OK. They didn't drop me," Charley said. He twisted his head backward. "Hey, you notice something funny about this bus?" he whispered.

"Yeah it's got bars on the windows," Tommy said.

"Not that, man," Charley said, "No Jim Crow. They're not separating us."

"It's not really integration," Tommy said. "It just means some of us are honorary Negroes."

"Welcome to the back of the bus," Charley answered.

The cops were bringing in the last few demonstrators. A young black man was carried out of the store and to the door of the bus. One cop dropped his feet into the bus and he stood to walk the rest of the way, led by the one who'd held his arms. They put the young guy on the seat beside Tommy. He was neatly dressed in a white shirt and blue slacks. He looked as if he were still in high school. Tommy started to offer a greeting, but the kid began singing at the top of his lungs the moment he hit the seat and didn't stop.

George Miller was the last one out of the store. The cops struggled with his huge body. As they tried to get him out the front door, they lost their grip and dropped him to the sidewalk. Miller lay with his eyes closed. The policemen squatted and grunted like sumo wrestlers and tried to hoist him again. "Can we have a hand with this one?" one of them called.

Another officer came and grabbed Miller by his belt. The three lugged him to the doorway of the bus and pushed him forward. Miller crumpled limp on the stairs of the bus. "C'mon guy, give us a break," one of the cops said, as they tried to push him forward into the bus. Miller didn't budge. A cop on the inside came to help. He grabbed Miller's arms and pulled while the others pushed.

Together they dragged the white-haired man along the floor until they reached the rear of the bus. They let go and left him lying there. The cop who'd pulled Miller's arms stepped on his belly as he walked back up the aisle.

Miller lay perfectly still. His skin was red and sweaty but he was breathing deep, steady breaths. His eyes were closed. People leaned over to look at him. "I think he's unconscious," somebody said. With his eyes still closed, Miller began to hum along with the singing and they knew that he was alright.

The bus began to roll and the passengers stopped singing and applauded. The bus was driven by a Jackson cop and another stood guard beside him. The applause died down as they rolled along backstreets on the fringes of the business district. Tommy looked through the bars of his window and watched the streets of Jackson pass. He felt as if he were leaving town for the last time.

When the bus was moving, George Miller sat up but remained cross-legged on the floor with his hands cuffed behind him, though there were empty seats. "You OK, man?" the black kid sitting beside Tommy asked.

"No damage," Miller answered.

"Why don't you take a seat? And get 'em to take those cuffs off you," the kid said, "your hands look kind of grey."

"It's OK," Miller said. "I won't ask anything of those men. That would recognize their authority over me."

Charley turned to join the conversation. "All respect, man, but what good does it do to hurt yourself like that?"

"That's a fair question," Miller said, "But the cuffs don't hurt that much. It's a spiritual thing. I try to follow the Spirit from moment to moment. For instance, I didn't know whether I would take a seat on the bus until they dropped me here. Then, when I lay on the floor, it seemed right, like this is where I belong right now."

"But why?" Charley asked, "This bus isn't segregated, what's to protest?"

"We're being held without charges or trial, for doing something protected by the U.S. Constitution. That's an illegitimate use of power. As a citizen and a human being, I am obliged not to cooperate."

"I hear they're going to do the legal stuff up at Parchman," Charley said.

"Maybe so," Miller said, "but that's police state tactics. In a free country, trials are held in public by the light of day."

"What you going to do at Parchman?" Charley asked.

"I won't walk, work, wear prison clothes or eat," Miller answered.

"No matter what?" Charley said.

"No matter what," he replied, "at least for a while. I'll reconsider if my life's in danger."

A heavy silence hung over the back rows for several minutes. The bus moved onto Highway 49, which was called Delta Drive on this stretch through West Jackson. They drove past the new black residential neighborhoods on the outskirts of town and into the countryside of cotton fields and cow pastures.

"This is the road to Parchman," Tommy said.

"How long will it take?" Charley asked.

"Three hours in this old thing, if we don't stop."

The prisoners settled in for the journey. Someone started singing "Down by the Riverside" and people joined in here and there, but after a few verses the singing faded into chatter. The bus reached the steep, roller-coaster hills that rise outside Yazoo City. Charley turned in his seat. "Is this the Delta, man? I thought it was flat up here."

"We're not in it yet," Tommy answered. "Wait till we pass Yazoo City." Yazoo City was the biggest town they'd go through on the way to Parchman. The bus rolled into the downtown area and, seeing an audience on the sidewalks, the prisoners began to sing. They did "We Shall Overcome" and "Woke Up This Morning With My Mind (Stayed on Freedom)." When the bus stopped at a red light, a crowd of white people gathered. The black people on the street stepped back into doorways, or turned onto side streets, and averted their eyes.

"Shut up, niggers!" yelled a white man on the street. The singing got louder. A Coke bottle bounced off the bars of a window. Another followed and it broke on a window near the front. People scattered to get away from the glass. Rocks began to fly at the bus. Most of them bounced off the side, but a few made it through the bars.

"Hey, look, there's a white boy with 'em, there in the back!" somebody yelled.

Tommy put his head between his legs. The people on the bus were still singing, louder than ever.

"Hey, nigger-lover!" a voice cried on the street. A rock bounced off Tommy's back. Finally the light changed and the bus started rolling again. The singing continued until they reached the outskirts of town and things were quiet.

Tommy tapped Charley on the shoulder. "This is the boundary," he said, and pointed out the window to their right. The two-lane highway ran along the edge of a steep, red dirt hill buried in leafy kudzu vines. "That is the hills." He pointed to the other side of the bus where rows of cotton plants, waist-high and bushy, stretched to the western horizon like a green, steaming carpet. "And that is the Delta."

"So this is your country, Jackson?" Charley said, squinting across the bus.

"Born and raised here," Tommy said, "My hometown's about 40 miles from Parchman."

"Do we pass through it?"

"Through Calhoun?" Tommy said. "No, thank God."

The bus was quiet as they started the long journey through the Delta. People talked quietly with seatmates. A few read paperback books they had brought along. Others used books or newspapers to fan themselves against the heat. Some people fell asleep. The kid next to Tommy was quiet at last, dozing with his head on the back of the seat in front of him.

Tommy fidgeted and tapped his feet and listened to the tree-frog murmur of conversations. The bus grew painfully hot as they drove along in the sun, but Tommy had a breeze on his face from the window. He felt the heat as a cleansing fire. He was tired from the night with Sheila and the morning's battle. But as they rode the tiredness burned away and left an intoxicated state of alertness.

Tommy watched the familiar landscape of fields and sharecropper shacks pass the window. He observed every detail, as if he were one of the strangers on the bus who had never seen this country before. But he saw things that the strangers missed. He saw the dogs hidden in shadows under the houses, and the round bolls on the cotton plants that would soon open into fluffy white. He also saw the familiar scene differently traveling in this prison bus filled mostly with black men. On the streets of the little towns, he saw hatred in the eyes of the white people, and he saw the mask of fear rise across the faces of the blacks.

Finally they turned off 49 onto another, narrower and bumpier, asphalt road. The cotton came right up to the edges of this road and the bus went more slowly. For a while they crawled along behind a farmer's tractor. The heat became stifling and breathing required effort. The tractor turned off on a gravel road, but before the bus resumed highway speed, the outline of a large gateway appeared on the right-hand side of the road.

The gateway was just two creosote poles on either side of a gravel drive, with a sheet metal sign running between them at the top. The sign was white with a green border. It had a red Coca Cola logo at each end and in the middle were thick, black letters that said "Mississippi State Penitentiary -- Parchman, Mississippi."

The bus turned right into the driveway and went under the sign. They drove about 100 feet and stopped at a locked gate in a barbed wire fence. A prison guard emerged from the booth beside the gate. He was a small man wearing a tan uniform and a straw cowboy hat. He carried a shotgun in one hand, pointed toward the ground, and a set of keys in the other. He unlocked the gate with a key, opened it, and, with the shotgun hoisted across his shoulder, waved the bus through.

Lewis Johnston started a song. It was "We Shall Overcome" again, but this time he went straight to the verse that said, "We are not afraid," and then added a new one, "God is on our side." They sang those two verses softly and slowly and continued to hum the tune.

The bus followed a narrow and winding gravel road through the penitentiary cotton fields. Scattered in the fields was a cluster of long, narrow wooden buildings. A dirt path barely wide enough for a single vehicle led from the gravel road out to the buildings. Alongside the dirt path was a hand-painted sign that said "Camp A."

The bus rolled on and wound through the cotton fields past the sign for "Camp B." The inside of the bus filled with dust from the gravel road. At a sign that said "Camp C," they turned. There was tall grass along the path and it rustled against the sides of the bus as they rode toward the barracks.

The bus stopped in a clearing surrounded by three shotgun buildings. The barracks had small holes in the walls and they had lost their paint years ago. They were empty and the doors were open wide. Inside were rows of metal bunk beds. There were small screened windows around the top of the walls and no bars. In the center of the clearing, between the buildings, was a wooden outhouse with a half-moon cut into the door. A white Parchman pick-up truck was parked in the clearing. A man wearing a cowboy hat sat inside.

Inside the bus the humming of the song stopped. "Everybody out, single file," the cop at the front said loudly, and people began to walk out. The ones at the back stepped carefully around and over George Miller's body. He was lying down again.

As the first prisoners filed into the clearing, the Parchman guard emerged from his truck. "OK, you boys form up in rows of six," he barked, "arms-length apart on all sides."

Tommy was standing in the aisle of the bus when he heard the guard's voice. It sounded familiar, and he stooped to look through the window, but the guard was hidden behind the lines of prisoners.

Tommy inched his way forward and stepped down from the bus. There were two people walking behind him, and then Miller. Tommy took his place in the back row of the formation. He still couldn't see the guard's face. The two officers inside the bus dragged Miller down the aisle. They grunted and cursed as they struggled with the load. The Parchman guard went over to see what was happening. The guard's body was short and thick and he seemed to be fairly young. He held a long billy club in one hand.

The guard went onto the bus to help the Jackson cops. A few seconds later George Miller tumbled down the stairs of the bus. He fell onto the ground and lay limp. The Parchman guard came down from the bus and kicked him hard in the stomach with a brown cowboy boot.

"Get up, motherfucker!" the guard stood over him and yelled. The guard was facing the other prisoners, he wore sunglasses, but Tommy saw him clearly. It was Barry Kimbrough.

- Twenty -

Kimbrough stood over George Miller and kicked again. Miller had curled into a fetal position and the boot glanced off his knee. "Walk, you Yankee son-of-a-bitch!" Kimbrough said. Miller didn't move or make a sound. Kimbrough raised the billy club above his head with both hands and slammed it down on the back of Miller's head. There was no reaction.

"Shit," Kimbrough hissed. He took a pair of handcuffs from his belt and held them out to the cops on the bus. "Y'all tote him into the first barracks there and cuff him to a bed," he said.

While the cops put Miller away, Kimbrough walked to his truck and removed a shotgun. He stood before the rows of prisoners with gun in one hand and billy club in the other. He fired the gun into the air. The prisoners jumped and gasped, and the shot echoed across the countryside. Kimbrough stood silently behind his shades for a long moment.

"Now that I got your attention," he said, "I want to welcome you assholes to Camp C. This is my little kingdom here. I give orders; that's my job. If you don't listen to the orders, you talk to this baby here." He raised the club above his head. "If you don't listen to her, you talk to the boss." He held up the gun.

Tommy stood in the back row taking sick, shallow breaths. He struggled to keep still on trembling legs. He bent his knees to hide behind the man in front of him, and turned his head down to conceal his face.

Kimbrough didn't seem to notice him. He put the billy club into a holster on his belt and continued to talk with the barrel of the shotgun pointed toward the ground. "We got orders not to mess y'all up if we can help it. So if you play along, I'll try and act like I don't hate your guts. You don't, and I'll fuck you up so bad your mama won't know you. Understand?"

He stopped and looked across the rows of men. "For now you'll be locked down in the barracks. You get meals delivered and I come around twice a day. You get a shot at the outhouse with every visit. Y'all missed dinner. There's some bread inside to hold you till supper, and a pot to piss in between bathroom breaks. We'll process you tomorrow, and after that you work the fields."

Kimbrough paused and shifted his gun from one hand to the other. "If y'all are good boys, you'll be treated like everybody else. You get lots of fresh air and sunshine, regular food, cigarettes, all that good stuff. If you're bad, things won't be so nice. Y'all understand that?"

There was silence. "Good. Now hit the john if you need it, and get into the barracks, with your buddy there." Kimbrough pointed his gun toward the building where Miller was chained. "All of you in the same one," he said, "You're all niggers to me."

Kimbrough put his gun in the truck and leaned against the hood while he waited for the prisoners to do their business. Tommy kept his back turned as he waited in line, but stole a glance going into the outhouse. Posed against the truck, Kimbrough looked exactly as Tommy remembered him from the high school parking lot.

Tommy made it into the barracks unnoticed and claimed a top bunk above Charley McGill. Kimbrough locked a padlock on the door and they heard the sound of his truck driving away. When he couldn't hear the engine anymore, Tommy jumped down from the bunk to talk to Charley.

"Remember," he said, "when I told you about that Darrell Farmer case in my hometown?"

"Yeah, what about it?" Charley said.

"Well, our guard is the son of one of the guys who did the killing," Tommy said.

"You mean you know that bastard?" Charley said.

"From high school," Tommy said, "Name's Barry Kimbrough. He used to spit on me and call me a nigger lover. I saw him beat a guy almost to death once. This summer he almost kicked my butt in a bar just for playing Little Richard on the jukebox."

"You think he was in on the killing?" Charley asked.

"Naw, he was too young," Tommy said. "Funny he landed in this line of work, though. Before he killed that kid, Barry's daddy did time here as a prisoner, for stealing."

"Think he'll do anything to you?" Charley said.

"I don't know. I hope he doesn't notice me," Tommy said.

"That can't be. Even if you stayed out of sight, they'll give him that list from the bus and he'll notice your name," Charley said.

"Barry's not the type to get real involved with paperwork," Tommy said. "Anyway, I don't think he'd mess with me, not bad anyhow, it'd get too complicated with my family and all."

They were interrupted by Lewis Johnston calling for attention. "Listen up, fellows," he said, "There's some things we have to talk about and we might as well start now." Johnston's white shirt was crumpled and grey with sweat and he had finally loosened his tie. He stood in the center of the barracks, between the two rows of bunks. The other prisoners quieted down and sat on the lower bunks to listen.

"We have to decide what we're going to do about work. Before we start discussing, let me give you some information. The last few groups up here have faced this. Some went to work, mainly for the contact with other Negro prisoners. Some refused; they didn't want to support the system we're here to fight. Good folks have gone both ways.

"Like the guard said, if you work you get prison clothes, food you can eat, open quarters, smokes, playing cards, chance to go to church, all that. If you don't work, they give you a pair of briefs and one blanket, lock you in solitary, and give you food so bad you can't eat it.

"I'm not going to take a position to start with; I want to hear from you all. But I do think we should come to a consensus and act together, whichever way we go." Johnston threw up his hands. "What do y'all think?"

"I didn't get into this movement to pick cotton for no boss man," a young black man said. Most of the group laughed. "Our people done that long enough." The young man's voice grew stern. "I say we don't give these crackers a goddamn inch."

Charley McGill rose to speak. "I understand the brother's point," he said. "But I'd like the chance to make some connections in here, maybe even do some organizing. We may be here for a while, so we might as well be useful."

"Non-cooperation is useful," one of the New Yorkers answered. "It exerts moral pressure on the system, and economic pressure. It costs more to keep us if we don't work, and they put us in single cells. It may also get publicity."

Several people started talking at once. Lewis Johnston stood. "I think we should hear from brother Miller on this," he said.

George Miller sat on a bottom bunk by the door with his left hand cuffed to the bed post. He held his other hand up with the palm out, as if taking an oath. "Friends, this is a conscience matter for me. I won't work. History shows that evil's only conquered when good people refuse to cooperate. I hope we can go into this battle together, in one spirit. But I know what I have to do."

Miller paused, and several voices jumped in. Johnston stood again. "Brother Miller," he asked, "does this mean you would break consensus if it came to that?"

"Yes, my spirit is clear on this," Miller said.

"Well, there you go people," Johnston said. "This is a brother we have a lot of respect for. If he hears the Spirit, I think we need to listen." There were "amens" around the barracks as he continued. "Let's do a show of hands, right now, just to see where we are. Who wants to work?"

Charley raised his hand. So did another black man across the room. Tommy sat on the bed beside Charley and hesitated. He didn't want solitary confinement or contact with the other prisoners. With no conviction of his own, he decided to support Charley and tentatively raised his hand.

"OK, who wants to refuse?" 28 hands went up. Johnston didn't vote.

"The brothers who voted to work," Johnston said, "can you accept consensus the other way? Or should we keep talking? Brother McGill?"

"I can go with it. Nothing wrong with refusing, and we got to stay together."

"Others?" Johnston said, looking at Tommy.

"OK with me," he said, in a barely audible voice,

"Me, too," said the guy across the room.

The meeting was over, and Tommy lay on his top bunk in the heat. He was dizzy and queasy from hunger. The discussion confused him, and he was afraid of each new minute as it came. He had thought he was taking a clear stand at O'Shea's that morning. But it wasn't clear anymore. He thought he was taking a stand for unity, for bringing everyone together. But this meeting drew lines within the lines.

Tommy was in the middle of a world with George Miller at one end and Barry Kimbrough at the other, and he felt pulled apart. He wanted to rest. He closed his eyes and felt the sweat run down his face and neck and onto the bare mattress. He felt the buttons of the mattress sticking in his back. He listened to the hum of voices in the barracks, and the hum of insects outside.

Sometime later there was noise in the barracks. Tommy opened his eyes, rolled over, and groaned. He'd been asleep and wasn't sure where he was. There was a dream in his head. In the dream he was back at JW's bar with Sheila. They were sitting where they had before, except Will wasn't there. The room felt cool and dark and wet. Sheila looked at Tommy from across the table, staring into his eyes for a long time. Then she said, "Tommy, find your feet."

He tried to ask her what she meant. But nothing came out, and she just said it again. "Find your feet."

Tommy looked down at the barracks. People were walking around. His mouth was dry and his head ached. He felt like he was hung over, but he hadn't had a drink for a week. Slowly things came into focus. It was suppertime. A black man in blue denim clothes was standing at a table by the barracks door. There was a number stenciled above the pocket of his shirt. On the table was a pot and a pan and a stack of tin plates.

Kimbrough appeared in the doorway as Tommy jumped down from his bunk. He stood behind the man with the food and held up a piece of paper. "Is there a prisoner here," he called out, "named 'Jackson, Thomas J.'?"

- Twenty One -

The other prisoners cleared a path to the door. As Tommy passed they looked at him with curiosity. Lewis Johnston stepped in front of him. "What's this about?" he whispered.

"I don't know," Tommy said.

Charley grabbed his hand. "Be strong, man."

Tommy reached the door and Kimbrough walked into the clearing without a word. Tommy followed. Kimbrough leaned against the side of his truck, still wearing his hat and sunglasses. A bulldog nose and a plug of tobacco protruded from his flat face.

"So you finally went all the way over with the niggers, huh, Jackson?" Kimbrough said with a chuckle. Tommy said nothing. "What is it with you and the niggers? Is it nigger pussy? Or nigger dicks?" Kimbrough continued.

"Neither. I got a white girlfriend."

"So what is it?"

Tommy looked at the ground and was silent for a long time. "I'm just trying to do the right thing," he said, still looking down.

Kimbrough laughed. "Jackson you always was crazy. But at least you got the guts to go all the way with it." He laughed some more. "Doing the right thing, huh? That's a good one."

Kimbrough stopped laughing, paused to remove his sunglasses, and squinted at Tommy. "Funny man," he said, "I'm here to tell you there's going to be big trouble if y'all don't hit the fields tomorrow."

Kimbrough looked at Tommy for a long moment. He was waiting for Tommy to say something. Tommy tried to think. Did Kimbrough want information? Did he want help on the inside persuading the prisoners to work? Did he just want Tommy to say he would work?

"Well, Barry," Tommy said, "they've already been talking about it and I don't think they're going to work. Some of them want to. But there's a few that are dead set against it, and there's a rule that we stick together on stuff like this. I wonder if you could consider that and hold off for a while..."

Kimbrough interrupted. "Which ones are against it? Maybe we could split them off..."

"Can't say exactly," Tommy said, "but it's not many."

"Uh, huh." Kimbrough spat brown juice onto the grass and put on his shades. He waited for Tommy to say more, but Tommy couldn't think of anything that wouldn't get him in trouble, either with Kimbrough or with his friends inside.

Kimbrough pushed away from the truck and stood upright, as if to end the meeting. Tommy moved to test the ground in another direction. "How's your daddy?" he asked.

Kimbrough stepped toward Tommy. "What's he got to do with anything?"

"Just asking," Tommy said.

"My daddy ain't got nothing to do with me and I got nothing to do with him. I'm on this side of the bars."

"I was just curious," Tommy said, "I wondered if maybe, with all this civil rights stuff kicking up, somebody might be looking at that Darrell Farmer case again."

Kimbrough took another step toward Tommy. His face was red and his hands were folded behind his back. "What do you mean?" he said through a clenched jaw.

"Nothing," Tommy said, "I just wondered if those new guys in Washington might look at some of the old cases again."

"That's over and done," Kimbrough said.

"Yeah, I guess it is," Tommy said. "Unless they find somebody that hadn't talked before."

"What you getting at?" Kimbrough said. His hands were still behind his back, but a vein popped out on his forehead.

"I heard that there might be another witness." Tommy was surprised at his own words. He didn't mean to go this far, but Kimbrough's reaction excited him and made him feel powerful.

"Where'd you hear that?" he demanded.

"Oh, just around," Tommy said.

"Around those Freedom Riders?" Kimbrough asked.

"Naw, just around. Probably nothing to it," Tommy said. "Tell you the truth, I was surprised anybody even remembered that mess."

Kimbrough relaxed a little. "Yeah, it's ancient history."

"That's right," Tommy said, "ancient history. Old as the dirt."

They stood looking at each other for a few seconds. Kimbrough stepped back toward his truck. "That's all, Jackson," he said, waving his arm toward the barracks. "Get back in there with your niggers. I'll see you in the fields tomorrow."

Tommy walked inside, took a spoon and a plate of beans and cornbread, and sat beside Charley on the lower bunk to eat. The beans were tepid and salty and the cornbread was crumbly and cold, but he was so hungry that it all tasted like Christmas. He stuffed his mouth full.

"So what happened, man?" Charley asked. "What'd he want?" Others gathered around waiting to hear from Tommy. He pointed to his mouth and they waited while he chewed.

"He wanted to tell me I was crazy, and that we'd be in big trouble if we don't work."

"So what did you say?" Charley asked.

"I told him I was just trying to do the right thing, and I didn't know what we would do about work."

"That's all?" Charley said.

"That's all. Rest was just hometown talk, nothing important."

After supper it was still daylight outside. The barracks had been collecting heat all day and was more miserable than ever. Tommy lay on his upper bunk again and sweated and tried to make sense of what was happening to him. He was surprised at how decent Kimbrough had been when they talked. He was mad, but he hadn't hit him or spit on him. Maybe that was because he was in uniform. Or maybe it was because they were two of the same kind, surrounded by outsiders.

He thought about Sheila. He remembered the dream from his afternoon nap and pictured her in that scene again. He pictured her in her bed at Freedom House. He rolled over on his side and closed his eyes. When he opened them again the sun was almost down. The sky was grey and pink through the narrow slit of the barracks window.

Below, a dozen conversations blended into background noise. In the center aisle of the barracks a single light bulb hung from a cord. Someone pulled the string and a few people sat on the floor beneath the light to read. In one corner people were singing. One of the New Yorkers was trying to teach the other guys a Yiddish song.

Tommy sat up on the bunk and took off his shoes. He took off his pants and rolled them around the shoes to make a pillow. He lay back with his head on the lump and closed his eyes again.

There was a loud motor running somewhere. Tommy lay on his bunk and told himself someone was mowing a yard. He put his hands over his ears and tried to go back to sleep, but the motor kept running. He opened his eyes a little. It was daylight. He remembered where he was and looked out the window. The noise was an empty grey bus with its engine idling in the clearing.

Kimbrough stood at the front door. "Up and at 'em, girls!" he yelled. "Get on that fucking bus. You're wanted for processing."

Tommy jumped down from his bunk, dressed and went outside. It was very early. The sun was still behind the trees, the air was fresh and cool, and the grass was soaked with dew. Kimbrough leaned against the bus. A black man in prison clothes sat behind the wheel. Tommy kept another prisoner between him and Kimbrough at all times and made his way to the back of the bus without speaking to him.

When everyone was on the bus, Kimbrough called to the black bus driver. They went inside the barracks and carried out George Miller. They dumped him in a pile inside the door of the bus. Kimbrough kicked him in the head as he passed to take the front seat.

The bus went out the dirt path and onto the gravel road. After a few minutes it turned onto another gravel road which ended at a paved driveway and parking lot outside a cinder block building. The bus stopped in the parking lot. Kimbrough ordered them inside and he rode away with the driver in the empty bus.

They were locked in a bare and window-less holding cell, about 12 by 20 feet. There was a double door made of bars and a toilet in the corner with no seat or lid. The cinderblock walls, the cement floor and the bars of the door were all painted the same shade of grey. From this cell they were called one at a time, by name, from the list the Jackson cops had made.

Each prisoner called went away for a few minutes and returned with black ink on his fingers. Photographs and fingerprints were the first piece of business. They were all kept waiting in the big cell for more than two hours. Tommy's turn came near the end.

One guard led him down a hall and into an office. Another guard pressed his right hand onto a blotter of thick, sticky ink and held it dripping over a printed sheet of cardboard. The guard put Tommy's fingertips onto the cardboard one by one, starting with the thumb. He touched the edge of the finger down first and then rolled it flat.

The same guard led Tommy to a blank wall in the same room. He held out a metal slate with removable numbers on it. Tommy took the board and held it in his left hand. A camera on a tripod was pointed at him.

"Stand on that mark with your back to the wall and hold that number on your chest," the guard ordered. The camera flashed and Tommy closed his eyes. "That's it for now," the guard said and led him back down the hall.

When everyone else was printed and pictured, two guards came for George Miller. They dragged him along the floor of the hallway. He was gone for at least 15 minutes. When they dragged him back in he had black fingerprint ink smeared across his face. "They can't get a clear print unless you let them," he said, "and I didn't. They were angry. The blackface is their idea of a joke."

Another guard entered the cell with a stack of brown paper grocery bags. He dropped them on the floor. "Everybody strip naked," the guard said. "Watches and rings included, and put everything into one of these bags."

Except for Miller, the men got naked. They stood, holding their paper bags in front of their genitals. The room was so crowded that each man's bag brushed against another man's bare butt. There wasn't room to sit down. They tried to laugh, tried to converse and tried not to look at each other. They tried to act as if they weren't naked. They were left that way for a long time.

The guard returned, opened the door and ordered them into the hall. Miller sat, still clothed, in a corner, while the rest walked naked in a single file line. There were offices with windows that looked out onto the hall. The men in the offices watched and laughed as they passed.

They came to the end of the hall and waited, still naked and holding their bags. One at a time they were taken through a door. Nobody came out the door, and the line got shorter. Tommy's turn finally came, and he passed through the door into a small room where a guard was waiting with a flashlight in his left hand and a rubber glove on his right.

"Put down your bag and hold your arms straight out," he ordered. Tommy did this.

"Now raise your legs one at a time." This was done.

"Raise your nut sack." Tommy lifted his scrotum with the fingers of his left hand. The guard stooped and shined the flashlight into Tommy's groin.

"Open your mouth," he ordered and shined the light into his mouth. "Lift your tongue." Tommy did that.

"Turn around and spread your legs." Tommy turned and spread. "Grab your ankles," the guard said. Tommy did this and the gloved hand abruptly entered his rectum. Tommy made a small moan, closed his eyes hard, and ground his teeth. The glove was cold and unlubricated and Tommy felt a rubber finger circle around his insides before the guard pulled out.

"Grab your bag and move on." The guard pointed to another door on the opposite side of the room. In the next room there was a barber's chair, and a black man in prison denims held an electric razor. The floor was covered with black hair and sprinkled lightly with brown and blond.

Tommy placed his bag of belongings on the floor and sat naked in the barber's chair. His skin stuck to the vinyl upholstery while the black man shaved his head down to a stubble. Hair fell from his head and stuck to the skin of his shoulders and back.

When the barber finished, he pointed to another door. "Across the hall," he said. Tommy looked around for a mirror to check the barber's work but there was none in the room. He took his bag across the hall through another open door. This led to a larger room with a bench along the wall and a six-headed open shower. One prisoner was in the shower. Another stood wet and naked between the bench and the shower while a prisoner with a can of bug spray squirted his head, armpits and crotch.

Tommy showered and was sprayed. The spray had a sickeningly sweet odor, so strong that Tommy could taste it. "Back in the hall and turn right," the prisoner with the bug spray said. Tommy walked down the hall. He wondered what time it was. There were no clocks in any of the rooms. The day had started without breakfast, and Tommy's stomach was grumbling. Down the hall he saw several naked prisoners lined up on the right, and he fell in behind them.

"What are we waiting for?" he asked a young black man in front of him.

"Jail clothes at the window up there," the man answered.

Tommy stood naked in the hallway with the others. The cement floor was cold on his feet, and he shifted his weight from one to the other for relief. Further up the hall a small, white prison officer, wearing a cowboy hat, came out of an office and walked toward the clothing line. He was a wiry and weather-beaten man, at least 50, with an unfiltered cigarette propped between yellow teeth.

"Hey, you, white boy," the officer called, "step out and follow me."

Tommy craned his neck and looked up the line. There were no other whites. He stepped out of line and looked at the officer quizzically.

"You're Jackson, ain't you?" he said. His voice was high, nasal and hard-edged.

"Yes, sir," Tommy answered.

"Then step out and follow."

Tommy followed up the hall and into a small, private office where the man closed the door behind them. In the office there was a desk covered with papers that were weighted down by rocks. There was a grey wooden swivel chair behind the desk and a four-drawer grey file cabinet beside it. In the corner of the room was a rotating fan on a metal stand. The wind from the fan rustled the papers on the desk. Tommy stood naked in front of the desk, holding the paper sack over his crotch, and felt the breeze from the fan run across him like a winter chill.

The officer sat in the grey swivel chair and looked up and down Tommy's body. He put out his cigarette and lit a fresh one. "You're Thomas J. Jackson?" he said.

"Yes, sir."

"Show me some i.d.," the officer said.

Tommy reached into his paper bag, fished his wallet from the back pocket of his pants, and placed the bag on the floor. His hands shook as he stood, completely exposed, and searched through the thick, brown leather wallet. His license was in one of the clear plastic sleeves, alongside his Social Security card. As Tommy tried to extract it, the wallet slipped from his hands.

It fell on the floor and several loose scraps of paper spilled out. Tommy kneeled on the cement to collect things. The first stray paper he saw was a business card with the bold words, "Ralph Powell, National Correspondent, *New York Times*" plainly visible on the floor. Tommy's whole body began to tremble and his stomach felt sick. He glanced up quickly. The officer was still seated and showed no sign of having noticed anything on the floor. Tommy quickly put his right hand on top of the business card and wadded it in his palm while he collected the other papers with his left hand. He stayed on the floor until he had extracted the license and stuffed all the loose papers back into the wallet. As he worked, the guard cleared his throat impatiently.

Standing, Tommy dropped the wallet back into his bag and the license onto the officer's desk. He glanced at it and handed it back, still seated.

"Get out of here," the officer said with disgust.

Tommy stepped toward the door of the office.

"No, I mean put on your clothes," he said.

"What?" Tommy asked.

"You're out of here," the officer said. "You're released."

Tommy was confused. Standing there chilled and naked, the possibilities leaped through his mind. Maybe this was a trick to get him away from the other movement people, or a trap to put him in jail for a long time. Or maybe Kimbrough had set it up as a joke.

"You got some kind of paper for this?" Tommy asked, pointing down at the desk.

"No paper. Don't need no fucking paper," the officer said, "I give orders and prisoners obey 'em. Put on your clothes, that's an order."

Tommy couldn't think of anything to say, and the impulse to cover himself was overwhelming. He fished in the sack and began putting on his underpants. He put on his shirt and stopped. "What about the rest of the group?" he asked.

"That's none of your business," the officer said.

"Yes it is. I'm with them, we're in this together."

"Not anymore," the officer replied, "now you're out and they're in. Get dressed."

"But I haven't been to court yet..."

"You ain't going to court," the officer said. "It's over."

"You mean charges are dropped?"

"Whatever," the officer said, with a wave of his hand. "You ain't staying here. You're going to hit the road and keep right on going."

"I'm not leaving," Tommy said, "until I've talked to a lawyer. I've got the number right here..."

"No." The officer slammed his fist on the desk. "No lawyers, no phone calls, and no more fucking backtalk."

Tommy pulled on his pants. "What if I refuse to leave?"

"We'll tote you to the road and drop you. You're going, either on your feet or on your ass."

Tommy sat down and put on his socks and shoes. "I'm not going," he said, sitting cross-legged on the floor.

"This is your last warning," the officer said. "Get up and walk or we'll do it for you."

"I'm not going."

The officer opened his door and called down the hall. "Buford, Frankie, y'all get in here. We got another non-cooperative."

Two white guards with tree-trunk torsos filled the small room. One grabbed Tommy under the arm pits and pulled up. The other grabbed his ankles and they carried him out the door and down the hall. The last prisoners were at the clothing window. At the far end of the hall two guards were dragging the pink, naked, ink-smeared carcass of George Miller from one door to another.

"I'm Tommy Jackson," he called loudly to the prisoners in the clothing line. "They're kicking me out of here. Tell Charley McGill, tell him what happened; tell him they carried me away."

The officers put Tommy in the back seat of a prison car. One of them sat behind the wheel and took him off prison property and up the highway a few miles to the tiny community of Jarvis. At the crossroads the officer ordered Tommy out of the car. Tommy got out and stood in the tall grass at the edge of the road. He watched the car drive back toward Parchman, and felt the mid-day sun bake away his prison chill. He was confused about what had just happened, and what would happen next, but mainly he was relieved to be out of Parchman.

When the car was out of sight, Tommy walked toward the crossroads store. There was a pay phone on the front wall. Tommy put a dime in and asked the operator for the district attorney's office at the Calhoun court house. She asked him to put in 25 cents; he did and the phone began to ring. A secretary answered, "Reed Glazier's office."

"May I speak to Jack Gerard?"

"One moment," she said.

There were a few seconds of silence then a familiar voice. "Jack Gerard, can I help you?"

"I hope so," Tommy said.

"Holy shit, where are you?"

"I'm at Jarvis, just up from Parchman," Tommy answered. "They kicked me out this morning."

"How come?" Jack asked.

"Hell if I know," Tommy said. "They just carried me out and dumped me here, nobody else, just me. It's weird."

"Want me to come get you?" Jack asked.

"Yeah, if you can," Tommy said, "I can wait till the end of the day, though. There's a store here and I've got a little money."

"Naw, I'm coming now," Jack said. "God only knows what might happen out there in the middle of nowhere."

- Twenty Two -

Tommy hung up the pay phone, turned around, and saw a McClellan County sheriff's car parked outside the country store. The deputy was talking into his radio microphone and staring straight at Tommy.

Tommy looked away and walked into the store. The place was dark and cluttered with creaking floorboards and dusty shelves. A very old white woman sat behind a counter next to a big hoop of cheese on a platter. The old woman watched as Tommy cut two big slices and wrapped them in butcher paper. He picked saltine crackers and peanuts from a nearby rack and selected a Coke from the cooler. "Pack of Camels, too," Tommy said, as the old woman bagged up his provisions.

He paid and took his brown paper bag outside. The deputy was still there. Tommy tried to ignore him and found a shady spot in front of the store. He sat on an upturned wooden Coke crate to eat, drink and smoke. The food was mostly salt and grease, but it strengthened him and the cold bubbly Coke lifted his spirits. The cigarette was his first of the long day and it made him drunk. He closed his eyes and rested. The sensations were so strong and pleasurable that for a while he forgot about the deputy silently watching his every move.

When he thought a half-hour had passed, Tommy walked to the road to watch for Jack's car. The deputy drove across the lot to keep him in sight. In about fifteen minutes Jack's old Plymouth came into view. He stopped at the crossroads and Tommy jumped in.

"Where you want to go?" Jack asked. "Back to Calhoun?"

"No, not there, not now. I'm not sure where I'm going," Tommy said. "Just drive for a while and let me think."

"This road ends up at Wellsburg," Jack said, "I'll head that way. You can always come to our house if you want." Tommy leaned back in the car seat, lit another cigarette, and tried to focus on the road before them.

"We knew you were out here," Jack said.

"Who's we?" Tommy asked.

"Me and Brenda.The movement people called us. Lot of people at the courthouse knew, too. Deputies come to Parchman delivering prisoners and stuff, and they hear all the news. 'Local boy turns nigger-lover.' It's a pretty hot story."

"You mean in the paper?" Tommy said.

"Naw, nothing like that. Just talk," Jack answered.

"Do my folks know?"

"Somebody might have told them. You know how people are," Jack said.

Tommy hadn't thought of facing his family. He'd planned to act on his own without involving them. They rode quietly for a few minutes. "What did they tell you when they let you out?" Jack asked.

Tommy tried to recreate the scene with the officer in his mind, but it was all a jumble. "Nothing much, just 'go.' It was all weird." Tommy followed the threads of memory back through the past 24 hours. "You'll never guess who our guard was in there. Barry Kimbrough."

"No shit," Jack said.

"Yeah, that's where he followed daddy's footsteps to. Funny, ain't it?" Tommy said.

"Yeah," Jack answered, "perfect job for a professional bully, though."

"Well, the evening we got there, Barry called me out for a talk. It was all about whether our people, the movement people, were going to do prison work or not," Tommy said. "But one thing led to another, and I ended up asking Kimbrough about his daddy, and if he'd heard anything else about the Farmer case."

"Tommy, you didn't..." Jack groaned.

"Yeah, I did. I said there was talk the case might come back up, something about a new witness."

"Where in the hell did you get that?"

Tommy looked out the car window at the cotton fields. Some of the plants were starting to show white. "I made up the part about the case coming back up," he said. "But there really is a witness." Tommy paused, and threw the butt of his cigarette out the window. He kept his eyes fixed on the green horizon. "I never told you, I never told anybody before this summer. But I saw Barry Kimbrough's daddy and some other man dump that kid's body in the Little Muddy."

"No, you didn't," Jack said, "That can't be..."

"I did, Jack. It was the night after we went to see Elvis in Greenville, right? And we had that wreck, where we ran off Moriah Road?"

"Yeah, I remember that."

"Well, the next night I was out riding around, just cruising, and decided to go check the scene where we wrecked," Tommy said. "I got out of the car to look at the tracks in the mud and all, and a pick-up with no lights on drove off the road and across the fields to the river. I laid down on the ground and watched and listened. It was a beat-up red truck like the one Kimbrough drove back then, remember?"

"Yeah, I remember that truck," Jack said.

"I heard the men talking to each other. I couldn't understand most of it, but one of 'em called the other one Billy. That's the daddy's name, right?"

"That's his name."

"They took a long skinny sack out of the truck, tied something to it, and pushed the whole mess out into the river. Then they drove back across the fields and off toward Moriah with no headlights. And that was it."

Jack rubbed his eyes with his left hand as he drove. "Give me one of those cigarettes," he said. He lit up and smoked. "How come you never told?"

"Come on, Jack," Tommy said, "I was scared. I was scared of getting killed. Remember the Klan put out that leaflet? And that rat on Hayden White's door when he said something in the papers?"

"Yeah, I forgot about all that," Jack said. He thought for a few seconds. "So why did you say something to Kimbrough now, when he's got you locked up in Parchman? That's even more dangerous. You know the stuff that happens in there."

"Shit, I don't know why I said it. It just popped out. Jack, don't you see, this is what I've been living with for the last six years, all the time. That and Wade and Dicky White." Jack threw away his half-smoked cigarette and clenched both fists on the wheel.

"I kept dreaming about it," Tommy said, trembling and swaying in his seat. "It all eats me up sometimes. That's why I got locked up, when you get down to it. Then Kimbrough was there, and it just happened. I don't know why. Maybe I thought it would scare him into treating us better or something. I don't know."

There was a long heavy silence. The sun was getting lower in the sky and Jack pulled his visor down to block the glare. He looked in the rear view mirror. "Maybe it did scare him," Jack finally said. "Maybe that's why they put you out. Maybe that's why a Highway Patrol car has been following us for the last ten miles."

Tommy looked over his shoulder and saw the car about 100 feet back. "Oh, shit," Tommy said. "I should've told you. There was a sheriff's deputy at that store watching me the whole time I was waiting for you."

"Son, I think they're sending you a message," Jack said.

"What do you mean? They're not going to arrest me again. They had me in jail if that's what they wanted."

"No, I think they want to run you out of the state," Jack said, "It's something cops do; I've heard them talk about it at the courthouse. Sometimes they don't like a guy's looks, but they don't have any cause to arrest him, so they just start bird-dogging him like this, and pretty soon the message gets over and the guy leaves town. They do it to drifters and guys with a criminal record that they can't catch at anything. Reckon they'd do it to a nigger-loving traitor, too."

Tommy looked back again at the police car and the blur of dark glasses and wide-brimmed hat behind the wheel. He looked over at Jack. "Is that what you think I am?"

"Don't start that shit," Jack said, "I put up with it every day from Brenda. I don't think anything except that you're my friend, and I wish you wasn't mixed up in this shit. I told you that before you did it, and I'm telling you now."

"Jack, I didn't go looking for this," Tommy said. "I didn't ask to be born here. I didn't ask to see what I saw. It all just happened. It was there, in front of me, and it wouldn't go away. I had to do something. Can't you understand that, at least a little?"

"Yeah, I guess, a little," Jack said.

They were quiet again. Tommy laid his head back on the seat and closed his eyes. When he leaned forward, he was ready to face the situation. "The first thing I've got to do," he said, "is call the movement people in Jackson to figure out what's happening."

"You can use the phone at our house," Jack said. "And stay as long as you need. I know Brenda'd like to see you. I called her from work right after we talked. She'll feed you, I'll drive you anywhere you need to go; we can give you a little money, too, if it comes to that."

A road sign said "Wellsburg 9 miles." Tommy lit another cigarette and tried to relax. "Could you turn on the radio?"

Jack hit the switch. There was a Coca Cola commercial playing, then Del Shannon's "Runaway." Eerie organ notes swirled around the car, cut by snare drum shots and a voice filled with pain and confusion. Tommy turned up the volume and felt the music in his bones.

The Highway Patrol car disappeared at the Wellsburg city limits. They drove to Jack and Brenda's house by the railroad tracks. Before they entered, Jack peeked in the window. "Better be quiet," he said, "looks like Zelda is napping."

Brenda was reading the newspaper in the living room. She jumped up and grabbed Tommy around the neck. "I'm so glad you're all right," she said. "I've been so worried since they called from Jackson. Are you going to stay with us?"

"I don't know where I'm going yet," Tommy said.

"Cops are following him," Jack said. "There was one watching where I picked him up, and another followed us to town. They'll probably turn up here soon." Jack looked out the living room window, but the street was still empty.

"What are they following you for?" Brenda asked.

"I'm not sure. Jack thinks they want to scare me into leaving the state," Tommy said. "Maybe that was the reason for putting me out of jail, to get me away from here."

"That figures," Brenda said, "a white person from down here is a lot more dangerous than the people who come from up North. They can't say you don't understand the way of life and all that."

"Yeah, that might be part of it," Tommy said.

"What else could it be?" Brenda said.

Jack interrupted. "It's a long story. Maybe we shouldn't get into it now. Tommy needs to make a phone call."

"Yeah," Tommy said, taking a seat on the couch, "it's a real long story, and it might not be good for you to know it."

"What's going on, Tommy?" Brenda demanded. "What's wrong?"

"Well, our guard in Parchman was Barry Kimbrough, you remember..."

"Sure, the moron whose daddy killed Darrell Farmer," Brenda said. "Y'all ran into him at a bar this summer, didn't you?"

"Yeah, then I ran into him in jail, and I said something to him about the Farmer case," Tommy said.

"What did you say?" Brenda asked.

"Oh God," Jack said, throwing up his arms, "do we have to get into this?"

"We're into it, Jack," Tommy said, "at least I am."

"Well, I'm getting a drink," Jack said, walking off to the kitchen. Tommy turned back to Brenda and finished the story.

"Did you tell Kimbrough all that?" she asked when he was done.

"No, no way," Tommy said, "I just told him that I'd heard there might be a witness. I don't know why I even said that."

"Tommy, you're right to be scared," she said. "Are you going to leave?"

"Maybe. I've got to call the movement people and figure it out. They'll have to help me if I do," Tommy said, "I don't know anybody outside the state."

"None of us do," Brenda said. "Well, there's the phone. Do what you need to and don't worry about the bill."

The phone was by the couch on an end table with a drawer. Tommy took a pencil and note paper from the drawer, dialed "0" and gave the operator the number.

"Freedom House, Phil O'Toole here, can I help you?"

"God, I hope so, Phil. This is Tommy Jackson," he said.

"Jesus Christ, Tommy, where are you?" Phil said.

"I'm with my friends in Wellsburg. They put me out of Parchman today..."

"Yeah, I know, I know everything."

"What do you mean?" Tommy asked.

"Some guys came a few minutes ago asking about you," Phil said. "It was a cop and a guy in a suit who said he was from the Sovereignty Commission. They said you were released from Parchman and they thought you'd turn up here. It was strange. They said they wanted to talk about your future, and they left a card. What in the hell is the Sovereignty Commission?"

"You are new down here, Phil," Tommy said, "it's a state agency to fight integration, like a secret police. They started it right after the Brown decision."

"What do they want with you?" Phil asked.

"I think maybe they want to run me out of the state," Tommy said. "That may be why they kicked me out of jail. There's been cops and Highway Patrol watching me up here."

"But why?" Phil said.

"Well, I am the only local white person arrested in this stuff so far," Tommy said. "Cops made mention of that from the beginning. They might want to make an example."

"That could be," Phil said.

"But that's not all. It might be about an old lynching case from my hometown..."

"Darrell Farmer," Phil interrupted. "Sheila told me about that before she left. She thought I ought to know, and maybe I could help you deal with it."

Something caught in Tommy's throat as he thought about Sheila out there somewhere caring about him. "Well," Tommy said, "turned out that our guard at Parchman was the son of one of the guys who killed Farmer. He called me out for a talk, and, I don't know what got into me, but I said I'd heard there was another witness who hadn't talked yet."

"Jesus, Mary and Joseph," Phil exclaimed. The sound of his fist banging the desk came across 90 miles of phone lines. "No wonder you've got problems. You're lucky you didn't end up under a swamp. We've got to get you out of here. You have any money?"

Tommy looked in his wallet. "Twelve bucks," he said, "my friends say they'll give me some, too."

"A bus ticket to Chicago will be at least $30," Phil said. "If you can't get that, call me back. I'll also wire some money ahead for when you get there."

"Chicago?" Tommy asked.

"Yeah, people I know up there'll take care of you. Hold on a second." He shuffled through things on his desk and Tommy held his pencil over a clean sheet of paper. "Here it is, Fred Berger, Catholic Worker Community, 1317 Racine Street, Chicago. The number is (312) 578-9634. Fred's a great man. I'll call him as soon as we hang up, and they'll be expecting you. You can call them collect from anywhere."

"I never thought of going that far away," Tommy said.

"You'll be fine," Phil said, "And it may not be for long, but you're not safe here now. I'll get Will to pack your stuff and mail it up there tomorrow."

"OK," Tommy said weakly.

"I guess you'll check in with your family before you go?" Phil said.

"Yeah, I guess so."

"Well, do that," Phil said, "and then get on the first bus North, and everything'll be fine."

"Can you tell Sheila where I am, and that I'll get in touch somehow?"

"Sure thing," Phil said, "I'll call California right away."

"Bye, Phil. Thanks for everything."

"No sweat, you hang in there buddy," Phil said, and hung up. Tommy sat with the phone receiver in his hand staring down at it. Jack walked back into the living room with a can of beer. Brenda stood in the kitchen door watching and listening.

"What's the word?" Jack asked.

"I'm going to Chicago."

"It's cold up there, man," Jack said.

"Yeah, I better take a coat. I can get one at my folks' house," Tommy said. "I need to go there, to see them, I guess. Then I'll get on a bus. That's what Phil said to do." Tommy put the receiver back on the phone. "Can you drive me to Calhoun?"

"Sure," Jack said, "You'll need money, too, man. I've been scrounging around the house and we've got $50 here." He held out a handful of crumpled bills. "Take it."

Brenda stepped into the room. "I can go to the grocery store and cash a check if you need more."

"No," Tommy said, "that's good. I can't take all your money. Give me $40."

He took a twenty and two tens from Jack's hand and folded them into his wallet. They stood awkwardly. Tommy looked at the door. "I guess it's goodbye, Brenda," he said, "maybe for a long time."

Brenda hugged him and choked a sob. "Stay in touch," she said. "Be careful."

Jack and Tommy walked to the car and Brenda stood in the door waving. Jack pointed across the street where a Wellsburg city police car was parked next to the railroad track. The cop followed Jack's car to the city limits and turned around. About five miles down the road, another Highway Patrolman appeared. He stayed with them the whole trip, into Calhoun and through the streets of the town to the Jackson house. There Jack stopped and the patrolman drove away.

Tommy and Jack sat in the car. It was the same old Plymouth Jack had driven to high school, the one that took them to Memphis. It was about three in the afternoon, there was no breeze, and the sun beat down hard on the roof. Tommy stuck out his right hand and Jack took it. "So long, old buddy," Tommy said, "it's been something so far, hasn't it?"

"Yeah. You'll be back for more, though," Jack said.

"That's right. I'll be back."

- Twenty Three -

Tommy left the car and stood in the shade of an oak tree while Jack disappeared around the corner. He was standing across the street from his family home. It had not changed in all the years he'd known it. It had the same white tile siding and green shingled roof, and the same front porch with white columns and green rails. But the house looked strange to him now.

Tommy's sister Josie, seven months pregnant, filled a rocking chair on the front porch. She watched five-year-old Jenny bounce a rubber ball around the front yard. They also looked strange to Tommy. They both had straight, dark hair tied in pony-tails with the same red ribbon. Jenny was laughing and singing to herself. Josie looked sour and grim. She seemed to be guarding the house, and Tommy dreaded confronting her.

They had never been close. Josie was five years older, and a girl, too. Tommy couldn't remember the last time they had spoken one-to-one, certainly not since she got married. On trembling legs, Tommy crossed the street. Jenny noticed him first. "Hey, Mama," she called, "it's Uncle Tommy."

"Yeah, I see, honey," Josie answered wearily, "Why don't you take your ball to the backyard for a while so me and Uncle Tommy can talk?"

"Yes, ma'am," the child said, gathering the ball to her chest, "Bye Uncle Tommy."

Tommy waved to her. When she was out of earshot, Josie leaned forward in the rocker. She was huge, and the weight was not just in her middle, but all over. Her face was round and her arms were thick. There were dark, sleepless circles around her eyes. "Thomas J. Jackson, what in the hell are you doing here?" she said.

"I guess y'all heard," he said.

"We heard," she said, "Every white person in Calhoun heard. How could you dare come back here after what you done?"

"I came to see Mama and Daddy," Tommy said, "to say goodbye. I'm going North, for a while."

"You're not going to see them," Josie said, leaning back in the chair, "I don't think they could stand it. You broke their hearts, Tommy. What's worse, some people in town blame them for what you did."

"Then I need to apologize," Tommy said, "I didn't want them to get hurt. I didn't think anybody would find out."

"Lord, Tommy," Josie said, raising her voice, "how could you do this to your own people? How could you turn against us like that?" She paused, but before Tommy could decide whether to answer, she was talking again. "You know, Jenny'll be in school next year. You want to put her in with those filthy nigger boys? Tommy, ain't no nigger boy getting near my baby, not ever. I know you're my brother, but I'll never forgive this. I hope you leave and stay gone."

"Damn it, Josie, you ought to move to the North Pole or something," Tommy said. "Haven't you noticed this town is 60 percent colored? You can't keep them away. We've got to live together down here."

A voice came through the window screen from inside the house. "Tommy, is that you?"

"Now you've woke up Mama," Josie whispered.

"Yes, Mama," Tommy said.

"Come on in, son," she answered.

Tommy went inside. His mother was sitting on a cushioned chair in the living room. She was crying, and her face was pale with deep lines he'd never noticed. "Tommy," she said, "We've been so worried about you. A deputy came and told us you were locked up with the niggers, and we've just been sick. Is it true son? Were you locked up? It's some kind of mistake, isn't it?"

"No, Mama, it's true. It wasn't any mistake," Tommy said. "I've been hooked up with the Freedom Ride people in Jackson this summer. I think they're doing the right thing, and I've been trying to help."

"Tommy, how could you do that?" she asked. "Mixing with the niggers? It's dangerous, son, and it's wrong."

Tommy said nothing. He stood with his hands behind his back, looking down at the shine of the polished wood floor.

"You're 21 now," his mother said, "so we can't stop you. But this is something we have to live with, too. People have said things to your daddy. I skipped work today because I'm afraid. I'm scared to go to church on Sunday." She sobbed and took a deep breath. "Tommy, we can't live like that. You've got to stop it."

"I'm sorry, Mama," Tommy said. "I didn't want y'all to get dragged into this. But I won't shame you anymore, Mama. I'm going away." His mother was silent for a while. She straightened her back and struggled to calm her emotions. "What about school?" she said.

"I guess I'll finish eventually, wherever I land."

"Where will you go?"

"Chicago," Tommy said. "Some people there'll take care of me."

"Colored people?"

"I don't know. The guy who set it up is white," Tommy answered. "Name I've got sounds like a white man."

"Well, you better take some winter clothes. It's cold in Chicago," she said.

"Yes, ma'am, I was thinking to pack right now. My other stuff will be shipped up from Jackson," Tommy said. "When does Daddy get home?"

"Little after four," she answered. "I'll get you a suitcase."

Tommy went to the closet in his old room and threw all the flannel shirts, sweaters and jackets onto the bed. He looked around at the pictures on his wall. There were St. Louis Cardinal baseball players and a picture of his family at the Memphis Zoo. There were pictures of his Little League Baseball teams, in uniform, and of his high school graduating class. There was a picture of Elvis with a nightclub dancing girl in a scene from King Creole. Tommy looked around the room again, and decided to leave it all behind.

When the clothes were packed, Tommy lay on his old bed and shut his eyes and listened for the sound of his father's footsteps at the back door. He was almost asleep when he heard them. Through the door he heard his mother's voice from the kitchen, calling his father's name. "Honey, we need to talk."

There was a scuffle of kitchen chairs and a murmur of voices. Tommy waited until they were quiet to rise from the bed. He walked down the hall and stood in the kitchen doorway. "Hey, Daddy," he said.

"Hi, boy," his father answered. He was seated at the kitchen table, staring at a half-empty glass of iced tea. He was wearing a white short-sleeved shirt and khaki pants. There was no life in his face, and he seemed very small and thin in the straight-backed chair. Tommy's mother had her back turned, working at the kitchen counter.

"Mama tell you what's happening?" Tommy asked.

"She told me," he said. There was a long silence. Finally his father looked up from the glass but he didn't meet Tommy's eyes. "I think it's best you go on your own," he said. "You're grown, and you've got your own things to do, and it's sure not going to work out around here."

"That's what I thought," Tommy said.

There was another long silence. "You taking the bus?" his father said.

"Yes, sir."

"I'll drive you when you're ready."

"That's OK, Daddy," Tommy said. "I don't want to involve you with this. It's not too far to walk."

"It's too far and it's too hot," his father said. "I'll drive you to the bus."

"Well, I'm ready now," Tommy said.

"Then let's go." His father stood up from the table and walked toward the master bedroom.

Tommy's mother turned to face him and held out a brown paper bag. "Here, son," she said, with her eyes fixed on the floor, "it's some cold chicken and cornbread. You can't live off bus station food."

"Thanks, Mama," Tommy said. He took the bag and touched her shoulder.

She threw her arms around him. "Goodbye, son," she said. She quickly pulled away and looked down again, to hide her tears. "Let us know where you are, and that you're safe."

"I will, Mama," Tommy said. "Goodbye."

His father reappeared and they went out the back door. Tommy put the suitcase in the back seat of the big green and white Ford and sat beside his father up front. "By the way, boy, where's your car?" his father asked as he started the engine.

"It's dead," Tommy answered. "Had a little wreck this summer and the frame got bent, wasn't worth towing."

"Reckon its time had come," his father said.

"Yes, sir," Tommy answered, "it was time."

They drove through the streets of Tommy's old neighborhood. Some people were out on their porches but they didn't offer the usual waves of greeting, and Tommy's father pretended not to notice. Tommy looked over his shoulder. A block behind them was a Calhoun police car.

They reached the downtown business district. The sidewalks were filled with office workers coming out from their jobs, and traffic slowed for a couple of blocks. The police car rode directly behind them. Tommy's father pulled over in front of the bus station and the police car parked half-a-block ahead. Tommy's father sat behind the wheel and looked straight ahead through the windshield.

"Tommy," he said, "I don't know what's happened to you, but I believe that you'll get over it. Just be careful till then, OK?"

"I'll be careful, Daddy," Tommy said.

"Here, take this," he said, and stuffed a $20 bill into Tommy's shirt pocket.

Tommy reached out with his right hand and his father shook it. "Thanks, Daddy," he said.

He got out of the car and walked into the Calhoun Greyhound station. He stood inside the door and watched through the glass as his father drove away. His lip quivered and his eyes were swelling. He stood for another minute until his emotions stilled, then he walked to the ticket counter.

"One way to Chicago," he said.

"Thirty-five dollars," the clerk answered. "Bus goes by way of Memphis and St. Louis. Don't come for another two hours, though."

"That's OK. I'll wait," Tommy said. He took a ticket and turned to the "white" section of the waiting room. There he sat beside a stack of magazines and picked up a copy of *Time* from back in April. He looked up a minute later, and a blue-uniformed local cop was settling into the chair directly across from him. The cop put his cap on his lap and started leafing through a *Field and Stream.*

- Twenty Four -

The sun was going down when the Chicago bus arrived. Tommy went outside the station and the policeman followed. He watched as Tommy climbed aboard and settled into a seat, alone, near the front, among the half-dozen or so white passengers. Twice as many blacks were seated at the rear. The bus began to roll and, through his open window, Tommy waved goodbye to the cop.

The streets of Calhoun were hazy and the sky was orange. On their way out of town the bus passed the hospital where Tommy was born, and the elementary school where he learned to read. A little further on, they passed the church where he'd been baptized and learned his Bible stories and gospel songs.

Inside the bus, Tommy bit his lip until it bled. At the edge of town he surrendered to the sadness and fear that overwhelmed him. He turned his body toward the window and buried his face in the back of the seat. The tears came, and he tried to muffle his sobs. He cried for his mama and daddy and sister. He cried for himself and the loss of all he'd known in his life, all he had loved or hated, or both.

The bus reached the cotton fields and picked up speed. There was nothing left to the day but a thin red stripe along the western horizon. Soon the stripe disappeared, and there was only a crescent moon and a million stars.

Tommy sunk back into his seat, limp with exhaustion. He smoked cigarettes and tossed the ashes and butts out the window. He counted his money twice-- $37 and change-- and wondered how long it would hold out. While counting the money, he came across Ralph Powell's business card again. It was crumpled and folded in half. Tommy took it from the wallet and smoothed it out and placed it inside the plastic wrapper on his pack of Camels.

The first part of the trip was long and slow. They went north from Calhoun to Wellsburg on the same road Tommy had traveled with Jack. From Wellsburg they took a meandering route through the heart of the Delta. Every fifteen or twenty minutes the bus stopped at some country crossroad. There, in front of a dark, padlocked general store, a few black people would stand by the roadside in the night, waiting for the bus. Nobody ever got off. They were all leaving the Delta.

The bus stopped at Jarvis, near Parchman, and Tommy got out to stretch his legs. The air was heavy, stagnant and damp. Tommy walked along the highway and heard his lonesome footsteps on the gravel shoulder of the road.

In the woods across the road there was a pack of wild, stray dogs. They howled like horror movie werewolves. There must have been 20 of them out there moaning inconsolably, each one trying to drown out the others. Perhaps, Tommy thought, they were howling at the evil spirits around this place. He'd heard that dogs could sense the spirits.

As Tommy stood at the crossroads and listened to the howling dogs, he looked out across the dark cotton fields, and thought about the people just up the road at Parchman. He thought of his friend Charley McGill, and all the others, out there in that haunted night. They might be lying cold and naked on the bare floor of some criminal cage. Tommy could see them in his mind, and he could hear them, clear as a bell, singing those freedom songs. He knew they were out there clapping that kidnapped rhythm that built this land, and bending notes around those ancient tunes which were its only solace.

Tommy heard those spiritual songs rising from the cotton fields before him. The sound mingled with the ceaseless howling of the dogs across the road. It made an awful racket in his head. It sounded like rock and roll. The sound roared in his ears as he climbed back on the Greyhound and settled in for the long ride North.

The bus pulled into Memphis at midnight on Highway 61. Tommy got out at the station to buy a drink. As they crossed the big steel bridge over the Mississippi into Arkansas, he ate his mama's chicken and cornbread and drank his Coke. Somewhere between West Memphis and Blytheville, Tommy fell asleep.

He was awakened several hours later by sunshine in his face and the amplified voice of the bus driver. The bus jerked to a halt. "St. Louis station," the driver repeated. "All out for St. Louis. It's an hour stop for breakfast and a new driver. Y'all have a good trip."

Tommy rubbed his face and tried to straighten his neck. He saw a young black man rise from the seat in front of him. He slowly stretched and rose and followed the black man off the bus.

The sun was already warm on the sidewalk, but the St. Louis Greyhound station was air-conditioned inside. Tommy stood in the lobby for a moment and looked around. Before him were several rows of chairs with black and white people sitting side by side waiting for buses. To his right there was a restaurant with only one section and no separate carry-out window. On the left were two rest rooms-- one "men" and one "women"-- and three phone booths. Tommy felt as if he had gone to sleep in one world and woken up in another one.

He took the pack of Camels from his shirt pocket, pulled one out and lit it. As he took the first drag he stared at the card in the pack's plastic wrapper.

Tommy blew a cloud of smoke to the ceiling, walked to the middle phone booth, sat down, and dialed zero.

"May I help you?" the operator answered.

"I want to make a collect call to a Ralph Powell in New York City. The number is 212-407-4136. My name is Tommy Jackson."

After a short wait there was a ringing sound on the line. He heard a distant male voice say, "Ralph Powell, here."

"Collect call from a Tommy Jackson," the operator said. "Will you accept the charges?"

"Your driver from Mississippi," Tommy said loudly, drowning out the operator's voice.

"Sure, I'll take it," Powell said. There was a click on the line, followed by silence. "You there, son?" Powell asked, raising his voice.

"Yes, sir, I'm here," Tommy answered.

"So what do you want? You called me, remember?"

"Yes, sir, Mr. Powell."

"And call me 'Ralph', you hear?"

"OK." Tommy stomped out his cigarette on the phone booth floor. Suddenly there was water in his eyes and his throat was so tight that he could hardly force the words through it. His voice came out thin and high-pitched. "Remember you told me to call," Tommy said slowly, "when I was ready to tell what got me into this civil rights stuff?"

"I remember," Powell said.

Tommy rubbed his eyes and took a deep breath. "Well," he said. "I'm ready now."

THE END

The future of publishing...today!

Apprentice House is the country's only campus-based, student-staffed book publishing company. Directed by professors and industry professionals, it is a nonprofit activity of the Communication Department at Loyola University Maryland.

Using state-of-the-art technology and an experiential learning model of education, Apprentice House publishes books in untraditional ways. This dual responsibility as publishers and educators creates an unprecedented collaborative environment among faculty and students, while teaching tomorrow's editors, designers, and marketers.

Outside of class, progress on book projects is carried forth by the AH Book Publishing Club, a co-curricular campus organization supported by Loyola University Maryland's Office of Student Activities.

Eclectic and provocative, Apprentice House titles intend to entertain as well as spark dialogue on a variety of topics. Financial contributions to sustain the press's work are welcomed. Contributions are tax deductible to the fullest extent allowed by the IRS.

To learn more about Apprentice House books or to obtain submission guidelines, please visit www.ApprenticeHouse.com.

Apprentice House
Communication Department
Loyola University Maryland
4501 N. Charles Street
Baltimore, MD 21210
Ph: 410-617-5265 • Fax: 410-617-2198
info@apprenticehouse.com
www.apprenticehouse.com

CPSIA information can be obtained at www.ICGtesting.com
Printed in the USA
BVOW08s0204050615

403373BV00010B/126/P